UNDERSTANDING CHILD DEVELOPMENT
Linking Theory and Practice

Jennie Lindon

LINDON, JENNIE

Understanding Child Development

-
London: Hodder & Stoughton,   0340886692

HODDER
EDUCATION
PART OF HACHETTE LIVRE UK

Orders: please contact Bookpoint Ltd, 130 Milton Park, Abingdon, Oxon OX14 4SB.
Telephone: +44 (0)1235 827720. Fax: +44 (0)1235 400454. Lines are open from 9.00–5.00,
Monday to Saturday, with a 24-hour message-answering service. You can also order through our
website www.hoddereducation.co.uk.

British Library Cataloguing in Publication Data
A catalogue record for this title is available from the British Library

ISBN 978 0 340 88669 4

First published 2005
Impression number   10 9 8
Year   2008

Hachette's policy is to use papers that are natural, renewable and recyclable products and made
from wood grown in sustainable forests. The logging and manufacturing processes are expected to
conform to the environmental regulations of the country of origin.

Typeset by Fakenham Photosetting Limited, Fakenham, Norfolk.
Printed and bound in Great Britain for Hodder Education, part of Hachette Livre UK,
338 Euston Road, London NW1 3BH by Martins the Printers, Berwick-upon-Tweed.

DEDICATION

To my family – thank you for everything

ACKNOWLEDGEMENTS

I am grateful to a large number of college tutors, early years managers, practitioners and advisors for their ideas and perspectives. Thank you to many 'colleagues' on the informal early years network, especially Jacqui Cousins (Early Years Consultant), Peter Elfer (University of Surrey at Roehampton), Penny Tassoni (Early Years Consultant) and the team at Community Playthings. I appreciate the information and tracking skills of Ann Robinson (Early Childhood Unit) and Jackie Boffin (Community Insight).

Thanks to Emma Woolf, Publisher at Hodder Arnold, who saw the value of a complete revision of *Understanding Child Development* when the previous publisher allowed it to go out of print. My thanks to Wanda Allen (Lecturer at Stamford College and High/Scope trainer), Veronica Francis (Senior Lecturer, Wiltshire College at Trowbridge), Annette Jones and Rachel Pryor (Pre-school Learning Alliance Eastern Region, Swavesey, Cambridge) for helpful comments on the book proposal.

I appreciate that my son and daughter are happy for me to quote from the informal diaries that I kept of them as young children, and to use photos from their childhood. They are both now adults and have been directly helpful on this book. My thanks to Drew for guidance with the section on page 52 and for compiling the index. Thanks to Tanith for her research tracking skills and for teaching me, a few years ago, how to use the internet. Many thanks to my partner, Lance, for all his technical skills, not least with the photographs.

The photographs were all taken by Jennie Lindon and Lance Lindon. I would like to thank the practitioners, children and parents of the settings where I took the photographs: Windham – a Partnership for children (Richmond), St Marks Square Nursery School (North London) and the Under Twos nursery in the East Leeds Children's Centre.

I also continue to learn a very great deal by watching children, listening to them and happily accepting an invitation to join them in play. They are the real judges of a sensible link between theory and practice.

Finally, I take the usual responsibility for this book, the ideas within it and any unintended errors. If you spot mistakes or misunderstandings, please let me know and I will correct them as soon as possible.

CONTENTS

1 Working as a reflective practitioner

Young children benefit from all those adults, practitioners and family carers too, who are willing in quieter moments to consider the possibilities. Young children are best supported by adults who are ready and able to reflect on what they do. Adults need to see themselves as people who make choices and could therefore change how they react. In the professional sphere this approach is called being a reflective practitioner and this description has a lot in common with the outlook of being a lifelong learner.

The main sections of this chapter are:

- What, how and why in child development.

- Key issues in trying to explain child development.

WHAT, HOW AND WHY IN CHILD DEVELOPMENT

This book addresses questions of, 'How do we think about children?', 'What do we know about child development?' and 'What is the basis for this knowledge?'. There are many practical sections in the book but, overall, it is less of a 'what to do' book and much more of a 'think about what you do' book.

The reflective practitioner

The last years of the twentieth century and the first years of the twenty-first brought many changes to early years and school practice within the four nations that comprise the UK. Some developments and initiatives have been very welcome – not least the recognition that early childhood is so very important. However, our society often still values very young children for what they will become, much more than who they are at the moment. Ignorance about early child development, combined with significant pressures to provide economic value, has sometimes created a kind of educational bullying that risks derailing good practice with young children.

Even experienced early years practitioners have sometimes been made to doubt the value of what they do and have felt a sense of headlong rush to move children at speed through crucial early skills and experiences. Early years practitioners need to find, sometimes rediscover, the sense of professional competence and knowledge that promotes the well-being of children. The foundation for such confidence has to be knowledge about child development – what are realistic expectations for young children? – and the theoretical framework that supports such understanding. Good practice includes reflection as well as action. Reflective practitioners are willing and able to:

■ Think over what has happened and allow for perspectives in addition to their own. Part of this open-mindedness is to acknowledge and recognise feelings: your own but also those of the children and of other adults (colleagues and parents).

■ Plan ahead but in a way that is flexible for the possibilities of the moment and children's interests. Useful forward plans all depend on applied adult thinking skills: what might the children learn, how will you recognise it?

■ Review, to look back and consider what actually happened: what did the children probably learn from an experience and how did they learn?

Practitioners who think they know everything are a hazard to children's well-being. When you are willing to reflect, you can learn, and that behaviour models a positive outlook for children. Finding scope for improvement is not necessarily a criticism of what has gone before; it can be much more about, 'Let's try another approach here'.

WHAT DOES IT MEAN?

Reflective practitioner: an outlook for early years, and other professionals, in which you are ready to think as well as to act and to be open to new ideas and approaches.

You will find many opportunities within this book to develop yourself as a reflective practitioner in action. Figure 1.1 summarises the main strands.

LOOK, LISTEN, NOTE, LEARN

Look at Figure 1.1 which shows the different strands of being a reflective practitioner.

■ Take one circle at a time and, over a few weeks, note an example of how you have worked as a thoughtful adult in that way.

■ Discuss what you have considered with colleagues.

■ Do you find some aspects to being a reflective practitioner more difficult than others? Any ideas why?

■ Make some specific plans about ways in which you could improve your own practice.

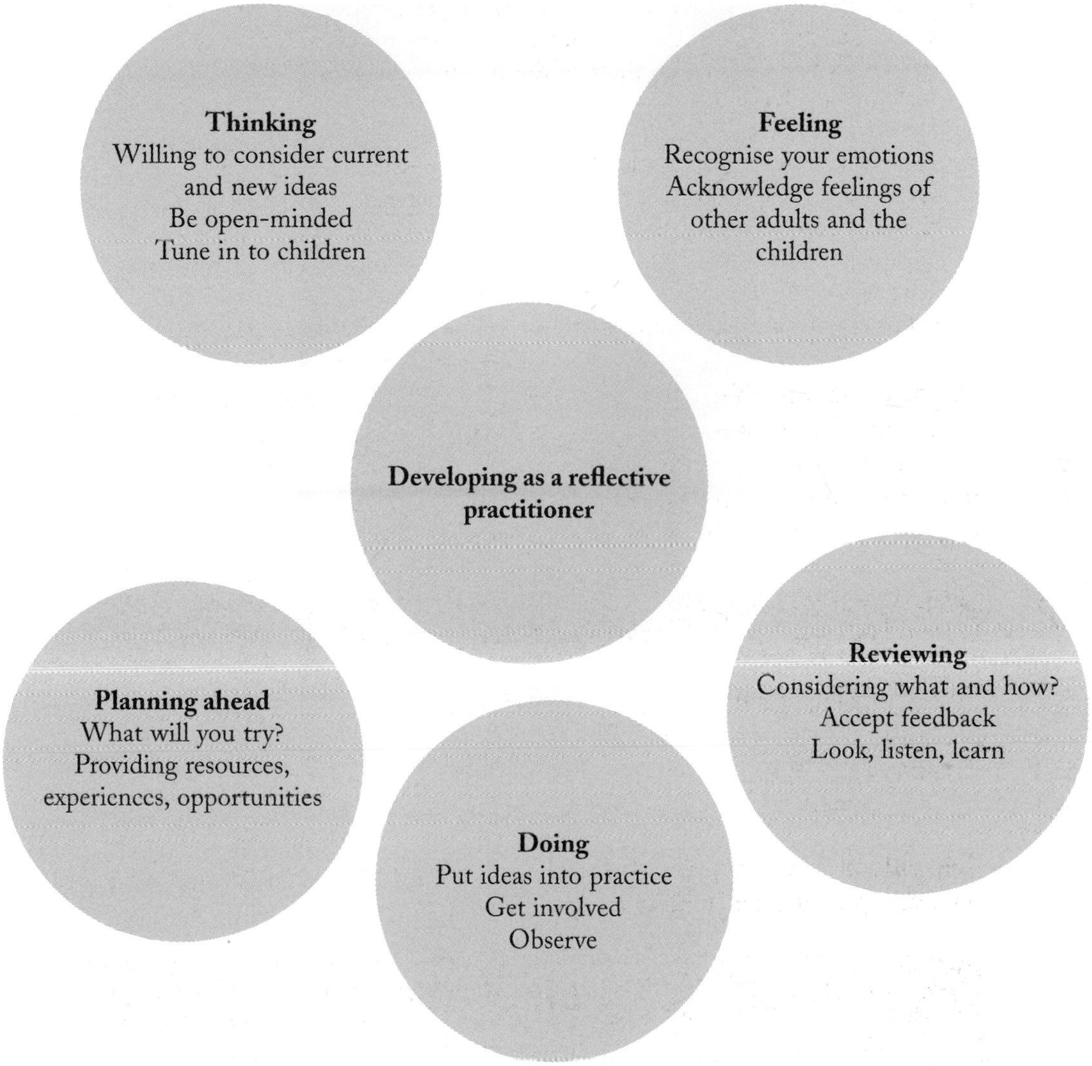

Fig. 1.1 *Being a reflective practitioner to support children*

The circles contain the following text:

Thinking
Willing to consider current
and new ideas
Be open-minded
Tune in to children

Feeling
Recognise your emotions
Acknowledge feelings of
other adults and the
children

Developing as a reflective practitioner

Reviewing
Considering what and how?
Accept feedback
Look, listen, learn

Planning ahead
What will you try?
Providing resources,
experiences, opportunities

Doing
Put ideas into practice
Get involved
Observe

Different disciplines and understanding development

Ideas about child development have been influenced, directly or indirectly, by several disciplines within the social and natural sciences, especially psychology, sociology, biology, medicine and philosophy.

Over several centuries, many books of advice for parents have been written by medical doctors, often from their experience as a general practitioner or a paediatrician. Only in more recent decades have developmental psychologists been regarded as the people to ask about children. The natural sciences have been important, not least because some of the

You will learn a great deal just by watching
what interests young children

recognisable 'big' names were not developmental psychologists at the outset.
Jean Piaget (page 35) was a zoologist with a passion for studying marine
life (who had had several papers published by the time he was 15 years of
age!) and the philosophy of knowledge. He wanted to find a link between
the two and decided to further his ideas by studying the development of
human children. His wife Valentine, a psychologist, made most of the early
observations and the rest, as they say, is history. Piaget was working on his
ideas throughout the 1920s and 1930s in Switzerland. At the same time,
Lev Vygotsky (page 39) was working in Russia. Vygotsky, a doctor,
also wanted to bring together biology and the fledgling science of
psychology.

In the second half of the twentieth century, boundaries between disciplines
became increasingly blurred. The 1960s wave of 'new universities' in the
UK took the radical step of bringing academic subjects together within
'schools of study'. This change created a large group of graduates, myself
included, who regarded it as normal to talk with people from other
disciplines. My undergraduate degree was an early 'blend' subject, social
psychology, and I worked alongside students of sociology, history,
geography, economics, philosophy and a few biologists. The experience left
me wanting to remain a psychologist, but open-minded about the source of
potential good ideas.

> **MAKE THE CONNECTION WITH ... SOCIAL CONSTRUCTIVISM**
>
> **Towards the end of the twentieth century, social constructivism grew to dominate early childhood studies as the theory of choice. This theoretical position is a conscious blend of several different disciplines (page 52). But this melting pot approach to ideas is relatively new in terms of the social history reflected in this chapter.**

Psychology has strongly influenced early years in terms of the theoretical background to what is viewed as good practice. For a long time, socio-cultural context was regarded as irrelevant in mainstream psychological research about children as well as about adults. More accurately, the particular socio-cultural context of western society, especially Europe and the USA, was taken as the template for 'normal'. Developmental psychology traditionally focused more on individual children rather than their social context, with the working assumption that what was observed or posed in theory was applicable to a 'universal child'. Some exploration was undertaken through cross-cultural psychology, a discipline that built bridges with anthropology.

By the late 1960s it was recognised that an excessive proportion of psychological 'knowledge' was based on experiments involving rats, psychology undergraduates and members of the US armed forces – all of whom were pressured to participate. Feminist re-working of psychology in the 1970s and 1980s challenged a discipline that had frequently operated as if males formed the template for normal behaviour. Social psychology formed a bridge to sociology, a subject traditionally more interested in social structures, with individuals in the background. Sociology diversified and some sociologists developed a strong interest in family experience and the sociology of childhood.

The natural sciences continue to be important for how we understand young children. Sources from biology have informed exploration of gender differences in behaviour and some aspects to children's play. Biological psychology has developed as a separate discipline. Neuroscience, and advances in computer technology, have pushed the boundaries of research into brain development.

What is meant by 'theory'?

The words 'theory' or 'theoretical perspective' are used in rather different ways and it is important to have clarity over meaning.

Theory in academic study

In the social sciences, a theory is a framework incorporating a set of ideas or principles that is used to guide the collection and interpretation of facts. Theories are sometimes developed from observations as the theorist strives to make sense of information that is already available. In a strict scientific definition, a theory should then generate clear-cut predictions that can be tested through research under controlled conditions (page 61). New information is gathered and interpreted to prove or disprove the theory.

WHAT DOES IT MEAN?

Theory: a set of ideas about experiences or events. As discussed in this section, 'theory' and 'theorists' can take on different meanings in practice.

Research: finding out about experiences and events. Researchers use a variety of methods (see Chapter 4). Some research plans rest upon theory.

Theory and academic practice

In reality, life is not that simple. Many theories within social science are not amenable to being proven one way or another, certainly not in the way meant by the physical sciences. Some limitations are properly placed by ethical considerations (page 65). However, all theorists and researchers operate within a time and place. Some research is easier to fund, and some theoretical concepts easier to promote, within one decade or cultural context than another. The main theories covered in Chapters 2 and 3 only make complete sense through their place on the social history time line.

Theorists are people too. The claims about objectivity and the reasoned weighing up of information do not always hold true. It is very tempting to make sense of information in the light of your own theory, rather than recognise that someone else's theoretical framework does an equally good or even a better job. Theory builders are creative thinkers and this process has a strong element of 'let's pretend':

■ *Let's pretend that the entire universe can be viewed as a kind of string* – a theory in physics that argues that physical matter consists of one-dimensional filaments that vibrate, a little like guitar strings, to create particles. No-one can see this 'string', but the concept was widely used over the last two decades of the twentieth century.

- *Let's pretend that all women experience penis envy* – the proposal of Sigmund Freud within his Psychoanalytic theory that female personal development is shaped by the realisation, at about four years of age, that they do not have this appendage.

Young children grasp the boundary between pretend and reality. They step away from 'let's pretend I'm a helicopter and my arms are those whirly things' in order to have lunch. Creative adult thinkers, whose theory is now enmeshed with their professional career, can find stepping away more of a struggle. The nature of academic debate around rival theories can surprise outsiders with the playground level of exchanges, despite the long words and complex sentences.

MAKE THE CONNECTION WITH ... CHILDREN AS THEORISTS

Everyone does some theorising, some level of abstract thinking, in order to make sense of the world and relationships. There seems to be a basic human need to bring some predictability out of an initially unfamiliar situation.

Young children try to work out what is happening and why. Partly they are fuelled by intellectual curiosity. However, children also feel more confident when there is tolerable certainty and reasonable predictability about daily life. It builds their sense of emotional security.

Children can work on the two broad patterns of theory building:

- *Inductive reasoning* – when you gather plenty of information and build your theory on that basis. Young children use this approach.

- *Deductive reasoning* – when you have a working theory and set up expectations on that basis. This pattern of theory-building is more typical of adolescents; children will only manage it in familiar circumstances.

See if you can identify simple examples of theory-building by children.

Why do practitioners need to know about theory?

Study of children and their development has included not only what happens as babies and children grow, but also an attempt to explain why and how development unfolds. The different broad theories of child development aim to show what is most important in that process.

Practitioners need a grasp of the range of theories that have been proposed to explain child development, otherwise it is easy to assume that one or two approaches you encounter are the whole range. Current theories are communicated to parents through advice and childcare books. Theory shapes educational philosophy and practice for school. In different decades, a dominant theory can become part of the cultural wallpaper and then basic assumptions are less likely to be challenged. By the start of the twenty-first century, the socio-cultural, or social constructivist, view has become prominent in early childhood studies and application to practice. There is much to value in this approach, but it is not the only way to explain child development or to approach good practice.

TAKE ANOTHER PERSPECTIVE

The word 'theory' is not always linked with its more academic meaning. In early years and school practice, the word is often used to mean:

- The developmental reasons for what is proposed as good practice.

- Information about child development: what usually happens at different ages and how that can be linked with realistic expectations.

- Ideas, anything that is not a suggested activity or requirement for action.

Different working definitions for 'theory' are not a problem – so long as it is clear which meaning is applicable right now. Chapters 2 and 3 cover more academic theories.

Readers who are college tutors will know that students are expected to link observations with some element of theory. This requirement is unworkable, especially before degree-level study, unless theory is defined loosely: key concepts and theoretical perspectives. Chapters 4–10 offer a range of concepts about good practice, with the underlying explanation.

WHAT DOES IT MEAN?

Theory of child development: a set of ideas proposed to explain how children develop and sometimes also to predict what will happen under certain circumstances.

Theoretical perspective: a particular angle on making sense of events or experiences.

Key concept: an idea, arising from a theory or theoretical perspective, that can be used to shape practice.

KEY ISSUES IN TRYING TO EXPLAIN CHILD DEVELOPMENT

Holistic development or different areas?

When you watch and listen to children it is very clear that they do not divide up their development. They move seamlessly from using their communication skills to question and speculate, using their physical skills to move from place to place and their thinking skills to work out how to assemble the materials they need to create a secret den. Children have no problem with holistic development: that all aspects of their current skills

Children operate within holistic development. What do you think they are learning?

work together with meaningful connections. Nor do children assign different values to the varied aspects of their learning, although they grasp very quickly if adults clearly value some skill areas, perhaps literacy, more than other abilities.

Anyone involved with children, for reasons of theory, research or practice, needs to keep a firm hold on holistic development. Often you will have good reason to focus on one aspect of development at a particular time. Good practice, and the task of a reflective practitioner, is to return frequently to the big picture of the whole child.

WHAT DOES IT MEAN?

A **holistic** or **whole child** approach stresses the importance of thinking about and behaving towards children as entire individuals, that all their skills are important and support their whole development.

For example, a more holistic approach through health psychology has shown that children's physical well-being cannot be separated from the rest of their development. Early psychological approaches to chronic illness treated children as if they were isolated individuals reacting passively to their illness.

- A child's illness affects their emotional well-being, but the impact is two-way. A depressed or frightened child copes less well with illness and medical intervention.

- Young children try to make sense of what is happening to them. In the absence of explanation and information, children may decide that illness or the need for surgery have been somehow caused by their 'bad' behaviour.

- Chronic illness or disability can affect family relationships and disrupt friendships. Children often need as much support for their social network as dealing with medical symptoms.

The balance between nature and nurture

A basic question asked about children is whether their development is determined by a pattern laid down before they were born, or whether children's reactions are the result of later experiences. This question sets the influence of nature (inborn reactions, heredity) in contrast with nurture (the impact of experience, their environment). The first answer is that matters are not as simple as, 'So, is it nature or nurture?'. Children's development is influenced by their genetic inheritance including how young brains develop. But there is ample evidence that direct experiences work on that biological base even before birth and certainly from the earliest days of infancy.

WHAT DOES IT MEAN?

Nature: a term used to mean all the influences separate from the impact of experience.

Biological programming: the basic materials with which babies are born, including how their brains work and body chemistry.

Nurture: a term used to mean all the influences other than genetics and biological programming.

Experience: what happens to babies and children, either through direct action by them, how they are treated by other people or how social circumstances affect them through their carers' behaviour.

Environment: usually means the physical features of the location in which children are raised, but is sometimes used interchangeably with experience.

A considerable amount of research has attempted to identify which individual differences are due to genetic factors, and to what extent. Until about the mid-1980s the balance was far more on considering how environment shaped children and the adults they became. This emphasis was a reaction against earlier approaches that had downplayed the impact of experience on children. No sensible psychologist or biologist talks any longer in 'either/or' terms about genetic and environmental factors. Patterns laid down through biological programming are only the beginning of the story of child development.

Computer imaging technology has allowed detailed study of the functioning of the brain. Young babies' brains are poised to develop and the early years are a time of impressive brain growth. However, detailed research has also shown the significant impact of experience on what and how babies and young children learn. New scientific and statistical techniques have also enabled a more sophisticated study of genetic patterns. Behaviour genetics is a relatively new area of research and studies have suggested that there is a genetic element in such varied areas as body shape, some aspects of cognitive problem-solving, reading disability, extreme anti-social behaviour and variations in temperament. This approach explores genetics as a possible explanation, talks about probabilities but not certainties.

TAKE ANOTHER PERSPECTIVE

Inequalities in society were a significant source of the resistance to biological explanations of developmental patterns and behaviour. Prevailing social values made a mockery of scientific claims of objectivity.

The feminist challenge was grounded in direct experience that male–female differences were so often interpreted in an evaluative way: that males were 'better'. Entrenched racial prejudice was entwined with attempts to track ethnic group identity and a genetic basis to intelligence.

Social inequalities are still a serious issue for contemporary society. But a more even-handed, less value-laden approach to the biological roots of development has allowed this important area of study to return.

Two periods in the lives of children seem to be particularly influenced by biological programming: the first year of life and puberty. At these times both babies and then adolescents experience substantial physical changes that happen without conscious effort on their part. However, even these powerful internal forces can be further shaped by the environment.

Development within the first year of life

Babies do not have to be taught to use their limbs, to crawl or walk; they naturally work on all the skills they possess. Yet malnutrition and severe restrictions on movement can limit babies' physical skills – a result of ill health and lack of necessary practice. However, even serious deprivation does not have the same impact on all babies. Studies of very poor practice in understaffed residential nurseries in the 1940s and 1950s produced distressing descriptions of babies in despair who lay silent in their cots all day. Yet, other babies, less than one year old, were trying again and again to climb out of their cot and attract attention. Similar desperate circumstances were revealed in the orphanages in Romania in the 1990s (page 87).

How do young brains develop?

Research into neuroscience over the last decades of the twentieth century has dramatically changed the view of babies and their capabilities. The brain of the human foetus develops rapidly, especially in the last three months before birth. The brain of a full-term newborn contains a staggering 100 billion neurons. The biological material is ready to use. However, the human brain is not fixed like a machine just waiting for birth to push the switch. On the contrary, the newborn's brain is poised to develop as a network of possibilities and direct experience creates those connections.

However, experience has already exerted an impact before birth. Neurons are active before birth and active brain cells generate minute amounts of measurable electrical activity. However, the brain cells of a human foetus do not fire at random. Activity seems to prime the system, especially in those parts of the brain that will deal with vision and hearing. This incredibly early learning through experience means that some newborns do recognise sounds they have heard before birth, such as a parent's voice or the song that a mother sang to the child who will be this baby's older sibling.

The brain of a full-term infant weighs about 350 g at birth. This weight trebles over twelve months to reach about 1000 g by one year old. Brain development continues so that the brain weighs about 1300 g at puberty and 1500 g in adulthood. This striking growth rate in early infancy is unique to humans. The difference in a human brain between birth and adulthood is not about sheer weight or volume; it is not simply more of the same. The brain cells have become heavier because of the many connections that have been made between neurons through experience.

The experience of puberty

Human brains continue to develop; we could not learn in adulthood otherwise. The early years are very busy, but there is another significant burst of brain activity in adolescence. Teenage brains are working hard to integrate the different functions and areas of the brain, especially those concerned with self-control, emotional judgement, organisation and planning. Teenagers can legitimately blame the emotional see-saw of adolescence on the frenetic activity of their brains!

Around the world young people experience puberty at some time between nine and sixteen years of age. The exact timing of the onset is largely a result of individual biological programming. However, puberty can be delayed by restricted diet and a great deal of physical exercise. The childlike appearance of some female gymnasts in the 1980s was caused by extremely vigorous training programmes, which have since been described as abusive.

In the first half of the twentieth century, the average age of onset for puberty decreased in the western world. The main reasons seem to have been a less physically active life style for many children, combined with sufficient food for physical needs.

As you yourself will recall, puberty is more than just physical changes. It is also an emotional experience and one which brings social adjustments. The individual experience of puberty for each boy or girl is affected by social environment. Biological programming does not determine the support, or lack of it, received from family and friends, nor how your social environment helps you to feel positive, or negative, about becoming more grown up.

Theory, evidence and wisdom

Theories can guide us in making sense of what is happening to children and offer useful explanations of how children develop. Key concepts can lead to practical ideas that will help you support children in their learning and puzzle out what they do not understand. You will soon realise that some theories take such diverse viewpoints that their respective supporters will never reach agreement. As a practitioner who is useful to children, you need to keep an open mind and look for what you can take away from the different perspectives. Contrary to what enthusiastic theorists will sometimes claim, there is no evidence that any one group has cornered the market in completely understanding young children in all their complexity.

In early years work, as in many practical professions, knowledge has been gained from two main sources:

- *Evidence* is gathered from the systematic use of research methods through which information is gathered and interpreted.

- *Wisdom* is gained through insights that emerge through daily practice, what seems to work best and learning from colleagues, often but not always more experienced in years.

Knowledge gleaned only from 'evidence' or from 'wisdom' can be of limited value on its own. When research knowledge is uninformed by the wisdom of practitioners, it can appear irrelevant to real dilemmas. However, well-planned research, when researchers take care to examine their assumptions, can test the 'everybody knows' statements about practice with children that otherwise continue unchallenged.

On the other hand, wisdom gained through experience, either directly or from that of other people, needs to be responsive to research findings. Otherwise, practice can stagnate. Experienced practitioners need to share the wisdom they have gained. However, their experience is most effective when they have reflected on the reasons for what they do and can share those as well as the details of practice.

USING THIS BOOK AS A RESOURCE

This chapter has addressed some broad issues about linking knowledge and practice. Chapters 2 and 3 explain the different families of theories that have shaped views on good practice: biological-maturation, environmental-learning, cognitive-developmental and socio-cultural. Like any categorisation, the division is not perfect, but I believe it creates a more helpful framework than taking one theorist at a time. Chapter 4 describes different ways of studying children and considers practical issues about making sense of research. Chapters 5–10 then take different aspects of child development and childhood. Each chapter considers some key concepts and approaches that can inform good daily practice.

My aim throughout is for readers to be able to consider and apply the ideas. So you will find some material set out of the main text, so that you can take an idea further in some way. These different features are:

- *What does it mean?* Definitions of words or phrases are placed close to where the concept is first mentioned. All terms are also listed in the index.

- *Make the connection with . . .* This feature will encourage you to link ideas or create a direct connection with your practice.

- *Take another perspective* will be an invitation to look at an idea, an activity or experience from another angle. Sometimes the invitation will include reflection on your own experience.

- *Look, listen, note, learn* will offer suggestions for an observation or specific activity, with the aim that you can then reflect on good practice.

Many readers will want to follow up ideas, right away or later. So I have provided more information in two ways:

- *If you want to find out more* gives the main resources for each chapter and is placed at the end of each chapter. If a reference is not there, you will find it in the main bibliography from page 257.

- *Using further resources* – a section from page 252 provides a range of sources of information and a full bibliography.

Sometimes I have summarised a large area of research and full references would stretch over many pages. Everyone needs a reliable child psychology textbook. You may have your own favourite, but these are my key sources:

▨ Bee, Helen and Boyd, Denise 2004 *The developing child* (tenth edition). Boston MA: Pearson.

▨ Cole, Michael and Cole, Sheila 2000 *The development of children* (fourth edition). New York: Worth Publishers.

2 Explaining child development: weighing up nature and nurture

In Chapter 1 you will have read that few theorists or researchers would now try to argue for a stark choice between nature or nurture. However, the social history of explaining child development includes some theorists with firm inclinations weighted towards biology or the impact of experience.

Many early years practitioners are aware of the ideas of Jean Piaget and Lev Vygotsky and these theorists are discussed in Chapter 3. Piaget and Vygotsky developed their theories over the 1920s and 1930s, but neither theory gained much attention outside their immediate circle for approximately 30 years. The first half of the twentieth century was dominated by the psychoanalytic theory of Sigmund Freud and the behaviourism of B. F. Skinner. Neither of these theorists made the detailed observations of children gathered by Piaget or Vygotsky. As Alison Gopnik *et al.* comment, 'Freud largely relied on inferences from the behaviour of neurotic adults and Skinner on inferences from the behaviour of only slightly less neurotic rats' (2001: 19). However, both theories have diversified since their infancy.

The main sections in this chapter are:

▦ Biological-maturation theories.

▦ Environmental-learning theories.

BIOLOGICAL-MATURATION THEORIES

Some theories focus especially on the impact of biological and maturational processes on human development. The focus of all biological theories is that the patterns of development that everyone shares and our individual differences are based in:

▦ The instructions laid down in the genes – an inherited pattern – and control exerted by hormones.

▦ The patterns of maturation triggered by messages from the brain, including human body chemistry.

▦ Inevitable patterns that arise from biological constitution and basic human drives.

Theorists who ground their ideas in biology do not usually claim that the environment has no part to play. They argue that genetic programming and the internal workings of the brain are a powerful influence and should not be discounted. Biological-maturation theories were largely out of favour by the mid-twentieth century, but there is now renewed interest in the biological basis to development and behaviour patterns.

A process of maturation

Arnold Gesell and his colleagues, working in the USA during the 1920s and 1930s, established a maturational approach to child development which still exerts influence today. Gesell believed that the sequence of development for babies and children was controlled by a process of maturation, which means the emergence of physical characteristics that are shared by all members of a species is triggered by the information in the genes. He believed that the environment has a supportive role, but that the push towards change was internal to the child.

Gesell and his team studied babies and children in great detail and their descriptions were very specific to particular ages. Their research work was extended into developmental tests for assessing babies and children. The ideas of 'milestones' and 'developmental norms' largely emerged from Gesell's work. The maturational approach, as developed by Gesell, influenced advice books for parents through the 1940s and 1950s. Some writers were very specific about what 'your child should be doing' at given ages. A related idea that passed into advice for parents was that babies and children would achieve the different developmental stages and skills when they were ready and that certain kinds of behaviour, such as two-year-old tantrums, were 'phases' that would pass.

WHAT DOES IT MEAN?

Maturational theory: the approach that there is a developmental sequence of changes, controlled by instructions in the genetic code that is shared by all children.

Developmental norms: statements about what a child is likely to be able to do or understand within a given age range.

Developmental milestones: term often used for what are seen as the more important achievements for children in different areas of their development.

The maturational approach to child development stimulated a tremendous interest in the detail of what children did. The focus on 'normal' development was a contrast with the psychoanalytical approach, also prominent at this time, which highlighted so much that could apparently go wrong. The maturational approach reassured parents that they were not personally responsible for every hiccup in their child's development. This removal of blame could be a relief. On the other hand, if development unfolded whatever adults did, the maturational approach did not generate ideas of how parents could help, beyond sitting out a phase like tantrums.

Do we need developmental norms?

A rigid approach to developmental norms failed to allow for the variety within a given culture. However, the early maturation approach to 'normal' child development was also strongly based in a western and Euro-centric context. The idea of a 'universal child' has been roundly criticised since the 1980s, at the same time as far greater awareness has grown of cultural variations in child rearing. An additional concern is that children with disabilities could seem to be invisible in terms of normal development and be defined largely by their failure to reach milestones on time.

LOOK, LISTEN, NOTE, LEARN

Consider and write down the main ways in your own practice that you use information about child development.

- How do you ensure that your expectations are realistic for this age group?

- How do you decide whether to be concerned about a child?

- How do you deal with parents' concerns when you judge they are expecting too much, or too little, of their children?

- How do you build awareness that a disabled child may be progressing well in one area of development yet struggling in another, or may be developing at a slower pace?

However, good daily practice with young children is impossible without some framework of knowledge to inform realistic expectations for children within a broad age range. This professional need was met for many years in the UK by Mary Sheridan's *Children's developmental progress from birth to five years: the Stycar sequences*. This booklet was first published in 1960 and went through many reprints with the National Foundation for Educational Research. Sheridan followed with *Spontaneous play in early childhood: from birth to six years* (1977, also with the NFER). These publications are still mainly reliable but, in a more diverse society, they increasingly looked mono-cultural in aspects such as dress and eating utensils. The need for information was met by publications such as Lindon (1993) and Meggitt and Sutherland (2000).

Of course, it is important to be flexible about using broad developmental expectations. Children vary in the age at which they manage all the different skills of their development. It is certainly not possible to make absolute statements along the lines of, 'At 14 months all toddlers will be able to ...'. Nor should practitioners focus only on those skills that are listed on a developmental profile. Even the longest record sheets cannot

Toddlers have a strong drive to use their physical skills

include every interesting development. Good practice is to be alert to children who are doing well for their age and may need more challenge in everyday activities. However, early years practitioners should also be aware, in a constructive way, of those children who are struggling and need some extra help. You need a sound basis to answer the question 'When should we worry?'. It is possible to build a flexible use of developmental norms without signing up to rigid maturational theory.

MAKE THE CONNECTION WITH ... REALISTIC EXPECTATIONS

- The Effective Provision of Pre-School Education (EPPE) project (page 68) raised the importance of knowledge of child development for good early years practice. You need reliable information to make sense of how best to relate to children and to hold realistic expectations.

- The pressing need to ground expectations in knowledge of young children is raised in some sections of this book, for example early literacy (page 155) and anti-discriminatory practice (page 245).

A biological basis for human behaviour

The development of attachment

Biologically, humans are part of the mammal family of creatures. A strand of theory and study has looked for connections between human behaviour and that of our closest animal relatives. Konrad Lorenz, a zoologist working in Austria from the 1930s observed animal behaviour and was the founder of the discipline of ethology. Lorenz showed that there were crucial periods in the early days of mammals, and some birds, when attachment had to take place between infant and mother. Some patterns of animal behaviour seemed to be innate, that is, animals were born with these tendencies, they did not learn the behaviour through experience.

In the later part of his career, Lorenz applied his ideas to human behaviour. John Bowlby, working in the UK from the 1940s used the studies to explain the early attachment behaviour of human infants. Bowlby believed that the development of attachment specifically between baby and mother was an innately driven set of behaviours that protected infants at a vulnerable time.

A biological basis for play

There has also been interest in the possible biological origins of children's play. Young mammals all show apparently spontaneous, playful behaviour with their peers. You will observe such activity if you watch young lambs in the fields or watch nature television programmes about the cat and monkey/ape families. Young mammals, besides human children, use props in their play: logs for jumping, materials that can be dragged by limb or jaw and sticks held by young apes or monkeys.

The biological explanation for playful behaviour is that it has a survival function for young mammals. They practise physical skills useful for adult life. The playful exchanges between youngsters build social connections that support troupe life for mammals who live in large extended groups. Immature mammals copy the actions of their elders, learning some skills that are crucial for obtaining food and for self care. Playful behaviour is common in young mammals raised in groups and only extreme social deprivation seems to prevent that development. The conclusion drawn is that playful and exploratory behaviour is part of the mammal and, therefore, part of human biological programming for life. Play is not instinctive, that is to say the behaviour is not automatically triggered, but young mammals seem to be predisposed to play.

LOOK, LISTEN, NOTE, LEARN

See if you can engage children in an exploration about 'is it only children who play?'. Three-year-olds may manage a conversation but this activity is far more likely to make sense to four- or five-year-olds. You might start with, 'I was wondering . . .' and explore:

- Whether children have observations of their own pets or animals within their extended family.

- Children living in, or who visit, rural areas may have watched lambs or calves in the fields.

- In partnership with parents you might weave in a nature and animal documentary programme on the television.

- What do children think? Are the animals playing? What games or toys do they seem to like? Do only children and animals play . . . do adults play?

The psychoanalytic approach

Sigmund Freud

Freud worked largely in Vienna, Austria from the 1890s, developing a clinical practice in neuropsychology. He worked from case studies and adult patients, and also, it would now appear, from his own personal traumas. Freud became convinced that energy from the libido, an unconscious sexual drive, was the force behind most human behaviour. His emphasis on biological motivation places him with this grouping of theories. However, his emphasis on the emotional life of children and adults led to the very different psychoanalytic tradition that began in the late nineteenth and early twentieth centuries. The theory was also linked with Freud's development of a form of therapy called psychoanalysis. This approach to therapy has diversified since that time and the general therapeutic approach is called psychodynamic.

Freud developed a theory of stages in children's development in which the libido exerted most impact in the part of a child's body that was sensitive at that age. Freud proposed five psychosexual stages: oral, anal, phallic, latency and genital. Freud believed that, at each stage, children needed sufficient stimulation for the area of their body in which key sensations were focused. He proposed that over- or under-stimulation led individuals to become fixated, by which he meant that they were stuck at that particular developmental stage, continuing to struggle in adult life with that unresolved emotional conflict. This theory claimed that the basics of adult personality were determined by the time a child reached five years of age.

Psychoanalytic theory moved on from biological drives to emphasise that behaviour was shaped by unconscious thoughts and feelings, as well as conscious processes. Some material in the unconscious can only rise to full awareness if people are prepared to explore the possibility either in personal introspection or through therapy. A further development in Freud's theory was that anxiety gives rise to conflict, which children and later adults manage through a range of defence mechanisms. These forms of self-protection work at the unconscious level. Freud regarded them as psychologically healthy, unless they led to a serious distortion of reality. The concept of defence mechanisms has entered much of ordinary conversation, for example, Freud's explanation of suppression, when an unhappy experience or uncomfortable dilemma is pushed to the back of your mind. Another defence strategy is that of projection: dealing with anxiety or inability to cope by claiming another person feels the same way – not you.

Psychoanalytic theory has a wealth of ideas but very few are open to proper testing through informal observation or research. Some ideas, such as the mechanism of denial or the idea of infantile sexuality, can be presented in such a circular way that they defy any challenge. The application of Freudian ideas to child development has sometimes led to a depressing view of childhood and family life as a minefield of problems. Some stages, for instance that of adolescence, have been presented as considerably more fraught than is the experience of many families.

The striking contribution of psychoanalytic theory was to highlight unconscious feelings and thoughts; that everything is not described by what we observe on the surface. This focus led Freud and his fellow theorists to be in continuous argument with the behaviourists (page 26). The importance of feelings, for children and their parents, was in striking contrast to the fierce training approaches to childcare of behaviourists such as John Watson. Benjamin Spock was very influenced by Freud and his best-selling *Common sense book of baby and child care* (published in 1946 and over 50 million copies sold!) brought psychoanalytic theory into ordinary homes from the 1940s. Spock changed the detail of his advice over the decades and the latest edition runs to 806 pages (co-authored with Stephen Palmer, 1997).

You may well feel that Freud and his ideas are ancient history. But psychoanalytic theory has exerted a significant influence on western thought, as much for the breakaway groups as for the original ideas. By the second decade of the twentieth century, there were fierce arguments within the group. Some theorists left on a permanent basis, to develop their own distinct approach. Many of the disagreements were about Freud's strong emphasis on the sexual drive as the main explanation of development.

Alfred Adler

Adler was a doctor who explored psychopathology, working closely with Freud in Vienna until 1911, when he left Freud's circle to develop what he called individual psychology. Adler and his followers emphasised the struggle against feelings of inferiority and increasingly explored children's life within their family, especially the impact of birth order on the experiences of childhood. Adler believed children's behaviour, and later that of adults, was shaped by their interpretations of what happened in social interactions. Children developed a belief system about themselves and their sense of self-worth, which in turn influenced their abilities to relate to other people in a sense of shared social interest.

Alfred Adler and another Austrian doctor, Rudolf Dreikurs, developed the first child guidance clinics in Vienna. These were all closed by the Austrian government in 1934 and Dreikurs emigrated to the USA in 1937. Alfred Adler had been visiting regularly since the 1920s. Rudolf Dreikurs developed Adler's ideas into a practical approach to guiding children's behaviour that has been influential in some parenting programmes. A key idea has been that adults can guide children's outlook and behaviour in a more positive manner once they recognise the purpose behind the child's behaviour. Dreikurs developed concepts to bring together emotions and behaviour, the importance of encouragement and using consequences rather than punishment (see Chapter 9).

Erik Erikson

Erikson was born in Germany and became interested in psychoanalysis in the late 1920s after meeting Anna Freud, who had joined her father in the psychoanalytic movement. In 1933 Erikson emigrated to the USA and by the late 1930s he began to study cultural influences on child development, especially the experiences of children from different American Indian groups. Consequently, Erikson developed his theory that all societies formulate a social response to deal with similar problems within personality development – yet the exact solutions differ. By 1950, he had finalised his view of psychosocial development: a sequence of stages that were strongly influenced by the society in which children were raised.

Erikson viewed behaviour as fuelled by the series of basic tasks, or dilemmas, that children face at different ages. Erikson made sense of development through how children resolved these tasks, sometimes presented as crises. He proposed that in the first year, babies face the dilemma of basic trust versus mistrust: of the predictability of the world, of their ability to affect events and the behaviour of key people around them. By the time young children reach two and three years of age, their dilemma is to weigh up autonomy versus shame and doubt. The toddlers' increased mobility enables them to act more independently, but this development is balanced against the reaction of others to their actions and the need to learn some self-control. By four and up to five years of age Erikson argued that children's main task was to resolve initiative versus guilt. Young children's physical and intellectual abilities allow them to be creative but this activity has to be balanced with learning limits, from a growing sense of conscience and boundaries set by adults.

In Erikson's theory, children's behaviour will be shaped by how they balance the competing possibilities of each dilemma and reach some degree of resolution. Balance is a key issue since young children need, for instance, some level of wariness. Total and undiscriminating trust would not be a psychologically healthy outlook. Erikson also diverged from original Freudian theory by taking a view of developmental change that stretched into young adulthood, rather than being essentially complete by five years of age. Erikson thought that middle childhood was the time for dealing with a dilemma between industry (or competence) versus inferiority.

Adolescence was the period when young people explored and re-examined their personal identity in a dilemma of identity versus role confusion.

Psychoanalytic theory in England

The psychoanalytic movement remained strong in Austria until Freud escaped from the Nazi occupation in 1938 with his youngest daughter, Anna. They settled in London and Anna Freud was irritated to find that the ideas of Melanie Klein were already well established. Klein, another Austrian psychoanalyst, had moved to London in 1926. She had diverged from traditional Freudian theory to focus almost exclusively on the very early years of the mother–child relationship, as the forum for powerful infant emotional impulses. Anna Freud had to use funds from the USA to set up her nursery and she established the Hampstead Child Therapy Clinic. In 1984, two years after her death, the Anna Freud Centre was established and continues to support children and their families.

Susan Isaacs worked in England from the 1920s and was initially influenced by the ideas of Melanie Klein. A common thread between Klein and Freud was that they both believed that the unconscious life of children, including the emotional conflicts underpinning the development of identity, was revealed through the themes and symbols of children's play, especially imaginary play. Susan Isaacs parted company with this psychoanalytic tradition once she came to believe that children's play had a broader developmental function than reflecting emotional turmoil. She set up the Malting House School (sometimes called The Maltings) in Cambridge, with a liberal philosophy that created local ripples at the time over the children's behaviour.

Susan Isaacs is significant because her ideas have affected early years theory and practice. She exerted a direct influence during the 1930s under the name Ursula Wise, when she answered readers' questions on the problem page of *Nursery World*. Through observation at her school, Isaacs became as interested in studying children's thinking processes as in their emotional life. She was very clear that her teachers should not try to act as analysts for the children. She continued to believe that symbolic and fantasy play could be a release for children's feelings and that children work through deep emotional problems within their play. However, she believed that children's play had an equally important educational function.

Isaacs drew on a range of theoretical sources, including the ideas of Jean Piaget (page 35). Susan Isaacs seems to be the source for the concept that children's play should be respected just as much as adults' work. She wrote that, 'play is indeed the children's work, and the means by which he or she grows and develops' (1929).

The ideas of both Anna Freud and Melanie Klein influenced the development of play therapy in the UK, although once again later ideas have diverged and many therapists do not subscribe to any version of Freudian theory. The psychoanalytic approach has supported very detailed observations of babies and children, with their families but also in out-of-home care, such as day nurseries. This tradition has promoted careful practice, the importance of personal relationships and the necessity of a key person system in group care (page 91). You do not have to agree with all the theoretical concepts behind some of this research (I certainly take issue with some!) to recognise the value of the application to practice and the emotional well-being of young children.

ENVIRONMENTAL-LEARNING THEORIES

Most theorists who focus on the impact of the environment and learning through experience do not deny the impact of biological factors. It is a matter of balance, of believing that the major causes of developmental change are located in the child's environment, or that such a focus gives far more scope for effective action to support development.

Learning theory developed as the major competitor with psychoanalytic theory in the first quarter of the twentieth century. Learning theorists focus on what children, or adults, learn through experience and the consequences of their behaviour. So this approach is sometimes called behaviourism. In basic terms behaviour is understood to change following patterns of reward and punishment. The extreme behaviourist stance, which few theorists now take, was that newborn babies start with biological reflexes, but everything else is then learned through direct experience.

Learning through conditioning

The principles of learning theory were first explored in work with animals and three names are most associated with this aspect of behaviourist theory:

- *Ivan Pavlov* was a Russian doctor whose research into the digestion of animals led him by the late 1890s to formulate his laws of the conditioned reflex. By the 1930s Pavlov worked to apply his ideas to explain human psychiatric problems. Pavlov's ideas are called classical conditioning.

- *John Watson* was a psychologist working in the USA from the early part of the twentieth century. By the 1920s and 1930s, Watson's theory of behaviourism dominated psychology. He asserted that human behaviour should, like any animal behaviour, be studied under exacting conditions in an experimental laboratory. Watson resigned his post as a professor in 1920 after adverse publicity around his divorce. He then promoted his ideas through books, including emotion-free childcare advice for parents. His firm ideas still echo in claims that babies are spoiled if you pick them up when they cry.

- *B. F. Skinner* (always known in this form – his first names were Burrhus Frederic) was a psychologist working in the USA from the 1930s. Skinner was strongly influenced by the ideas of Pavlov and Watson. He developed ideas that were known as 'instrumental' or 'operant' conditioning (the term operant is now more usual).

The simple, rather mechanical-sounding explanations of the early work based on dogs, rats and pigeons do not make much sense when applied directly to humans. Much like the psychoanalytic tradition, the diversification of ideas in the following decades has led theorists a long distance from the first theoretical perspective. However, you need to understand the basics, in order to make sense of how learning theory then developed.

Classical conditioning occurs when a new signal or stimulus brings out an existing behavioural response. A simple example would be that, if you stroke a young baby gently on the cheek, she will automatically turn and begin to suck. She does not have to learn to turn and suck. It is an automatic reflex with which babies are born – and a very useful one if you are trying to get a distracted baby to feed. Classical conditioning involves an involuntary response – the response is not chosen, but is an in-built physical reaction.

In classical conditioning terms, the touch on the baby's cheek is the unconditioned stimulus and the turning and sucking is the unconditioned response ('unconditioned' because the baby does not have to learn either of these). Now, other events (stimuli) can become associated with the unconditioned stimulus of touch. For instance, perhaps the mother talks gently as she picks the baby up for a feed or some babies seem to recognise the mother's familiar smell and the baby starts to turn and try to suck without the touch on the cheek. The sound of mother's words or her body smell have become a conditioned stimulus and the sucking is now a conditioned response to learned patterns.

B. F. Skinner explored a second type of learning through direct experience, called operant conditioning. This process involves linking a new response to an existing stimulus. In contrast, classical conditioning links an existing response to a new stimulus. The change is achieved through the principles of reinforcement. Any behaviour (response) that is reinforced is likely to be repeated in the same or similar situation in which the reinforcement (stimulus) previously happened. In contrast with classical conditioning, operant conditioning involves a deliberate action as response.

LOOK, LISTEN, NOTE, LEARN

- Classical conditioning makes sense as a process of learning when feelings and senses are involved. People and places can become associated at the most basic, and non-rational way, with both pleasant and unpleasant events for children. These reactions are personal and can last a long time.

- My stomach still churns in reaction to a distinctive aroma of institutional cooking. The smell brings back an unhappy memory of being forced to eat a 'disgusting' school dinner at the age of five. On the other hand, the smell of coal dust has positive associations for me. It triggers happy memories of playing in my grandparents' garden in a Welsh mining village.

- Think for a while and you will almost certainly come up with similar personal examples of an association.

Through these processes, Skinner trained laboratory birds and animals to perform complex actions, including getting pigeons to play a kind of table tennis. He applied the ideas to human learning processes to propose the efficiency of programmed learning by teaching machines, by which children or adults could learn at their own pace, rewarded for correct responses.

MAKE THE CONNECTION WITH ... STEP-BY-STEP LEARNING

There have been practical applications of the behaviourist approach in carefully structured learning programmes for children, including those for children with physical or learning disabilities. It is possible to use the ideas without the queasy lack of emotion proposed by Skinner or Watson. A focus on the step-by-step learning has been valuable in illuminating all the finer developments that are very important to notice, teach and reward when children's development may be slower or different from that of their peers. An example would be the practical ideas behind the Portage system, a home-visiting educational programme first developed in Portage, USA, during the early 1970s. See their website http://www.portage.org.uk

TAKE ANOTHER PERSPECTIVE

It is intriguing to note that the logical ideas of B. F. Skinner depended partly on chance and human error. The story, allegedly behind his discovery that reinforcement did not have to happen every time, was that one night the equipment went haywire, or possibly a hapless research assistant failed to check. The next morning the pigeons were performing bizarre movements for no apparent reason. Investigation showed that the equipment had been delivering the reward food pellets in an unpredictable way. The pigeons were now repeating actions they happened to be making when the food arrived. It did not matter that this movement did not work every time; it worked often enough for a pigeon. The concept of partial reinforcement was born.

Social learning theory

Early behaviourist theory depended on research with animals but soon the ideas were applied to explain and predict human behaviour, including that of children. There are two basic propositions in behaviourist learning theory:

1   Behaviour is strengthened by reinforcement.

2   Behaviour that is reinforced on a partial schedule is stronger, more resistant to stopping altogether, than behaviour that has been reinforced every time.

However, explanations of children's learning do not work well if they depend entirely on classical and operant conditioning and the kind of rewards attractive to dogs or rats. Through the 1960s, Albert Bandura, a psychologist working in the USA, developed his theory of social learning.

He noted that a powerful predictor of children's behaviour was what they could directly observe of other children's or adults' behaviour. Bandura added the significance of personal feelings of reinforcement and the link between thinking and observational learning. The more sophisticated approach of social learning theory provides explanations with greater flexibility. The ideas make more sense applied to the lives of children, as opposed to pigeons, even those who can play table tennis!

Bandura's social learning approach added two more key propositions about the process of learning:

3   Children learn new behaviours mainly through the process of modelling – adults' showing through their behaviour what is wanted.

Internal satisfaction starts young

4 Children do not only learn actual behaviours, they also learn ideas, expectations and develop internal standards.

The basic explanation of behaviourism is that reinforcement increases the likelihood that behaviour of children or adults will be repeated. Behaviour may be strengthened by positive or negative reinforcement.

▨ **Positive reinforcement** is the addition to the situation of something pleasant. Reinforcement might be tangible rewards, such as sweets or a prize. However, with children, it is just as likely to be a smile or hug and words of praise. When positive reinforcement is present after an action it increases the likelihood of that action.

▨ **Negative reinforcement** is the removal of something unpleasant or unwanted from the situation. For instance, perhaps a child does not want to go to bed. She whines and finds excuses to stretch out the bedtime routine. Her parent persists for a while in saying 'hurry up!' and shouting 'get upstairs, it's bedtime' but soon gives up and lets the child settle on the sofa. The child's strategy has been strengthened because the unwanted going to bed has been postponed.

▨ **Partial reinforcement** is a pattern in which behaviour is not reinforced (positively or negatively) every single time. Ordinary life for children tends to follow this pattern, since even adults who try to be consistent do not achieve total consistency. Learning on the basis of partial reinforcement is stronger, since individuals sometimes persist with patterns of behaviour. Experience has informed them that reinforcement does not occur every time (positively or negatively), but the pattern is sufficiently frequent to support perseverance.

Reinforcement strengthens a pattern of behaviour – increasing the likelihood. On the other hand, punishment may weaken the pattern.

- **Punishment** is the removal of something pleasant from the situation (refusal of sweets, cancelling treats or privileges) or the addition of something unpleasant (criticism and nagging, making children do disliked chores, insisting on silence or physical punishment such as hitting). In human interactions, punishment is used with the intention of stopping a given behaviour, although the results are unpredictable. Children, and adults too, may simply become secretive, ensuring that they are not observed.

- **Extinction** is a term that describes the complete removal of a pattern of behaviour; it no longer occurs.

PLEASE NOTE: A COMMON MISREPRESENTATION

Punishment is **not** the same as negative reinforcement. I stress this point because it is now common to find writers of general childcare and early childhood studies books who wrongly state that negative reinforcement is the addition of something negative. In behaviourist theory, reinforcement always increases the likelihood of a given behaviour. Unfortunately this misinformation is now being repeated, as readers understandably trust a textbook. You will find more about negative reinforcement on page 201.

Intrinsic reinforcements

Albert Bandura emphasised that feelings shape behaviour through internally experienced rewards such as a sense of personal satisfaction and pride in managing something. These feelings are unlikely to emerge spontaneously and familiar carers have an important role to play. Adults not only share their own delight in what children manage but, through their own adult behaviour, can encourage children to relish a sense of personal achievement and to work for that, not just for tangible rewards. Indeed, an over-emphasis on rewarding children for specific 'good' behaviour can persuade them they are only working towards the tangible reward and internal satisfaction reward is lost (page 200).

Thinking and observational learning

Bandura further extended his version of learning theory to cover how children are not passive observers, or unthinking imitators, and began to refer to his approach as social cognitive theory. Bandura's ideas are a reminder that many theories of direct relevance to work with children are a blend of different approaches. In some ways Bandura has more in common with the family of cognitive-developmental theories than with behaviourism.

MAKE THE CONNECTION WITH ... ENDURING PERSONALITY TRAITS

Albert Bandura believed that human learning does not always require the kind of direct and visible reinforcement described in operant conditioning. His ideas were also shaped by a 1928 study by American psychologists Hugh Hartshorne and Mark May. They created an experimental situation in which 10–13-year-olds had the choice to yield to the possibility of cheating and stealing, or to be honest and considerate of their peers. The study showed that the children were not consistently honest or dishonest (the idea that honesty would be a fixed trait of character by this age). The best prediction for the children's choice of behaviour was the actions of the other children around them.

Bandura developed his ideas that children learn through observation of others, familiar adults and other children: they look for a model to imitate. Over the period when he was working, Bandura was also able to note that children observed others through the medium of television.

If you watch children you will be struck by the extent to which they copy others; the motivation to imitate seems strong. In family life especially, the wish to copy is fuelled also by the strong attachments made by many children to their parents.

Bandura proposed that the extent to which children learn through observation of others does not depend only on what there is to observe around them. The end result will also be affected by:

- The exact focus of children's attention.

- What they are able to remember.

- What children can physically copy, given their skills at the time.

- What they are motivated to imitate. Children are far less likely to copy an adult whom they dislike, unless it is in mockery.

Bandura also proposed that children develop abstract ideas from observational learning: working out what is admired or disliked behaviour, developing attitudes and a sense of their own worth.

WHAT DOES IT MEAN?

Behaviourism or learning theory: a set of theoretical propositions that focus on the impact of experience in shaping how animals, including humans, behave.

Social learning theory: a development of behaviourism to recognise that human behaviour is further shaped by feelings, direct observation and thinking about experiences.

Modelling: learning through imitation of another child or an adult whose actions are then copied. This term is also used to mean deliberate actions to provide a model to imitate.

If you want to find out more:

☆ **Gopnik, Alison; Meltzoff, Andrew** and **Kuhl, Patricia** 2001 *How babies think: the science of childhood*. London: Phoenix.

Readable account of what has been discovered by careful research with very young children and the ideas behind making sense of early development.

☆ **Lindon, Jennie** 1993 *Child development from birth to eight: a practical focus*. London: National Children's Bureau.

Helps with information about developmental norms and links to good practice. But Meggitt and Sutherland have better photographs!

☆ **Lindon, Jennie** 1996 *Growing up: from eight years to young adulthood*. London: National Children's Bureau

Continuing the information into the teenage years.

☆ **Meggitt, Carolyn** and **Sutherland, Gerald** 2000 *Child development: an illustrated guide – birth to 8 years*. London: Heinemann.

With information and illustrations, updating the ideas of Mary Sheridan to meet practitioners' need to know about what usually happens and when.

☆ **Riley, Denise** 1993 *War in the nursery: theories of the child and mother*. London: Virago.

Tracks how the psychoanalytic ideas of Melanie Klein and John Bowlby affected national policy and nursery practice, especially around the second world war.

3 Explaining child development: from cognitive-developmental to socio-cultural perspectives

The cognitive-developmental family of theories focuses on how children think and make sense of their world. Theorists place considerable emphasis on children's experiences with play materials, the evidence of their senses and how they build knowledge from those experiences. There has been an increasing emphasis on social relationships with adults or other children. Development of social constructivist theory has gone further to incorporate a socio-cultural framework. The main sections in this chapter are:

- Cognitive-developmental theories.

- Socio-cultural theories.

COGNITIVE-DEVELOPMENTAL THEORIES

Jean Piaget and Lev Vygotsky are both significant names in the development of this family of theories. However, in terms of the social history time line, the spread of their ideas was relatively limited, until Piaget's ideas were translated into English from French and Vygotsky's from the original Russian.

Piaget and stage theory

The ideas of Jean Piaget have exerted a very strong influence on early years philosophy and practice in the UK. Piaget initially developed his theories from observations made by Valentine Piaget of their own three children from babyhood. This resource was extended to include children of his research team at Geneva, in Switzerland, from the late 1920s onwards and through a series of experimental studies designed to test his propositions about what children understood at different ages.

Piaget developed his theory of developmental stages from observing that children of an equivalent age made similar mistakes and appeared to develop very similar concepts to explain how the world worked. The essence of his stage theory of development was that the process of learning was not just more of the same, a quantitative build-up of information. Once young children's thinking had been provoked to move to a qualitatively different stage, there could be no return.

> ### MAKE THE CONNECTION WITH ... OTHER THEORIES
>
> Jean Piaget proposed that children were not just small grown-ups, but that they learned in a qualitatively different way from adults. He described children as active participants in their own learning, constructing their own understanding and furthering their own knowledge.
>
> Piagetian theory has been such a strong influence on early years practice and education in the UK that it is easy to overlook that his ideas were very radical at the time. Piaget's image of the child as little scientist was in stark contrast with other perspectives in Europe and the USA over the same period. The prevailing educational belief about children was that they were essentially empty vessels who needed to be filled up with adult-given knowledge. One main theoretical position was the behaviourist approach of John Watson and his fierce training schedules, devoid of emotional distractions (page 26). The alternative was the Freudian approach of emotional turmoil, with psychological health being the absence of significant trauma (page 22).

Adaptation through schemes/schemas

Piaget explained that young children construct their understanding of the world through their use of schemes or schemas. I use the word schema, since this term is familiar in the UK because of the work of Chris Athey (page 124).

A schema is more than a mental category; it is a word to explain ideas in action and the grouping of a set of actions linked with an idea. During the first two years of life, which Piaget called the sensori-motor stage, schemas are very physical. Babies and toddlers use their physical skills and senses. Piaget proposed that for a baby an object was the same as its feel or taste. So an adult observer can refer to a baby's holding or sucking schemas. Piaget proposed that, from about 18–24 months of age, toddlers develop schemas that go beyond physical sensation and have an intellectual content linked with the actions. He interpreted observations of very young exploratory behaviour as evidence that the children had made cognitive connections supported by the physical exploration within their current schema(s).

Schemas support active development because they change in response to experience. Piaget proposed three processes of adaptation to explain how young children learn:

- *Assimilation*: objects, events and experiences are drawn into and made a part of an existing schema. For instance, a baby incorporates a new rattle into her grasping and shaking schema. In this way, existing schemas can become more varied.

- *Accommodation*: children encounter experiences that will not fit an existing schema. Piaget theorised that a new schema is then created through physical experimentation, thinking out loud through spoken language or silent thought for older children. Children's schemas (and our own adult ones) are re-organised, and if necessary changed, through this process of accommodation.

- *Equilibration*: in order to explain why children make this effort, Piaget proposed that they have a powerful desire to make sense of their world. It is also uncomfortable to persist with inconsistency and the imbalance of a schema that does not work. Through equilibration, children make the significant leaps of childhood learning, as they abandon schemas that cannot cope with new information.

Piaget's stage theory of child development rests on three very significant equilibration points in childhood. At each time, Piaget claimed, schemas undergo a major re-organisation and children shift to a qualitatively different phase in their development.

- When children are about 18–24 months, the dominant sensori-motor schemas change to incorporate the first use of symbols: an object standing for something else and the symbolism of the use of spoken language. This major change brings children from Piaget's first developmental stage, the sensori-motor, into his second, called the pre-operational stage.

- Children from about two to six years of age extend their use of symbolism and explore a wide range of abstract concepts and mental ways of organising and understanding the world. Piaget described their thinking as egocentric. He meant that young children could only make sense of the world from their own perspective and were unable to take alternative perspectives into account. It is important to realise that Piaget meant that children were self-centred in a cognitive way; he did not imply they are 'selfish'.

- Between five and seven years Piaget proposed that children made the shift into a whole new level of thinking, that of operations. These are the mental activities such as categorising, use of number and early scientific concepts such as conservation (that an amount remains constant regardless of how it appears). This new level of understanding took children into the concrete operational stage, that Piaget believed lasted up to about 12 years of age.

- By the brink of adolescence, children have gained such a broad and thorough understanding of ideas in action, concrete operations, that they were able to deal with increasingly complex ideas in their head and move to the stage of formal operations.

TAKE ANOTHER PERSPECTIVE

The detailed theory of Jean Piaget is now seen as the foundation of a constructivist approach. However, Piaget had common ground with some of the biological theories. He proposed a 'genetic epistemology': a timetable established by nature for the four stages of child development.

WHAT DOES IT MEAN?

Stage theory: an explanatory approach that proposes there are distinct stages of development through which all children pass in the same sequence.

Schemas: repeated patterns of behaviour that characterise how children explore and understand their world at a given time.

Adaptation: Piaget's theory of how children's schemas change in response to experiences: through assimilation, accommodation and the drive for equilibration.

Deficit or incompetence model: an approach that focuses more on what children cannot yet do rather than on their level of competence.

Challenge to the stage theory

Few theorists now hold to original Piagetian theory, but the ideas have been the source of much creative research and re-thinking. Divergence of opinion was clear from the 1920s. Lev Vygotsky (page 39) took a different route in Russia, but Susan Isaacs in England was also doubtful about Piaget's evidence for pre-operational thought.

The practical problem is that Jean Piaget defined young children, particularly the two- to six-year-olds, mainly in terms of what they could not yet do. This view of young children has been called a 'deficit' or 'incompetence' model. In her observations at Malting House School, Susan Isaacs drew upon much the same research as Piaget, but reached different conclusions about children's ability (see also page 71). Isaacs took more of a bottom-up than a top-down perspective. She offered positive descriptions of cognitive competence in young children: what they could do and how, rather than what they could not yet do.

By the 1970s, researchers, such as Margaret Donaldson in Scotland, were challenging the validity of Piaget's experimental approach (page 71). In subsequent decades there was a steady move away from the more solitary learners of Piaget's theory towards how children learn within their social and cultural context.

MAKE THE CONNECTION WITH ... PRACTICE

Piaget's ideas, and interpretations of those ideas, have exerted a strong influence on UK early years and school practice. Think about how you may encounter those ideas in practice.

- Piaget's insistence that children constructed their own understanding and were active learners led him to emphasise that adults should create environments in which children could discover for themselves. This approach has sometimes been interpreted within early years practice that 'learning through play' means a strict non-interventionist role for adults. Margaret Donaldson challenged this approach with her ideas of children's enjoyment of the role of novice (page 186).

- Piaget's ideas about early mathematical concepts led to an underestimate of what children understood about number. Penny Munn and other researchers have explored a more accurate balance between concepts and the means to support young learning. You can follow up these ideas with the support of Dorothy Caddell (1998a, *Numeracy in the early years: what the research tells us*) and Effie Maclellan, Penny Munn and Victoria Quinn (2003, *Thinking about maths: a review of issues in teaching number from 5 to 14 years*).

The influence of Lev Vygotsky

Lev Vygotsky worked in Russia through the 1920s and 1930s. He was one of the first people to disagree with Piaget's theory of child development. However, Vygotsky's premature death meant that he could only respond to Piaget's early publications. So, it is important to realise that much of what is presented now as a Vygotskian model of play and learning is the result of continued reworking of his ideas, especially in the 1980s and 1990s. Unlike Piaget, who had a very long academic career, Vygotsky had only a decade of generating ideas before he died at 38 years from tuberculosis. The Stalinist purges took over in Russia, developmental psychology was banned and most of Vygotsky's research team ended up in prison.

Vygotsky's work was inaccessible outside Russia until the political climate changed and his working papers were translated into English (*Thought and language*, in 1962, and *Mind in society: the development of higher psychological processes* in 1978). These publications provide Vygotsky's discussion of theoretical concepts, relatively informal experiments and his practical suggestions for how children learn.

Vygotsky placed far greater emphasis than did Piaget on the social context in which children explored and learned. Vygotsky also viewed language as a vital social tool. He did not believe that children operated as the 'lone scientist' of Piaget's view and Vygotsky described learning as far more a process within social interaction. If Piaget is described as the pioneer of an approach of individual constructivism, then Vygotsky is seen as the founder of the social constructivist approach. This perspective is also the reason why Vygotsky is sometimes placed with the socio-cultural family of theories.

Vygotsky felt that early language, during the years when children speak out loud to themselves in play, should not be dismissed as immature or egocentric, since it was an instrument of thought. The whole feel of Vygotsky's approach is much more a competence model, that young children already have skills and add to these through experience. Vygotsky felt play was significant, but did not see it as the only way that children learned. Interestingly, he warned against the drawbacks if adults intellectualise play and overlook the significance of the emotional content for the children themselves.

Vygotsky used his concept of the zone of proximal development to explain how children's learning could be supported (page 178). 'Proximal' is the English translation of a Russian word meaning 'nearby'. Vygotsky felt that play could create positive conditions for learning within the zone and he was interested in how adults could best help children to learn. But Vygotsky also proposed that children helped each other within the zone, through social and play interactions.

WHAT DOES IT MEAN?

The zone of proximal development: the area of potential learning for an individual child at a given time.

Jerome Bruner

Jerome Bruner is an American psychologist who has mainly worked in the USA but who also led a large UK research project at Oxford in the 1970s. Bruner developed Piaget's ideas but was also influential in bringing Vygotsky's ideas to the English-speaking academic world after the 1960s.

Bruner disagreed with Piaget's view that children's development should be left to unfold without intervention. Bruner believed that development could

be accelerated, when adults took a more active role in children's
Bruner was especially concerned that children whose circumstai
provided poor intellectual stimulation would be seriously disadv
without an active role for early years practitioners and school te

Piaget stressed the importance of children's physical environment in
stimulating them to learn. However, Bruner saw language as an important
medium for adults to stimulate children to think and understand beyond
their current grasp. He was in favour of a child-centred environment and
learning through discovery, but believed that adults should actively
anticipate difficulties and help children directly.

Bruner further developed Vygotsky's theoretical perspective into the
concept of the spiral curriculum, of how children learn through discovery,
with the direct help of adults, and by returning again and again to the same
materials or ideas. Bruner proposed that children were able to extend their
understanding over a period of years because later learning could build on
what they had learned previously and through sensitive help from adults.
Jerome Bruner's concept of learning as cyclical is shared by writers such as
Lillian Katz (see also page 104) in that children need to revisit ideas and
experiences. The practical implication is that supportive adults need to
provide a flexible learning environment in which children can easily access
and use resources.

DEFINITION

The spiral curriculum: the idea that children will revisit play
materials and activities over the years, but then use them
differently because their cognitive development has progressed.

Scaffolding: supportive technique used to offer verbal or non-
verbal guidance to children in the process of gaining a new
skill or understanding.

Jerome Bruner felt that young children learn most easily through the
medium of their play. Familiar play materials could remain of interest to
children, as the months and years passed, but older children used the same
or similar materials in qualitatively different ways. Bruner developed the
concept of scaffolding to explain how adults could use their greater
experience appropriately to help children to understand and to think. He
used the visual parallel of scaffolding on a building site to explain how
observant adults can provide temporary guidance to a child who is in the
process of gaining a new skill or understanding. Once the child feels
competent, this particular bit of scaffolding support can be removed.

You can never have too many blocks!

LOOK, LISTEN, NOTE, LEARN

An example of the spiral curriculum in action is how a rich array of building bricks or wooden blocks is a creative source of learning for all children.

■ Babies like bricks to hold, look at and drop. But as they become toddlers, the same children relish bricks as a simple build up and knock down resource.

■ Three- and four-year-olds use a good store of bricks as the construction material for buildings. But they also use bricks to create boundary lines essential for other games, to make enclosures for toy animals or cars. They use blocks for stepping along or over or for delicate balancing games. Different sizes and shapes may serve as props in their pretend play.

■ Five-, six-year-olds and older children may still enjoy building impressive structures with bricks. But they may also use them deliberately as the raw materials for counting, weighing and relative weight, exploring mathematical concepts that now make sense to the children.

At any point in these years of exploration and learning, the supportive adult input could work within the zone of proximal development, with adult skills of scaffolding. What might be appropriate kinds of support?

- You could build up current and past observations of children you know and explore the building blocks example. If you would like to focus on blocks, contact Community Playthings for their video, Foundations: the value of unit block play (free – call 0800 387 457).

- Other possibilities are to gather observations of the different ways in which children use the potential of dressing up clothes: from the very simple hat-on-head or scarf-over-the-face game of toddlers through to complex pretend play of the older children.

- Combine your observations with those of colleagues or fellow-students who work with children of a different age, or who knew these individual children when they were younger.

SOCIO-CULTURAL THEORIES

Practitioners of the discipline of developmental psychology spent decades studying children as if it were irrelevant where and how they lived, or even the context in which they were observed or asked questions. Cross-cultural psychology developed through the 1960s largely in order to test whether propositions, for instance from Piaget's ideas, applied outside western society. The discipline moved closer to anthropology with an interest in documenting ways of raising children, searching for common themes as well as contrasts. The socio-cultural approach developed through the last decades of the twentieth century and has aimed to place children in context, without losing their individuality.

Systems theory

Systems theorists argue that every system, whether biological, economic or psychological, has wholeness and an order to how it works. The whole consists of the parts and their inter-relationship. So, change in one part of the system will affect other parts; it is not possible to separate them. Arnold Sameroff applied the theory to understanding family dynamics: family life is created by the relationships between parents, children and any other close relatives. The experiences of individuals within any family are influenced by the way this family operates. Sameroff takes the analogy of music: you cannot possibly appreciate a melody if you only listen to a series of single notes. The unique tune is created by how those musical notes are set together, whether they merge in harmony or clash.

WHAT DOES IT MEAN?

Systems theory: an approach emphasising an interaction between the whole and the parts in any system. Applied to families, systems theory argues that family life cannot be understood by focusing only on individuals.

The other defining feature of a system is that it adapts to change in the same kind of way that Piaget described for children's cognitive development (page 37). Families can be resistant to change – some more than others – and, if possible, they will absorb some new feature into family life without major re-adjustments: Piaget's idea of assimilation. But sometimes, family life becomes very stressful unless particular re-adjustments are made that shift how the family runs: Piaget's idea of accommodation. Such change is challenging, but may be painful and resisted by families who have a strong vested interest in the current situation.

- Families are seen as self-balancing systems: they establish a way of coping that for them defines normal family life. (Young children assume that every family operates like their own, until social interaction provides a contrast.)

- All families act so as to achieve a balance in their relationships and family communication patterns help to maintain this balance. Changing the balance, or having change thrust upon a family, can be stressful.

- If equilibrium seems precarious, family members exert effort to restore it. Sometimes, equilibrium may be maintained largely because one family member or a sub-group imposes on others in the family.

MAKE THE CONNECTION WITH ... FAMILY SUPPORT

- The development of family-oriented therapy, rather than therapeutic intervention focused solely on the child, was a recognition that family dynamics can be key in bringing about positive change for some children.

- Family members help to maintain the balance overtly and covertly. For example, parents may resist help with the 'problem' they regularly present about their child. It may be very important that family troubles can be attributed to the disruptive behaviour of their child. If the child's behaviour is resolved, then the adults will have to find another reason to explain why they are so unhappy.

Alfred Adler (page 23) made the point that each child is, in effect, born into a 'different' family because they face a different configuration of people and existing roles than either an older or a subsequent child. Children are themselves active family members, responding and reacting to the family system. They make alliances with or feel resentment towards individual parents, siblings or other relatives in the close family. Of course, families do not operate in a social vacuum. Adults are affected by the ways in which the surrounding community judges their actions. Cultural traditions may create expectations that are a source of conflict within families and/or may be a strong source of support.

TAKE ANOTHER PERSPECTIVE

- Systems theory applies to any social group, so the ideas are just as relevant to the social interaction and roles within a working team.

- Reflect on how the dynamics of your own team or study group operates. What kind of roles do individuals take on or have thrust upon them? What changes when someone is absent or a new person joins the group?

- Take your time over these concepts. It can be unsettling to apply the ideas to oneself rather than other people.

An ecological approach

Urie Bronfenbrenner, a psychologist based in the USA, travelled to observe children in other countries and developed a theory to take account of childhood in a given time and place. He saw his approach as a way to study the ecology of human development and the theory is sometimes known as the ecological systems theory. From the 1970s Bronfenbrenner worked to describe the impact of children's environment, without downplaying the uniqueness of individual children.

The ecological approach is a reminder that children do not develop in isolation. Bronfenbrenner's approach offered a balance to theories that continued to focus on individual children, at most in the context of their immediate family. One advantage of the ecological approach is the attempt to grapple with parts of the social system that indirectly affect children. The details of culture or faith, of current economic policy or the demands of adult employment influence children as they trickle down through the layers and into personal relationships.

Bronfenbrenner developed a model that is presented visually as a series of concentric circles. The concepts are also represented as a set of Russian dolls, the kind where each doll nests within another and the set can be taken apart until all are revealed, down to the very smallest doll.

■ The innermost circle of the microsystem encompasses children's direct, daily experience with family, peers and friends. It also includes settings of which the child has direct experience: early years setting, schools or places of worship. Children's socialisation occurs within this circle (page 223).

■ Bronfenbrenner calls the next layer the exosystem. This circle, or doll in the set, includes the social system that affects children. The impact may be their own direct experience but can also be filtered through their family. Important aspects can be the neighbourhood, local social networks including their parents' friends and the world of work, which affects children through parents' experiences of job pressure or unemployment.

■ The outer layer is the macrosystem. This circle includes broad social structures: education, economic systems and cultural values. Economic policy may result in relative wealth or poverty in the child's family. Ethnic identity gains meaning from the predominant cultural values of the society.

TAKE ANOTHER PERSPECTIVE

Bronfenbrenner recognises the impact of time as well as place and in some discussion of his theory he talks of the chronosystem. Broad social changes affect the nature of childhood over the years.

■ Consider the significant changes for a child growing up in the UK during the early twenty-first century, in contrast with a 1970s or 1950s childhood.

■ For example, what about familiarity with computers, video or television?

■ What was the likelihood that children in other decades attended some kind of early years setting and what difference might that have made?

■ What about the numbers of cars on the road or the likelihood that the family would own a car?

■ What else could be reasonably seen as broad social changes that affect childhood over time?

Bronfenbrenner acknowledges that the richness of the model, reflecting the genuine complexity of ordinary life, makes it hard to design research that could test the ideas. It seems a price worth paying for such a thoughtful approach. The effects of environment are complex and the most likely influences are of interactions rather than linear patterns of cause and effect. In later re-working of the theory, Bronfenbrenner worked to redress what he felt was an imbalance away from the impact of children's individuality.

LOOK, LISTEN, NOTE, LEARN

There is good reason to be concerned about rising levels of clinical obesity in childhood and the health consequences of a more sedentary life style for many children now. But what is to be done? Use Bronfenbrenner's ideas to identify the strands of this practical problem.

■ For example, what is the role and responsibility of the children themselves or their family?

■ What about responsibility for the content of nursery or school dinners and that some schools generate funds from selling crisps and fizzy drinks?

■ Companies who sell snack food, and advertisers who promote the goods, say it is inappropriate to control sales or ban the adverts. What do you think?

■ Discuss your ideas with colleagues and build up a model of what you judge to be the strands of cause and effect in this area of practical social concern.

Social construction of childhood

During the 1990s Berry Mayall, and other sociologists in the UK, became interested in how social structures and dominant social values shaped the way in which childhood was viewed and the daily experiences of children. Berry Mayall was involved in several large-scale studies of children in the UK and she brought together insights from psychology and sociology into an area of study now described as the sociology of childhood.

WHAT DOES IT MEAN?

Sociology of childhood: a branch of sociology that has focused on children and childhood in the context of social groups and society as a whole.

Social construction of childhood: the idea that there is neither an absolute, nor a universal image of a child and childhood. The image is created by social attitudes grounded in time and place.

A key concept is that of social construction of childhood: that childhood experience is neither universal in the details, nor fixed within a single society over time. Childhood may exist as a permanent social category in society, as distinct from adulthood, but social circumstances determine children's experiences and the boundaries to their daily life. Current attitudes and social values within any society shape the prevailing childhood and ways of talking about children. For example:

Family experience tells children what is valued

- Are children important in themselves or only for what they may become?

- Economic pressures, for an entire society or families who are under the greatest stress, exert an influence on how children are viewed. Is children's economic labour crucial to family survival? Is their involvement in household chores part of a family or community philosophy about ways to raise competent children?

- To what extent are children seen as legitimate targets for commercial interests, as young consumers or purchasers?

How should children be raised?

Christina Hardyment is a social historian who has described the changing views in Europe of how children should be treated, from 1750 up to the end of the twentieth century. Her examples of advice to parents are a timely reminder that opinion has changed dramatically and continues to circle. Hardyment also shows that experts can disagree, even within the same decade.

MAKE THE CONNECTION WITH ... THE CULTURAL CONTEXT

Melvin Konner spent time with the !Kung San, a hunter-gatherer community living in Botswana. He translated a passage for a !Kung mother from a 1985 edition of Benjamin Spock's best-selling *Baby and child care*. The section was about how to avoid spoiling infants by being busy with your own tasks.

The mother listened with increasing disapproval and asked in a bemused tone, 'Doesn't he understand he's only a baby and that's why he cries? Later, when he grows older, he will have sense and he won't cry any more'. Konner points out that the !Kung San also raise children within a theory of child development and 'it is the opposite of our own theory of development, that says that if you pick the baby up you will train him to cry more and more. The !Kung bet on maturation — and they have never yet had a child who didn't outgrow crying' (Konner, 1991: 111).

- Gather examples of how you, or your colleagues, have experience that diversity of cultural background can question assumptions that everybody follows particular childcare advice or that it is all 'common sense'.

TAKE ANOTHER PERSPECTIVE

Christina Hardyment comments that families do not always follow the advice of their era. Popular advice manuals of the past cannot tell us what all parents actually did with their children. Advice also varies within an era. When do you think these two excerpts were written?

1 '... even very small babies like to look at simple books and interesting toys. For your baby to enjoy these things it is important that you do them at the right time. The best time is usually approximately one hour after he is awake and not hungry. He should never be played with or over-stimulated 20 minutes prior to his nap ... Even from a very young age babies should be encouraged to occupy themselves for short periods. This is much more likely to happen if the baby is left playing alone on a playmat or under his cot mobile, as he will be much more likely to kick and move around than when he is being held.'

2 'Many of the troubles of management which arise in childhood are due to the persistent refusal of grown ups to regard a child as a proper human being. Some persist in calling the child "it", others talk about him to his face as if he were not there ... Say "naughty" as little as possible. It is not naughty to shout and romp, to fidget about, to be "always on the go". Mischief is only a sign that the child needs more to do. It may be exasperating for the grown up but it's perfectly natural to him. Forcing a child to be quiet or inactive will only cause his pent-up energy to overflow into bad behaviour, tantrums and irritability.'

Answers on page 52.

Social role and status

Berry Mayall has argued that, in the UK, children are often assigned 'minority social status', that their views are frequently judged as less important than adult priorities. The development of children's rights and consultation with children has been a practical way to address this inequality (page 244). Studies have explored the importance of children's own views of their daily experience, how they view their social world or experiences at school or when ill in hospital.

The sociological concept of role is that adults, as well as children, have different parts to their life, in which they have a qualitatively different social position and relationship. For example, you may be a daughter or son but also have a longstanding family role as sister or brother. You may have a more recent role as a parent and be a colleague or a manager to another set of people. You may have experienced the temporary role of patient when in contact with medical services. The sociological approach to childhood looks especially at the roles for children, for instance as a school pupil. Mayall describes what she calls the 'scholarization' of childhood, by which she means the way in which the school experience has come to dominate family life. Children and young people spend many hours in school but parents are also told how to use family time, especially with homework given in English primary schools.

MAKE THE CONNECTION WITH ... FAMILY AND SCHOOL POWER RELATIONS

Consider Berry Mayall's ideas about the scholarization of childhood. To what extent are children and the years of childhood defined in terms of the educational experience of school?

- My particular annoyance is the way that young children are regularly called 'pre-schoolers', rather than babies or three-year-olds. I draw the parallel and say do we call teenagers pre-workers? Are people in their 50s or early 60s regularly called pre-retirees? Is it only young children whose identity is defined by the next 'stage'? And what does that communicate about the relative importance of early childhood?

- Most discussion around the transition into primary school is about how families and early years settings can prepare the children for school – a lot of 'getting them ready for ...'. Hilary Fabian (2002) is unusual in calling a whole section of her book 'Preparing schools for children'.

- Look also at the discussion about early years services and partnership with parents in Chapter 10.

WHAT DOES IT MEAN?

Role or social role: a way of describing the social position of being in a particular relationship with other people and social institutions such as the family, school or paid work.

LOOK, LISTEN, NOTE, LEARN

Here are the answers to *Take another perspective* on page 50.

■ Excerpt 1 is from 2002, Gina Ford *The new contented little baby book*, page 106. Gina Ford brings back the definite routines that were pushed out by advice that was strong in the late 1970s and early 1980s to follow demand feeding and baby's wishes.

■ Excerpt 2 is from 1950, from John Gibbens *Care of children from one to five*, pages 121–22. Gibbens first wrote his childcare manual in 1936 and it was so popular it went through many reprints. I have the fourth edition on my shelf because my mother consulted Dr Gibbens in raising me and my brother.

Take a look at the range of current childcare advice books for parents.

■ What kind of advice is offered? How much agreement, and disagreement, can you identify between authors?

■ How might social historians in 2050 describe 'typical childcare in the early twenty-first century' if they only had one or two of these books?

The socio-cultural perspective

The theoretical stance of social constructivism is very strong now within early childhood studies in the UK and has developed into a socio-cultural model. The approach has drawn from theorists in early developmental psychology, such as Lev Vygotsky, but there are also important sources within sociology, cross-cultural studies and also philosophy.

The socio-cultural approach draws on the traditions of cross-cultural psychology and anthropology, aiming to avoid the evaluative comparisons that were sometimes part of earlier academic traditions. Certainly, cross-cultural psychologists and anthropologists did not all describe non-western cultures in a demeaning way. But reports sometimes gave a feel of the 'interesting' or 'exotic', as contrasted with the more 'normal' western template. Academic discussion of social constructivism or socio-cultural theory uses terms such as 'postmodern', 'poststructural' and 'discourse'. This section explains the origins of the approach and provides definitions.

Postmodernism

This concept comes from a radical re-think in sociology. The argument is that sociology as a discipline started with the analysis of modern society. 'Modern' is defined as the changes brought about by the industrial revolution. Sociological analysis was in terms that make sense to an industrial kind of society: that social class was significant, family was an important social structure and that adults gained their personal identity from work.

Sociologists proposed that from the 1970s onwards the whole social situation changed. The nature of society in the western world had altered and so an alternative way of analysing society was required: the postmodern approach.

- One of the changes, it is argued, is that personal identity cannot be summed up accurately in large groupings. Social change is widespread, so identity is much more fluid. One person could have a multiplicity of identities and make active choices to take on an identity, for example, by changing their accent or style of dress.

- There was a reaction against the grand narratives and a move towards the individual narrative as a perspective to be respected, even valued over broader social concepts. There is a sense of pluralism: that a range of personal narratives will offer a full and meaningful explanation.

- There was also a reaction against the big myths: that science was objective and would be a source of progress and well-being. This perspective also drew from the philosophical position of existentialism (page 54).

Poststructuralism

The poststructuralists overlap with the postmodernists. The movement was a reaction against the previous dominance in sociology of structuralist principles and theories such as Marxism. There are two broad ways to think and talk about society: action (through personal decisions and perceptions) and structure (institutions which became autonomous, such as religion).

- The key idea of structuralism was that these social structures were like the puppet master and more powerful than individual actions. People could only wield power through the structures, as puppets on the strings.

- The structural approach to analysis was challenged, with the claim that the exercise of power is more a matter of interpersonal relations. Some people are in a better position to wield power and work the puppet strings. It is possible to gain power, especially with greater fluidity of personal identity (link with the postmodernist analysis).

So, this form of sociological analysis was called poststructural. The new approach placed a great emphasis on language and that use of words can be seen as a barometer for the power relations.

- Forms of analysis from linguistics, including semiotics, proposed that words can be fluid and are separate from concepts. The same words have an infinite possibility of meanings and are always open to interpretation.

- It is possible then to analyse spoken and written words to reveal the meaning and power relations behind the words. For example, use of language within the medical profession, such as calling people 'patients' and 'cases' reflects the balance of power.

Patterns of language, linked with ideas, are particular to a given socio-cultural group and can be analysed as a whole, as discourse, and can be challenged. An example is how the social model of disability was used to confront the words and linked concepts of the medical model (page 232). Another relevant example would be the discourse that underlies the promotion of hitting children as a form of discipline (page 205). In order to understand the use of this term in the early childhood studies academic discourse, we also need the strand of philosophy.

Deconstruction

By the twentieth century philosophers in France and Germany, but not in the UK, had developed a philosophical position called existentialism. A central theme of this philosophical approach is that meaning cannot be found unless you recognise that humans are engaged in the world. Their experience of objects and events provides them with meaning. The assumption is that humans seek to understand anything because they are involved with it. So there will always be a particular point of view and complete objectivity is impossible, even in the pure sciences such as physics and chemistry – let alone the social sciences.

The existential position values concrete and personal experience more highly than general and abstract. So, existentialism stresses that, in the search for understanding, it is more important to be involved than to be detached. The impossibility of scientific objectivity is not therefore a problem. In fact the traditional scientific values and methods – a positivist approach – were dismissed as misguided and irrelevant to valid inquiry.

The existential tradition led to further explorations of how meaning was always embedded in context. Jacques Derrida was influential in promoting the process of deconstruction, that of stripping bare an event or a piece of writing in order to reveal the structure of assumptions and finally reach what is unique about it. You could release social meaning by analysing discourses.

Discourse

So, the term 'discourse' means much more than the words alone. For example, the word 'stress' is grounded in a context of meaning and is different along many dimensions from the word 'nerves', which was common in the mid-twentieth century. Discourse is a collection of ideas, practice and of power relations in society. If you analyse scientific discourse, you are able to define the explanations and power relations that are mediated through language. Because language itself constructs people's ideas, the process of deconstruction, it is argued, releases meaning and illuminates context. The analysis also proposes that you have to have the word for a concept in order to bring about any change

TAKE ANOTHER PERSPECTIVE

- Gather examples of how the way in which people talk about an experience or an area of practice shapes and may restrict possibilities. Look at the discussion about partnership with parents on page 231 and consider how words and outlook can create very different meaning for this phrase.

- Some discourses incorporate rigid and mutually exclusive opposites: if you are A, then you cannot be B. You may be able to think of some ways of talking, and arguing, that are underpinned by this pattern.

- A predominant discourse can be challenged. For instance, in the USA some young adults challenge the discourse around ethnic group identity that says you can be either 'black' or 'white' and nothing in between. A new approach to identity has arisen in which some young men and women claim an ethnic group identity that blends different sources.

Applications to childhood

Discourse is a key concept for the sociology of childhood and the social constructivist approach. This idea rests within a theoretical framework that children are born into a pre-existing society in which the dominant culture(s) have shaped attitudes about values and priorities. The prevailing pattern of discourse determines from childhood what we regard as natural, normal, obviously the right choice or priority. Discourse is manifested through verbal and non-verbal behaviour. The choice of words shapes thought and the details of how people talk about an issue or area of practice communicate a great deal about attitudes, priorities and values.

Young children construct meaning from their experiences and learn spoken language to express their ideas and feelings. However, they learn the meanings and values that dominate their socio-cultural group and deal with the clash of values between groups to which they belong.

WHAT DOES IT MEAN?

Socio-cultural theories: approaches to explanation of adult and child experience through social interaction and the context provided by social and cultural group.

Social constructivism: a focus on how children, or others, make meaning from experience with full attention paid to the context of experiences.

The social constructivist position argues that few young children learn the same things at the same time. Therefore, support for early learning cannot proceed as if all children pass through the same experiences in sequence. Children construct their own view of reality from personal experiences and use this outlook to deal with new information. Consequently, adults' most important task is to understand individual children's understanding and strategies for learning. The approach therefore stresses the context in which children learn and that adults need to seek ways to make learning meaningful for each child.

The social constructivist movement in the UK has been influential in encouraging an adult role as enabler or facilitator of children's learning. A more active directing role is seen as potentially disruptive of early development – because of the importance of children's own concepts. The power of the approach is in stressing the pointlessness of adults' pushing on with their own plans for children's learning when there are no links to children's current understanding.

The theoretical ideas have been applied in research through the concept of pedagogy: that of the whole approach of adults whose aim is to support children's learning. The word pedagogy describes the craft of teaching and the interactive process between adult teacher, child learner and the learning environment. So the term does not mean curriculum, although a particular approach through a curriculum could be part of pedagogy. The term is not restricted to early years practitioners, nor to early years settings and can be applied to parents with their own children, as home-based pedagogy.

International links have furthered the socio-cultural base of this broad theoretical perspective. Alternative cultural traditions are used to give context to the experiences of childhood, family life and early years or schools services. There have been especially strong links between the UK and the early years approach in New Zealand and Australia and the particular approach of the centres in the Reggio Emilia region of Italy.

WHAT DOES IT MEAN?

Pedagogy: the actions and outlook of practitioners in direct interaction with children and the learning environment, that can be seen to include family and community.

If you want to find out more:

☆ **Bronfenbrenner, Urie** 1979 *The ecology of human development*. Cambridge MA: Harvard University Press.

Description of the ecological approach.

☆ **Bruner, Jerome** 1990 *Acts of meaning*. Cambridge MA: Harvard University Press.

Consideration of how young children's oral language supported their thought processes.

☆ **Hardyment, Christina** 1995 *Perfect parents: baby care advice past and present*. Oxford: Oxford University Press.

The survey of a couple of centuries of childcare advice to parents. The discussion shows how ideas appear and re-appear.

☆ **Kehily, Mary** (ed.) 2004 *An introduction to childhood studies*. Buckingham: Open University Press.

A range of chapters that provide socio-cultural perspectives.

☆ **Mayall, Berry** 2002 *Towards a sociology for childhood: thinking from children's lives*. Buckingham: Open University Press.

Sociological perspectives on childhood and children's experience.

☆ **Sutherland, Peter** 1992 *Cognitive development today: Piaget and his critics*. London: Paul Chapman.

A useful resource for summaries of different theories in this area – more manageable than some of the original writings of the theorists covered.

4 Research as a source of information and ideas

Research has extended our understanding of how the different parts of children's development relate to one another: of the whole child that we see day by day. Studies, recent and not so recent, have given greater awareness of how events support or block children's psychological and physical health. However, research teams do not have all the answers, anymore than do experienced practitioners. I started my career in child psychology as a full-time researcher and developed a blend of respect for and healthy scepticism about research. I believe that is a wise combination.

The main sections of this chapter are:

- Different ways to study children.

- Planning and interpretation in research.

- Linking research with practice.

DIFFERENT WAYS TO STUDY CHILDREN

In the early decades of research into child development, methods were largely experimental and researchers strove to meet scientific standards for objectivity. Interesting ideas still emerged, sometimes through open-ended observation. The work of Piaget and Vygotsky are two significant examples (pages 35 and 39). However, both these influential figures also tested their ideas through more controlled, experimental methods.

Standards for research

H. Rudolph Schaffer identified five qualities of well-organised research. He stated that studies should be:

- *Empirical*: the conclusions of the research are based on direct observation, not on hunches or some variation of 'everybody knows that . . .'.

- *Systematic*: the data are collected according to a clear plan, explained in the research report. Methods are not altered at individual whim.

- *Controlled*: good research is designed so that explanations or patterns of cause and effect can be deduced as reliably as possible.

- *Quantitative*: results can be measured accurately and reliable statistics presented.

- *Public*: details of methods and findings should be open to scrutiny. It must be possible to compare studies and make supported generalisations.

Social scientific research was first established within a tradition of numerical measurement and statistical analysis. Quantitative analysis was seen as the sound basis for concluding that one group was different from another and to track patterns of cause and effect. The descriptive case study tradition belonged more to therapy, where information was gathered in detail from individual experiences or sequences of events.

It is important to understand the traditions described by Schaffer, because such studies have contributed to our understanding of children. A proportion of research about children and childhood is still undertaken in this way. However, through the last decades of the twentieth century, some researchers within the social sciences, including those who study child development, challenged the value of objectivity and quantitative methods.

WHAT DOES IT MEAN?

Quantitative: analysis of the results of an experiment or observation in terms of numbers, percentages or further statistical analysis. There are mathematical rules for use of different statistical methods.

Qualitative: analysis of observational material in terms of descriptive themes or patterns.

It is not a stark either/or choice; some studies combine both methods.

The development of more subjective methods, including participant observation and narratives, was part of the social constructivist movement (page 53). Supporters rejected the illusion of objectivity in the scientific method, also known as positivism, arguing that social phenomena do not have meaning independent of social actions. Social constructivists present a subjective approach not only as equally valid, but more meaningful than detachment through objectivity. There is an emphasis on qualitative, descriptive information, with the fair argument that much of interest in child development does not reduce to quantitative analysis and statistics.

Careful research conducted within a constructivist framework still addresses quality. Glenda MacNaughton *et al* propose similar standards to those outlined by Schaffer, although they choose different terms. For example, they stress that research should, among other qualities, be:

■ *Ethical*: research should be based on informed consent of those involved and do no harm.

- *Transparent*: a standard that is similar to Schaffer's 'public' point, in that any research report should enable other people to follow decisions about how the research evolved; what they call the 'research trail'.

- *Contextualised*: there are clearly stated descriptions of the philosophical, theoretical or policy context in which the research was planned and undertaken.

- *Equitable*: research should acknowledge the bias, interests and concerns of researchers.

Different research methods

A considerable amount of research has been undertaken with children and their families and many different approaches have been used. All of the different methods have some inbuilt drawbacks, as well as advantages.

Some studies are planned under controlled conditions, perhaps in a psychological laboratory, which can be an ordinary room with a one-way mirror and usually video recording.

- Experimental designs are an attempt to control some of the many factors in the variety of children's ordinary lives. In the traditional method there is an experimental and control group – only the former has a specific experience and the control group is supposed to be the comparison. The whole experimental–control group method is a researcher's nightmare when dealing with real children and families.

- Controlled observations may be made in a specially designed room in which children and adults can be observed and recorded. The room may be set up with play materials, a researcher may go through a set of activities and questions, or parents may be asked to interact with their babies.

Some studies involve a mix of methods, perhaps observations but also interviews and different types of psychological assessment. The time span also varies.

- In a longitudinal design the same children are studied over a period of time. Kathy Sylva, Alan Stein and Penelope Leach in Oxford are following 1200 children and their families from birth into primary school (details at http://www.edstud.ox.ac.uk/FELL/fcc.html). Michael Rutter is leading an ongoing study of children brought out of the Romanian orphanages in the 1990s and adopted into English families (the English and Romanian Adoptees (ERA) project, page 87). In the USA the National Institute for Child Health and Human Development is tracking more than 1300 children over ten towns and cities (details at http://www.nichd.nih.gov).

- A cross-sectional research design enables study of different ages, without waiting for the same children to grow up. For example, research into children's moral development has studied how children in different age groups are able to reason about a moral dilemma (page 213).

- Cross-cultural or cross-context designs include children from more than one social class, culture or country. A meaningful cross-cultural study can be hard to plan: it may make no sense to ask the same questions in a different setting.

- Socio-cultural studies tend to step aside from direct comparisons. Researchers may look in detail at child-rearing patterns or the approach to early years education in different cultures. They aim to understand the ideas in place and perhaps to consider what can be learned for another socio-cultural context.

MAKE THE CONNECTION WITH ... WHAT CAN THE STUDY TELL US?

- Consider each of the different approaches described in this section. What might be the advantages and disadvantages of each method? For example, longitudinal studies can gather a great deal of information, but long time spans encounter the problem that society has changed since the study began. So, how far can the lessons of this research be applied now?

- A small study or narrative approach may provide meaningful descriptions, but how much can the study tell us about other children or settings?

- You could return to this activity when you have completed the chapter.

From the 1970s and 1980s more researchers aimed to observe as naturally as possible events and behaviour that occurred. Studies were undertaken in settings that were part of children's daily life: nurseries, schools or their own home. There was concern that the desire for experimental control could remove most of the variation of genuine interest.

- Jerome Bruner, for instance, led a major research study based in Oxford through the 1970s that developed a target child method of observation. Similar studies gathered observational data on children or adults and then analysed the information by categories, such as kinds of play or adult behaviours. Judy Dunn developed ways to observe in children's own homes.

- Some observational studies moved away from a quantitative approach altogether and used qualitative methods: identifying themes and supporting

Some researchers observe how children choose to use their time

this interpretation by examples of events and conversations. Such an approach takes a more narrative method.

▣ In either approach, observers aim to remain uninvolved, although they are aware that the behaviour of children, and more often adults, can be different because of their presence.

TAKE ANOTHER PERSPECTIVE

Researchers are people too and many are unwilling to reject children who are persistent in wanting a chat, and even more so when children are upset.

▣ Joyce Robertson made the written observations while James Robertson held the camera for their influential 1950s films about separation (page 77). In the film of a young boy staying in a residential nursery, you can see clearly one point where Joyce Robertson cannot stop herself from hugging the boy as he leans against her in total distress.

▣ Peter Elfer has written (in articles about his research during 2003–2004 for *Nursery World*) of his unwillingness (very reasonable in my view) to be rude to a young child who is demonstrably pleased to see him as a familiar visitor in the nursery.

- Some narrative studies are undertaken by a participant observer: someone who is also directly involved in the setting. One example is the reflective reporting by Vivian Gussin Paley. Action research is often undertaken by practitioners who remain part of daily life in a nursery while documenting a change. An example is Penny Holland's observations of the removal of a ban on weapons play in her centre (page 217).

- Some researchers have made detailed longitudinal observations of individual children, sometimes with whom they have a family relationship. Robin Campbell (page 156) described in detail how Alice, his grand-daughter learned her early literacy skills.

WHAT DOES IT MEAN?

Participant observer: a development of the observational method in which the person observing may remain active in what happens – playing or talking with a child, although ideally not over-influencing what happens.

Narrative approach: a variation of observation in which there is an attempt to document the detail and flow of events as they happen, often from the perspective of individual children.

Evidence-based practice: an approach that values making clear links between information gained through research and actual practice. The term is often also used to mean good daily practice in which practitioners are able to put into words the rationale for their choices.

Some practical researchers have involved children more directly in the gathering of information.

- Margaret Carr's approach of 'learning stories' has been adapted for use in early years settings. Children's learning and current interests are explored through photographs, children's memories and reflections and the comments that they wish to have written down.

- The Mosaic approach, developed by Alison Clark and Valerie Wignall (page 243), involved young children as researchers, enabling them to express their views, use cameras to take photos and to lead the researcher on a nursery tour.

Some research projects have developed a strong link into practice, with the wish to provide reliable evidence to back advice about the best approaches to supporting children and their development. The EPPE project, for example, has aimed to document the impact on children of different kinds of early years settings. However, the team have also worked to identify the most effective pedagogical approach – what adults do with children in nursery or pre-school.

PLANNING AND INTERPRETATION IN RESEARCH

Carefully conducted research can open our eyes to what children can do or how we can best support them. But the lessons of research, and the concepts generated by studies, must be seasoned with wisdom. Questions need to asked of any kind of research: 'What leads you to say that?', 'Does this apply to everyone?' and my favourite question, 'So what?' – a query that does not have to sound as confrontational as it looks on paper.

Ethics and values

Research in the social sciences, including psychology, has become more respectful of the people involved in observations and experiments who are not the researchers. It is symbolic that my own professional organisation, the British Psychological Society, from the 1990s required that articles for its house journal no longer used the impersonal term 'subjects'. People have to be described as children, students, parents and so on. This shift in terminology was evidence of a change in attitude and power relations (remember discourse from page 55).

The ethics committees of professional organisations or universities are far more concerned than they were, say, 30 years ago, that anyone involved in research is able to give their informed consent. People need an honest description of the study they are being invited to join, or asked to allow their child to join. Information can only be withheld from them if there is a good and safe reason to do so. Then, participants in a study must be given an information debriefing after the work is complete.

WHAT DOES IT MEAN?

Informed consent: that people have enough information to be able to agree or disagree about taking part in a research study. Parents give consent on behalf of young children.

Debriefing: when people are given results, or a full explanation of their participation after a study is finished.

In past decades, researchers were very concerned about ethics and values, but the priorities were different. What really mattered were the scientific standards of objectivity, appropriate statistics and not cheating on the data. For example, in 1920 John Watson, the founder of behaviourism (page 26) and Rosalie Rayner published a series of experiments with a nine-month-old baby known as Little Albert. Watson and Rayner used the techniques of classical conditioning to make the baby scared of a white rabbit. Albert was happy to play with a series of animals, until the researchers hit a steel bar with a hammer right behind the baby as he reached for the rabbit. Albert very soon associated his fright at this racket with the rabbit and began to panic as soon as it appeared. Watson and Rayner reported that Albert's fear then spread to other white fuzzy objects, including a dog, a fur coat and a Santa Claus mask. They used the study to argue that fears are learned through direct experiences and so could also be removed.

Watson and Rayner were challenged by their contemporaries because their conclusions rested on a sample of one baby, they had no control group and were inconsistent in their reporting of procedures and results. Current readers are more likely to be shocked by the description of a desperate baby: crying and trying to escape the white rabbit and presumably also from the researchers (who in the grainy photographs appear to wear a very scary Santa Claus mask). Watson and Rayner claimed that learned fears could be removed by similar procedures, but there is no published report that they ever tried to dissipate Albert's terrors!

MAKE THE CONNECTION WITH ... CHILDREN'S FEARS

- The ethics of the study with Little Albert are unacceptable, but the point about learned fears is valid. Young children, and adults to an extent, often make sense of a situation that induces fear by linking key elements.

- I am not the only parent (sample of my two-year-old son, hospital experience in 1983) who has had to support a very young child through extreme wariness of anyone in a white coat resulting from a single frightening, although not painful, procedure carried out by only one person.

Interpretation and generalisation

Any research study has to tackle the major issue of interpretation: what sense can be reliably made of the findings and what conclusions can be drawn? Then, how far it is justified to generalise those conclusions beyond the precise time, place and individuals involved in this study?

Some of the interpretation issues are about decisions made when a study is set up. For example, suppose a research team chose to observe children in their nursery during the hours of 'free play', but not during tidy-up time or over lunchtime. They cannot then conclude that the most valuable early mathematical activities occur through the medium of play activities. The research plan has specifically excluded the possibility (a real one, in my view) that tidying up or laying the table provide a meaningful context for basic mathematical concepts.

LOOK, LISTEN, NOTE, LEARN

Gather some examples of how research about children or families is reported in the media. What claims are reported, what is the basis for statements such as 'over 50 per cent of children don't like reading'? Use this section to guide the kind of questions you ask and discuss with colleagues or fellow-students.

- For instance, suppose in a study of television viewing that most of the children who watch violent programmes at home are also rated as 'aggressive' in their playground behaviour. Newspapers are swift to pick up: '7 out of 10 children who watch television violence are bullies!'.

- But, how many children were involved in the study? Suppose the neat '7 out of 10' comes from a sample of 20 children, 16 of whom were boys, from the same disadvantaged community. What if the study was a sample of 2000, selected to balance for sex, age and socio-cultural background?

- Even then, we should ask whether the researchers have allowed for the variable of family dynamics, that explains both the aggressive strategies in the playground and being allowed indiscriminate television viewing.

Control group and variation

When you study children and families, it is not possible to control all possible sources of variation and good research has to recognise any difficulties. For example, researchers interested in the effects of different types of early years group experience do not have, nor should they have, the right to direct families to use nurseries, pre-schools or childminders, according to how it suits the research design. Families have their own reasons for choosing or avoiding different options. Research teams have to attempt to assess how this variation may create groups that are different at the outset.

The EPPE research team wished to compare children who had some kind of early years group experience prior to reception class in England and children who had stayed at home. However, in the late 1990s it proved very difficult to find children who had experienced no early years setting at all. The research report is clear that this 'home' group was very different in socio-cultural background from the 'pre-school' groups. There is no basis for saying the research proves that attending any kind of pre-school provision is always better than learning at home, although some media and political coverage has made this interpretation.

Admitting and checking assumptions

Sometimes researchers need to check their assumptions. One study of night waking in early childhood had to re-organise when the team realised that some parents in the 'no problems' group were up most nights. However, these parents had not sought help at the sleep clinic, where the team found the 'problems' group.

Assumptions also need to be checked at the interpretation stage of a study. Some observational research in the 1970s and 1980s focused on adult behaviour, often in an attempt to distinguish the interactional styles of teachers from nursery nurses. Some studies had an unchecked assumption that any differences between the groups must indicate the more beneficial style of the teachers. No study that I encountered at the time began by defining clearly what was appropriate practitioner behaviour to support young children. Had it done so, then it would have been possible to plan observations to determine who was behaving in this way and whether differences could be explained by professional qualification.

Several research projects from the late 1990s, including EPPE, have worked to address that difficulty of interpretation through blending a clearer statement of values, measures of children's developmental progress and observation of adult behaviour. This approach has supported the possibility of evidence-based practice, that recommendations for what is done day by day with children need to be grounded in information that is open to challenge.

A problem of interpretation still remains, as hard as the EPPE team have worked to distinguish the strands of explanation. There is often an assumption in studies of attendance at early years settings that all the developmental progress made by children over that period can be attributed to the group experience. But of course it is practically impossible to distinguish what has been contributed by early years practitioners and the continuing contribution of children's parents or other family members. The EPPE research has shown that children's developmental progress was affected by supportive activities happening at home. This pattern arose because parents already chose to interact with their children in these ways, not that early years practitioners had requested this kind of involvement.

Cause, effect and the control group

The experimental method is supposed to ensure objectivity. However, researchers are people and commitment to a particular theory can sometimes close minds to other possible interpretations.

Sara Smilansky explored what she called socio-dramatic play as part of her challenge to Piaget's conviction that children younger than six or seven years of age could not handle abstract ideas. She stressed that sophisticated levels of thinking could be observed in socio-dramatic play, and that it was therefore important to promote such play in early childhood, especially for children from socially disadvantaged families. Smilansky developed a method called 'play tutoring' and set up research to demonstrate her theoretical proposition. Children in the play tutoring group, in comparison with a control group, increased their level of socio-dramatic play and showed an improvement in their social and intellectual skills. Smilansky presented the findings as an endorsement of the power of play tutoring and the essential nature of socio-dramatic play for children's learning.

TAKE ANOTHER PERSPECTIVE

A large study of morale at work identified what has since been called the Hawthorne Effect. Elton Mayo and his team were trying to identify what factors would improve productivity at the Hawthorne works of the Western Electric Company. To their surprise, whatever changes they made in the working environment improved productivity: for instance, whether they increased the lighting level or decreased it. The explanation was that productivity rose because worker morale had improved. The workforce appreciated being consulted about changes. The study is also a reminder about time and place. The research was undertaken in Chicago in the early 1930s, a time of thug rule by Al Capone and his gang. Anybody in that city at that time was grateful to be treated with consideration!

In the 1980s, Peter Smith and his team undertook research to check Smilansky's claims. They contrasted three groups of nursery children: one group received play tutoring, a second group had a more general skills training session but with the same amount of adult attention and a third group had nothing additional to their normal nursery session. Children showed equivalent improvements in intellectual and language development in both of the extra sessions. Generous adult attention and friendly communication was key; there was nothing special about play tutoring.

MAKE THE CONNECTION WITH ... CLAIMS ABOUT RESEARCH

Recall the importance of proper control groups whenever you read, in the newspapers or on the promotional literature for play resources, that 'research has proved' that such and such an educational experience has made children more 'intelligent', or similar words. See page 127 about the so-called 'Mozart effect'.

Are the conclusions valid?

Jean Piaget's cognitive developmental stage theory (page 35) exerted significant influence on views of child development. However, even at the time, some researchers challenged the conclusions that he drew from his interviews and experiments with children. Two examples of research, reported in Cole and Cole (2000), highlight care about conclusions. Piaget drew support for his pre-operational stage from interviews he held with young children about how bicycles work. During the interview a bicycle was propped against a chair, so the child could see it. An interview with five-and-a-half-year-old Grim shows the kind of response that made Piaget say that children of this age operated with pre-causal reasoning. The interview went like this:

So how exactly does a bike work?

Piaget asks: 'How does the bicycle move along?'. Grim replies: 'With the brakes on top of the bike'. The interview continues with . . .
P: 'What is the brake for?' . . . G: 'To make it go because you push'.
P: 'What do you push with?' . . . G: 'With your feet'.
P: 'What does that do?' . . . G: 'It makes it go'.
P: 'How?' . . . G: 'With the brakes'.

In the late 1920s Jean Piaget visited Susan Isaacs' Malting House School, where she was conducting observational research. She was sceptical of the evidence apparently provided by interviews with children like Grim. Cole and Cole quote from Isaacs' observation of Dan (aged 5 years 9 months):

At that moment, Dan happened to be sitting on a tricycle in the garden, back-pedalling. I went to him and said, 'The tricycle is not moving forward, is it?'. 'Of course not, when I'm back-pedalling', he said. 'Well', I asked, 'how does it go forward when it does?'. 'Oh well', he replied, 'your feet press the pedals, that turns the crank round, and the cranks turn that round' (pointing to the cog wheel), 'and that makes the chain go round, and the chain turns the hub round, and then the wheels go round – and there you are!'.

Of course, you cannot take Susan Isaacs' observation of Dan and say it proves all five-year-olds understand how bicycles operate. But Isaacs did not generalise from Dan to the knowledge of all his peers. She put a fair challenge to Piaget's claim that five-year-olds in general are unable to make causal links about the workings of a familiar item such as a bicycle.

Children try to make sense of a situation

Several decades later Margaret Donaldson and her team in Edinburgh challenged Piaget's interpretation of young children's replies as 'wrong' and evidence of immature thinking. Margaret Donaldson had started her career in developmental psychology when behaviourism was very strong in the UK. She spent several months in 1957 working with Piaget in Geneva. Donaldson was impressed with his methods and the scope of his theory, but was unconvinced that Piaget was correct in the detail. During the 1960s and 1970s, Donaldson set up a nursery in the Psychology department at Edinburgh University and began research with the children who attended. Through the 1960s and 1970s Margaret Donaldson also had strong links with Jerome Bruner in the USA, who was working to identify the educational implications of his theoretical concepts (page 40).

Margaret Donaldson and her team were interested in early language and thinking and they considered how Piaget's classic experiments might look to children: the sense they might have made of the situation. Her team worked from the assumption that what children said to researchers made sense to those children. It was not inevitably 'wrong' and was often as 'right' as they could make it, given the oddities of the research situation and the questions that adults had asked them.

MAKE THE CONNECTION WITH ... PRACTICE

The work of Margaret Donaldson and her team reminds us that any adults can easily decide that their perspective is the only or most sensible one. Piaget proposed that young children were egocentric: unable to take the perspective of other people. However, often this term could be applied to adults. As a reflective practitioner, you will consider play and other daily situations in which you are closely involved with children.

- Take a moment to reflect ... are there routines or less-than-easy situations in which it is tempting to believe that the children's perspective is much the same as yours – of course they know or understand ...?

- In conversations, especially if you are keen to help children learn an idea, you need to watch and listen. If children look confused, perhaps from their point of view the adult has asked odd questions that make no sense.

- Responsible practitioners are ready to consider what sort of answer a child is giving to a question, rather than simply deciding it is the wrong answer.

- Sometimes you need to use your adult thinking skills to work out what question a child is trying to answer: what they think you want to know.

Donaldson's team ran many of Piaget's experiments with minor changes. They made an important shift in interpretation and assumed young children did not switch off their thinking skills because they were in an experiment. Despite adult intentions to control the setting for research purposes, of course children bring in social expectations about how adults behave and what they usually want if they ask you questions.

For instance, the team experimented with Piaget's three mountains scenario. In the original method, children sat by a model of three mountains and the researcher placed a doll at different locations. Children had then to say, or show from a selection of photos what the doll could see. Young children usually said or showed the doll as having their own visual perspective.

- Donaldson's team first gave three- to five-year-olds some experience of a layout in which a toy figure can see another figure from some positions but not others. Then they introduced the three mountains layout. Children could mostly say correctly when the first figure can see the second and when the latter is hidden from view.

- They tried several variations on a blocked view experiment and reported that children made more sense of the situation when it was explained as 'hiding'. A naughty boy might be hiding from a policeman or a mouse from a cat. Given a believable scenario, the children were far more able to 'look through the eyes' of one of the figures in the setting.

The team also varied the conservation experiments that Piaget used to support his view that children younger than about five years could not understand that number remained constant even if objects were moved into a different pattern.

- The Edinburgh group found that children were far more likely to say that two rows of the same number of toys were still the same when a soft toy, Naughty Teddy, had pushed one row up tighter, than when the adult researcher had brought about the same change.

- One possible explanation is based on children's sophisticated social understanding of relations between children and adults and how the latter usually behave. It is very possible that, when an adult makes a change and then asks a question about whether 'It's still the same?', children are misdirected into thinking that something must have happened. Otherwise why would an adult ask that kind of question?

It is important to know that, even with Naughty Teddy messing up the rows, some children still concluded that a more stretched-out row made more in terms of number.

LINKING RESEARCH WITH PRACTICE

Research, following any method, does not offer a clear-cut answer to all the questions posed by practitioners or policy makers. H. Rudolf Schaffer sums up the problem with

> Practitioners generally want straightforward answers: yes or no, good or bad. Research rarely provides such answers. Instead its conclusions are (or at any rate ought to be) full of constraints, hedged in with conditions and caveats and marked by a reluctance to indulge in unjustified generalizations ... Conclusions are generally of the 'it all depends' rather than 'good or bad' variety. To the practitioner (and perhaps the average man or woman) this may sound like an infuriating refusal to commit oneself; to the research worker it is an essential caution that does justice to the complexities of life events. (1998: 14)

MAKE THE CONNECTION WITH ... DIFFERENT PRIORITIES

- Charles Desforges neatly summed up the potential research–practice gulf when he asked whether 'Researchers have got lost in thought whilst practitioners have gone missing in action'. Desforges raised key issues about the need to link what I have called evidence and wisdom (page 14).

Charles Desforges was writing in the National Educational Research Forum (NERF) Bulletin on 'Evidence for teaching and learning' (Issue 1, summer 2004) http://www.nerf-uk.org/bulletin/current

- I will add my own opinion based on a great deal of reading and attendance at conferences and seminars. Problems arise not because researchers follow a theoretical position based on positivism or constructivism. Academically inclined speakers enthused by the narrative approach, and the power of socio-cultural theory, are as likely as their more traditionally scientific colleagues to fail to connect with early years practitioners.

Research in a time and place

In his review of how research could, or could not, inform practice, H. Rudolf Schaffer describes how the ideal of properly conducted research (page 59) can rarely be met, because of the complexity of most social issues of any interest. However, the social priorities of the era often determine the questions that shape a research plan, the interpretation of findings – even whether the team can get funding in the first place.

Schaffer points out how studies of children and the effects of divorce were first undertaken when social attitudes towards divorce were hostile. The research plans focused on finding negative effects. A similar pattern was followed in the early research into day care. The experience was believed to be harmful, so the job of research was to quantify those inevitable negative effects. In case any readers are thinking that bias is a problem of the past, there is a genuine risk now over day care in the UK that we have swung to the opposite direction. Political priorities have defined childcare as the block to getting mothers back into the workforce and to reducing child poverty. In some quarters, there is confident repetition that research proves time spent in any early years setting delivers measurable benefits for children's development – when the accurate picture is more complex. Research that shows that very young children may be harmed by long hours in day care, especially of doubtful quality, has sometimes been dismissed.

Prevailing social values can determine what is studied. Alison Gopnik and her colleagues describe how, for decades, most developmental psychology in the USA was uninterested in babies and very young children. Partly this omission seemed to arise because babies and very young children tend not to cooperate in controlled experiments. But it was also relevant that young children were seen as women's work and therefore irrelevant to almost exclusively male academic departments.

Over the last quarter of the twentieth century, it was largely unacceptable to study male–female differences and certainly to allow that there could be a biological explanation for differences, at least as important as the explanatory power of socialisation. Even at the beginning of the twenty-first century, Simon Baron-Cohen describes his extreme caution about presenting his ideas that male and female brains work differently – not better or worse, just in a different way on average.

Short- and long-term consequences

Policy makers wish for research to deliver swift and clear-cut answers. However, effective interventions sometimes work with a slow burn effect.

During the 1970s, many programmes were designed to help children from socially disadvantaged backgrounds through early educational intervention. These projects were assessed by differences in measures of intelligence (IQ tests) between children who had attended special programmes or had been in the control group. A boost for IQ in the intervention group did not last longer than the early years of school and the gap between the two groups typically closed. This apparent 'wash-out' of the IQ difference dashed hopes that children's early educational experience could counteract social deprivation. These findings spread a high level of gloom over a section of early years research during the late 1970s and early 1980s. (If your career does not stretch back to that time, please believe me, people were very depressed!)

However, some of the best-organised, and well-funded, American projects continued to follow children through their schooling and they found a long-term impact of the early experience. The successful programmes, such as the High/Scope Ypsilanti programme, had a clear structure for children's learning, an active role for children in the day and parent involvement. Children from such programmes showed greater competence in school and stayed in education. They were less likely to be assigned to remedial classes or to be kept down a year – a common option in the USA when children are struggling. By early adulthood the young people had higher aspirations for employment, the girls were less likely to have become pregnant as teenagers and both sexes were less likely to be in trouble with the law.

The high quality pre-school programmes seemed to have created a positive outlook in the children, and their parents. They viewed school as a useful experience and themselves as people who could achieve and overcome difficulties. The IQ difference faded; positive attitudes lasted, along with a drive to persevere and succeed. The longitudinal EPPE research in England is showing that a good quality early years setting can contribute to closing the gap between children from socially more, and less, advantaged backgrounds.

Does research ever affect practice?

Some research over the years has demonstrably affected practice and a few examples are given here. You will find further examples in other chapters. The ease of access to information seems likely to increase the links (page 253).

Maternal deprivation theory

John Bowlby documented the genuine distress of children separated from their families through the evacuation of children from UK cities during the second world war. The evacuees, and children he studied in residential orphanages, had often been separated from their families, even siblings were sometimes separated. However, Bowlby's psychoanalytical basis led him to interpret the impact of separation on children as maternal deprivation: the temporary or permanent loss to a child of a mother's care and attention. His practical conclusions were that, unless children had the exclusive attention of their mother, especially for the first three years in childhood, then children would be permanently emotionally damaged.

John Bowlby's approach was convenient when the war ended and the government wanted to persuade women who were mothers back into the home, out of the jobs they had occupied for the war effort, and to close down the day nurseries. The maternal deprivation theory continued to be very influential and shaped views about employment of women who were also mothers and the lower age limits for children to enter nursery class or school. Fresh approaches to attachment have led to a re-think, including of the legacy of John Bowlby (page 86).

Children in hospital

The research of James Robertson and Joyce Robertson brought about changes in hospital practice for children and their families. Until the 1950s and 1960s, medical practice was to treat children in hospital as if they were any other patient: small bodies that were ill, but cried a lot at the outset. Medical opinion was that children had short memories, so there could be no lasting effects, even when parents were made unwelcome because they allegedly upset their children.

The Robertsons made two films: *A two year old goes to hospital* in 1953 and *Going to hospital with mother* in 1958. The documentaries show the genuine distress felt by children on separation from their family combined with the strange situation of a hospital stay. The children's distress was interpreted by the Robertsons in terms of separation from their mother, in line with John Bowlby's maternal deprivation theory (page 76). The view now would be that children had been separated from a network of family relationships. A shift away from the exclusive focus on the mother–child relationship now does not reduce the significance of the research.

James Robertson was very active in using their material to try to change hospital practice, but it took time and a considerable amount of pressure. By 1959 they managed to get government guidance to recommend that medical practice recognise the full emotional and social needs of sick children. However, many medical teams continued to resist change. The turning point came in the 1960s, when excerpts of the films were shown on television. A group of mothers in Battersea, South London, formed Mother Care for Children in Hospital (now Action for Sick Children). This organisation put sustained pressure on medical teams to acknowledge the distress of children and to enable easy family contact to sustain key relationships.

Challenging assumptions in practice

From the 1990s onwards some researchers became committed to bringing the children's perspective to the fore.

- The narrative method of Vivian Gussin Paley (page 169) has been influential, as have the consultation methods that arose at least partly from a focus on children's rights.

- The Mosaic method developed by the team from Thomas Coram Centre in London (page 243) has been used and adapted for early years practice. One example is where teams have wished to develop outdoor play and consultation with children, led in some cases by the Learning Through Landscapes (page 242) early years development team. In this kind of work, the research–practice links are viewed as two-way.

- Penny Holland (page 217) undertook action research in a North London nursery centre to track the experimental removal of the ban on what adults judged to be war and weapons play. Holland's research, supported by practical reflections about the tradition of banning 'aggressive play', has been influential in leading some nurseries to re-think their practice.

- Tina Hyder and colleagues at Save the Children have combined action research with the development of advice and support materials with, for example *In safe hands*, a resource pack to support practitioners working with children from refugee and asylum-seeker families (Hyder, 2004).

Research can be wrong; experts can be mistaken

It is not only practitioners who would like a straight answer to a straight question. The media want information, and even the quality end of the media can struggle with the 'ifs', 'buts' and 'it all depends'. Increasingly the legal system has looked towards expert witnesses to provide some definite answers in cases of child protection. Early years practitioners need to be aware that 'experts' can be egocentric, unable to see alternatives to their own theory and can be proved wrong.

Unexplained infant deaths

During the 1970s and 1980s, parents in the UK were told that lying babies on their back put them at risk of choking and that the safest position was on their stomachs or their side. This very firm advice was based on research with premature babies which was then, with no further justification, generalised to care of full-term babies. By the 1990s, statistical tracking showed a rise in unexplained infant death, often called cot death. Further research identified the stomach sleeping position as a risk factor in what became called Sudden Infant Death Syndrome (SIDS). The advice to parents was reversed and the level of unexplained infant deaths dropped significantly.

Careful tracking, before and after the reversal of advice, showed that behaviour change by parents had reduced the level of unexplained infant deaths. This episode is a sober warning about the risks of generalising from small-scale research findings. However, the link between sleeping position and infant death is not an absolute cause and effect. Many parents who followed the 1980s instruction did not face the tragedy of losing their baby. Sleeping position was a significant risk factor but research continues to look at other factors, such as smoking in the family home and genetic vulnerability.

MAKE THE CONNECTION WITH ... PERSONAL EXPERIENCE

The back sleeping position seems so 'obvious' to practitioners who have trained since the 1990s, that I have heard doubts expressed that parents were ever told to put their babies on their stomach. To this reservation I must reply in true pantomime style, 'Oh yes they were!'.

I raised my babies in the early 1980s and could not reconcile this instruction with information that young babies could suffocate if given a pillow. My son and then my daughter slept on their side – alternating left and right each sleep – until they were agile enough to change their own sleeping position.

During 2003–2004 Professors Roy Meadow and David Southall hit the headlines with their claims that multiple infant death in a family could be explained through Munchausen Syndrome by Proxy in the main carer. Both professionals had extended their clinical research to accept expert witness work for legal cases. Other clinicians and researchers accept that the syndrome exists in a minority of disturbed adults, who gain a sense of self-importance as the carer of an apparently very sick child. However, both Meadow and Southall have been criticised because they extended their theory to support claims that accused parents had most likely deliberately killed their babies.

In criminal and civil court it became extremely difficult for parents to disprove the professional opinion, since it was presented as highly expert. Some of this confidence in a professional knowledge base was more about repeated assertions of being right, when there was no clear independent evidence for specific families. In some legal cases, equally qualified professionals had disagreed with the conclusions. In September 2004 an inquiry led by Baroness Kennedy published a report, *Sudden unexpected deaths in infancy*. The report included guidelines to control the use of expert witnesses and to counteract dependence on 'medical belief' rather than a body of scientific evidence.

What causes autism?

In the 1970s, expert opinion agreed that the pattern of child behaviour we now call autistic spectrum disorder was caused by emotionally cold and unresponsive mothers – offensively called 'refrigerator mothers'. The mother-blaming theory sat comfortably with the strong post-Freudian influence in much of psychiatry and a male-dominated profession. This theoretical perspective caused considerable distress within families and most likely delayed the more constructive approaches now available to support parents.

Research can be confusing; experts may not agree

The idea of hyperactivity in children gained a hold in the late 1970s and early 1980s. Even at that time, some researchers expressed doubts about a significant syndrome and alarm about normal childhood exuberance being inconvenient to adults, who might press for solution through medication. There remains considerable disagreement around the definition and causes of Attention Deficit Hyperactivity Disorder. If practitioners, or parents for that matter, only encounter one strand of the available research or application into practice, they can be forgiven for believing that what they have heard or read is the whole story.

Advice on a healthy diet has become progressively more confusing as small-scale research projects seem to suggest that this food is beneficial or that another food has risks to health. An important issue for early years practitioners, and parents, is that advice suitable for a healthy adult diet cannot simply be transferred to diets for infants and young children.

TAKE ANOTHER PERSPECTIVE

- Sometimes it is useful to discover what was actually done in a research study. One piece of folk wisdom is 'research has shown' that, left to their own devices, children will choose a balanced diet over the days, even if their choices are unbalanced within each day.

- I passed on this information as an inexperienced child psychologist, until experience as a parent made me question it. I found a description of the original research in Christina Hardyment's *Dream babies: child care from Locke to Spock* (1983, re-issued in 1995 as *Perfect parents*).

- Clara Davis undertook a study in the USA in 1938 about 'self-selected feeding'. Children in a group setting were given a wide array of food from which to select their meals. All the choices were good quality, freshly cooked food and no snacking between meals. It was true that some children ate nothing but bananas for one meal or were very enthusiastic about potatoes one day. Their food intake and health was monitored carefully and they were healthy, energetic children. However, the children's choices did not include crisps, fizzy drinks or chocolate bars.

- The study does offer practical implications for parents and practitioners. But what in your opinion should be the link to practice now?

Research into diet for children is demonstrating that children are not small versions of adults. Children's diets have to fuel their growth as well as maintain health. But children also appear to have different nutritional requirements from adults because their bodies work differently. For instance, low-fat, high-fibre diets are not suitable for the very young. Babies and children need three to four times as many calories per day in proportion to their body size, in comparison with adults. Low-fat adult diets are unhealthy for children because they need the fat content, for instance from milk. Children can be missing vital nutrients and be malnourished amidst plenty of food. Children's bodies seem to be designed to use fat more efficiently than adults, but children are not yet well equipped to process fibre. Excess fibre can also interfere with their bodies' absorption of zinc and iron.

TAKE ANOTHER PERSPECTIVE

We need respect for social history to avoid the assumption of 'we know it all now!'. Past mistakes seem easy to identify, with the luxury of hindsight. It is easy to say now, 'How could they?' or 'Wasn't it obvious?'. Current dead-ends or serious misapprehensions will take time to be revealed. It is deeply unwise to think that now (whenever 'now' is) that we know it all.

If you want to find out more:

★ **Baron-Cohen, Simon** 2003 *The essential difference: men, women and the extreme male brain*. London: Allen Lane.

Discussion of ethical approaches and consistent male–female differences. The paperback edition is titled *The essential difference* 2004. London: Penguin.

★ **Bryman, Alan** 2004 *Social research methods*. Oxford: Oxford University Press.

The detailed coverage of different types of methods will support you to understand how research can be planned and undertaken

★ **Clough, Peter** and **Nutbrown, Cathy** 2002 *A student's guide to methodology*. London: Sage.

The practical approach of this book grew from the authors' research teaching sessions for postgraduate students.

★ **Cole, Michael** and **Cole, Sheila** 2000 *The development of children*. New York: Worth Publishers.

The fourth edition of this good source book for following up more detailed psychological theory and research.

- ✭ Effective Provision of Pre-School Education – the EPPE project
  http://www.ioe.ac.uk/cdl/eppe/ and www.ioe.ac.uk/schools/ecpe/eppe

  Research project tracking the effects of different types of early years
  settings on the learning and behaviour of young children across
  England.

- ✭ **Gopnik, Alison; Meltzoff, Andrew** and **Kuhl, Patricia** 2001 *How
  babies think: the science of childhood*. London: Phoenix.

  Readable account of what has been discovered by careful research with
  very young children and the ideas behind making sense of very early
  development.

- ✭ **MacNaughton, Glenda; Rolfe, Sharne** and **Siraj-Blatchford, Iram**
  2001 *Doing early childhood research: international perspectives on theory
  and practice*. Buckingham: Open University Press.

  A practical book that explains research methods from different
  theoretical perspectives, especially relevant for research about and with
  children.

- ✭ **Maybin, Janet** and **Woodhead, Martin** (eds) 2003 *Childhoods in
  context*. Milton Keynes: Open University Press.

  Chapters show different ways to approach childhood, acknowledging
  time and place. The book has a wealth of examples, activities and
  readings.

- ✭ **Paley, Vivian Gussin** 2004 *A child's work: the importance of fantasy play*.
  Chicago IL and London: Chicago University Press.

  Reflective account of the author's work as a teacher and of sharing her
  perspective with other professionals.

- ✭ **Robertson, James** and **Robertson, Joyce** 1989 *Separation and the very
  young*. London: Free Association Books.

  Description of their research and the practical implications.

- ✭ **Schaffer, H. Rudolf** 1998 *Making decisions about children: psychological
  questions and answers*. Oxford: Blackwell Publishing.

  Standards for good quality research, the link between research on social
  topics and possible application to practice and policy.

★ **Shore, Rima** 1997 *Rethinking the brain: new insights into early development*. New York: Families and Work Institute.

Illustrated, very practical book about the brain research and information on US long-term intervention projects. Currently out of print, so look on a library shelf (and hold on tight if you have your own copy!).

★ **Smith Peter** 1994 'Play and the uses of play'. In Moyles, Janet (ed.) *The excellence of play*. Buckingham: Open University Press.

A thought-provoking chapter about how play has been regarded and the care needed in apparently objective research.

★ **Sylva, Kathy** 1994 'The impact of early learning on children's later development'. In Ball, Christopher (ed.) *Start right: the importance of early learning*. London: Royal Society of the Arts.

Summary of research into early learning in group settings. Information on the long-term effects of early intervention.

5 Social and emotional development – the foundation

The importance of social and emotional development is strongly emphasised in each of the early years curriculum documents for England, Scotland, Northern Ireland and Wales (also the Welsh Foundation Phase, in process at the time of writing: Autumn 2004). Guidance packs about good practice with under threes, including *Birth to Three Matters* in England, all stress that emotional security and warm relationships underpin healthy early development. The necessity of supporting the emotional development of young children cannot be in doubt. However, it is too easy to skim over what may appear to be a fuzzy area and to focus in daily practice on apparently greater priorities of intellectual development. This chapter covers key concepts that can help to ground a crucial concern with feelings.

The main sections of this chapter are:

■ The importance of attachment.

■ Emotional literacy.

■ Dispositions – where feeling meets thinking.

THE IMPORTANCE OF ATTACHMENT

Attachment is a central idea in any discussion of children's social development. Ideas and perspectives have varied since the mid-twentieth century. The consistent theme emerging is that early experience matters.

What is meant by attachment?

Attachment is a bond of affection between two people in which a sense of personal security and commitment is bound up within that relationship. Secure attachment within very early childhood seems to be a crucial building block for healthy development. Attachment is a set of internal feelings, so it cannot be observed directly. You can, however, see the presence or absence of attachment behaviours. For example, young children may greet their parent with enthusiasm, after even a short separation, and may cling tightly, especially in times of stress or uncertainty. Attachment, like any relationship, is a process and not a single event.

■ A first bond can be formed in the period immediately after birth providing the mother, and father, are able to have this very early contact with the child. The close relationship of affection starts from the very early days. For this reason, special baby units encourage parents to spend time with and hold premature or sick babies who cannot yet leave hospital.

■ The early days are not a one-off, use-it-or-lose-it bonding opportunity – a concept that was dominant in the 1970s and early 1980s. Attachment strengthens through the early months of a baby's life through time spent together in play, communication and through the routines of physical care.

WHAT DOES IT MEAN?

Attachment: feelings of emotional closeness and commitment between children and significant people in their daily life.

Mothers are important and …

From the mid-1940s to the mid-1970s the prevailing view on children's social development was that of John Bowlby, supported by Mary Ainsworth and Donald Winnicott. Bowlby's maternal deprivation hypothesis rested on psychoanalytic theory and his views shaped research, policies and practical advice to families in the UK over several decades. Mothers were seen as the most crucial ingredient in young children's early life; fathers or siblings scarcely rated a mention, except possibly as rivals for mothers' attention.

From the beginning, some psychologists challenged parts of Bowlby's theory – not least that young children needed the almost constant presence of their mother for psychological health. From the 1970s onwards, the stream of criticism became a tidal wave. Research reviews, such as that undertaken by Michael Rutter, challenged the interpretation of the data underlying the basic theory. The social movement of feminism meant that beliefs about 'normal family life' were also challenged. A greater awareness of cultural diversity undermined the highly Euro-centric view that mothers were exclusively responsible for childcare.

Research, as well as daily observation, shows that many young children demonstrate a strong attachment to their mother. But, there is consistent evidence that infants and very young children also develop strong attachments to others within their family, often to their father but also to siblings and other relatives. The key factor seems to be, not surprisingly, that other family members spend time to get to know the young child and to build an emotional rapport. There is no evidence in these situations that very young children are confused by multiple attachments, nor that family attachments to figures other than the mother are 'second best'. On the contrary, children seem well able to distinguish the objects of their attachment and to anticipate and enjoy different care and playing styles.

Early experience matters

However, there was merit in much of what John Bowlby said about the pressing emotional needs of very young children. Barbara Tizard argued in her overview in 1986 that the focus on rebutting Bowlby's over-emphasis on the role of the mother had led people to overlook the important implications of his analysis of mothering. Tizard pointed out the immense importance of the research of James Robertson and Joyce Robertson (page 77) in changing hospital practice, despite their acceptance of the maternal deprivation hypothesis. Now in the early part of the twenty-first century, we have reached a new plateau in views about attachment.

Barbara Tizard had been active in research in the 1970s into the experiences of children in residential care and the negative consequences of a high turnover of carers. In one study Tizard reported that the sample of children had, between four months and four-and-a-half years of age, experienced an average of 50 carers in their residential home. The continued disruption of attachment seemed to disturb the ability of some of the children to make relationships later in childhood.

MAKE THE CONNECTION WITH ... SERVICES FOR LOOKED-AFTER CHILDREN

- In some of the criticisms of Bowlby in the 1970s, there was great optimism about the ability of children to recover fully from even very harsh early experiences. Certainly we do not need to return to the Freudian view that later patterns are utterly fixed by five years of age. However, the experiences of early childhood do matter, because they shape how children, and later adolescents, make sense of, and therefore react to, their social world.

- Make contact with professionals within your local residential or fostering service. Of course, you will not ask about the confidential experiences of individual children or teenagers. However, fellow-professionals who work directly with looked-after children, in fostering or residential care, will be able to give a sense of how much hard work can be needed when early experience has been harsh and disruptive.

Michael Rutter and his team are undertaking a longitudinal study of Romanian children adopted from the impersonal orphanages of their birth country into UK families. The research has documented significant improvement in the serious cognitive delays of the children at adoption. However, the degree of 'cognitive catch-up' was better for those children who had left the orphanages by six months of age. Children who left at between 12 and 18 months of age had experienced serious emotional deprivation and physical harm through malnutrition. The team assess that the psychological deprivation has led to developmental consequences that are harder to alleviate, even when children are adopted into a loving family. The ERA study, other research with adopted Romanian orphans and with children in residential settings shows that serious psychological deprivation in the very early years affects children's emotional security and ability to make relationships.

Young brains and early experience

Children can be resilient through minor troubles and they do not require parents and other carers to be perfect in every way (fortunately!). However, there are limits; young children are affected by harsh treatment and unpredictable daily lives. Research on early brain development supports concerns long expressed by early years professionals. Repeated experience of emotional harshness (it does not have to be also physical) and unpredictable adult behaviour (not the odd 'off day') creates elevated levels of cortisol in young brains. This chemical is present in saliva and consequently changes in its level can be measured with a simple test.

Cortisol is a steroid hormone secreted by the adrenal gland and, like all hormones, it circulates through the body via the bloodstream. Cortisol reaches the brain where it regulates response to stress. Human brains need cortisol but too great a level, caused by stress, can actually destroy brain cells and reduce the density of the synapses, those crucial connections between the cells. High levels of cortisol block children's ability to learn in positive ways. But, equally important, their brains make other connections that show through their behaviour, including anxious or aggressive actions. The young children have become hard wired for trouble and are swift to interpret the actions of others as a potential threat.

In contrast, babies and young children who have experienced warm and consistent nurturing, have lower levels of cortisol than those babies whose daily lives have been highly stressful or traumatic. The other significant difference is that, when the nurtured infants experience stress, the natural elevation of cortisol reduces more rapidly. The brain connections of secure infants are telling them that this is a blip or a bad day, rather than further proof that life is dire and people are not to be trusted.

MAKE THE CONNECTION WITH ... YOUR PRACTICE

- Strong emotional states create chemical changes in the brain. So, anxious parents or early years practitioners do not help very young children by putting them on a treadmill of 'stimulating' intellectual activities. Such frenetic activity, however well intentioned, is far more likely to backfire.

- Young learning unfolds best of all when positive emotions experienced by young children facilitate chemical secretions in the brain that help the messages to cross the synapses. These substances, called neurotransmitters, help learning when children feel rested, able to make their own choices and are feeling emotionally secure.

- On the contrary, feelings of exhaustion, anxiety and pressure can make it impossible for the neurons in the child's brain to send or receive the necessary signals.

- What are the practical applications of this finding to your own practice?

Developing close relationships within childcare

The research and theory on attachment and separation is a complicated, and often emotive, area. However, it is clear that out-of-home childcare must be organised to enable children to form attachments, and that these should not be disrupted without warning. Social pressures have changed from the time when John Bowlby developed his ideas about attachment, but children have not changed. They are still distressed if important attachments are disrupted, just as John Bowlby himself was apparently devastated at four years old by the loss of his nanny.

What matters for quality care?

Research reviews have generated very similar key issues that focus on the importance of close, affectionate relationships to ensure quality in out-of-home care for young children.

- Margaret Henry focused on the importance of responsiveness: a warm and affectionate relationship with children that demonstrates the adults' high regard for the children. Involvement was an active support of children's learning, which encourages exploration and achievement. The third dimension was a positive approach to control, characterised by consistency and explanations, which encourage children to independent action. Positive control in action works through both responsiveness and involvement.

■ Barbara Tizard highlighted familiarity, responsiveness and attachment. These three themes are the focus of the discussion of the key person system by Peter Elfer, Elinor Goldschmied and Dorothy Selleck.

■ The Scottish *Birth to Three* guidance has been built around the three Rs of: relationships, responsive care and respect.

Several writers emphasise the concept that young children need to feel that they are 'kept in mind'. This theoretical perspective has very practical implications. The idea most likely originated with W. R. Bion (*Learning from experience* 1962 – thanks to Jane Elfer for this bit of detective work). Bion described how babies become able to summon up the idea of someone who is important, but not physically in front of them. Babies are then less desperate that someone has gone forever. He described how their emotional security depends upon feeling that they are held in mind by an important person in their life, as much as held in body through caring physical contact.

LOOK, LISTEN, NOTE, LEARN

Please focus on the concept that young children need to feel that they are 'kept in mind' by the important adults in their life. The Scottish *Birth to Three* guidance describes the relationship as that 'even in the busiest times of the day, young children feel secure that they have not been forgotten, by being given a smile, by being talked to, by being noticed' (2005: 17).

Reflect on your own practice:

■ In what ways do you behave so as to assure babies and young children that they are 'kept in mind' during the day?

Then reflect on ways that you let young children know that they are kept in mind by their important adults when those people are not there.

■ Think first – what do you say and do that lets young children know that you recall what you did together or what they told you yesterday or last week?

■ In what ways do you help to make close links between children's home and your care? How do you reassure young children that they are kept in mind by their families, when children are with you?

Share your observations and reflections with colleagues.

MAKE THE CONNECTION WITH ... HOLISTIC LEARNING

Emotional warmth and secure relationships in out-of-home care are not only crucial for the very youngest children. In the EPPE research it became clear that outcome measures for behaviour and cognitive development with three- to five-year-olds were most supported by early years teams who showed emotional warmth and were responsive to the individual needs of these, still very young, children. As Judy Dunn has strongly argued, it makes no developmental sense to attempt to study cognitive progress as if it is separate from emotional development and social relationships.

The key person system

Quality in work with babies and young children can only be delivered through a caring, personal relationship between baby or child and practitioner. In nurseries, a key person system needs to link an individual practitioner with individual children and with their parent(s).

- One practitioner is responsible for settling in both the child and parent, or other family carer. The key person role is not simply about filling in records; it is a personal relationship.

- Ideally, the key person is the one who attends to this child's physical needs. Very young children need to be able to recognise the face of the person who changes and feeds them or to whom they wake from a nap.

- The key person really gets to know an individual baby or toddler. The adult then understands the child's preferences and develops personal rituals of songs, smiles and enjoyable 'jokes'.

- The key person can develop a friendly relationship with the child's parent, sharing ideas about the young child and communicating important information about the day or the baby's state of health.

WHAT DOES IT MEAN?

Key person system: a way of organising within group settings that assigns a named practitioner to develop a close relationship with a young child and his or her parents.

Peter Elfer and colleagues discuss carefully the reservations expressed by practitioners who worry that affection for young children is somehow incompatible with professional standards. Such concerns have to be resolved for the sake of the children. Otherwise the result can be 'multiple indiscriminate care' – a phrase used by Alastair Bain and Lyn Barnett (1986)

MAKE THE CONNECTION WITH ... YOUR PRACTICE

Babies and toddlers need to develop close and enduring relationships. They cannot be 'too attached' to familiar adults who are key in their daily life and some young children spend many hours in out-of-home care. They need to develop an attachment to their key person and then to, at most, one or two other familiar practitioners.

Adults, practitioners and parents, need to resolve the mixed feelings that undoubtedly exist. Parents who work long hours may well be worried if their young child is clearly fond of her key person. But these understandable feelings need to be discussed between the adults and not 'solved' by disrupting young children's attachments in out-of-home care.

- Reflect on how you are able to make a personal, supportive relationship with young children in your work.

- If you work in a group setting, does your team operate a key person system? If yes, then exactly how does it work?

- Consider some of the 'Ah but ...!' concerns recognised by Peter Elfer and his colleagues in *Key persons in the nursery* (2003). To what extent do these reflect your own concerns, or those of your colleagues?

For further information look at Julia Manning-Morton and Maggie Thorp (2001) *Key times: a framework for developing high quality provision for children under three years old* 2001, pack including video.

Relationships between children

The focus in this section has been on affectionate relationships between adults and children. However, babies are essentially social in nature and show interest in other children as well as adults. Older babies and toddlers seek to make social contact with others of their own age as well as with older children. An important feature of supportive out-of-home care is that children get to see each other on a regular and predictable basis, so they can discover the shared games and interests that build friendships. This aspect to social development is discussed from page 152.

Young friendships can be supported in relaxed groups

The importance of touch

Look back over the key issues raised in this section. You will see that such qualities cannot emerge without a relaxed atmosphere in which adults touch and cuddle, and children feel able to ask for physical contact by word or gesture. Reviews of good practice with young children, for example Colwyn Trevarthen and his team, describe emotional and other developmental needs that cannot possibly be met without touch.

Research into the workings of young brains has shown that physical contact is part of the whole social and emotional experience for babies and children. A sense of emotional security creates strong connections within children's brains. A positive environment is created chemically in the brain and this balance supports learning and happy exploration. Touch is a powerful non-verbal message, reassuring children that they are liked and welcome. Restrictions on cuddling, for whatever reason, undermine children, creating a sense of emotional insecurity. Young children may redouble their efforts to gain personal attention, and see their peers as direct competitors in this effort.

MAKE THE CONNECTION WITH ... YOUR PRACTICE

Young children should be confident of your physical comfort in times of distress or uncertainty. But a cuddle, a friendly lap, a hand-hold are all important messages that say, 'I missed you yesterday' (being kept in mind) or 'What a building! Haven't we done well!'.

The *Birth to Three Matters* pack (published through Sure Start in England) uses the phrase 'snuggling in' to mean the need for babies, toddlers and young children to have easy access to a lap, to be cuddled and close. Misplaced concerns about child protection have created doubts in some early years teams about touch. Do you face such issues in your own mind or in your team?

Young children learn about appropriate touch and boundaries when they experience warm and affectionate touch from familiar adults, and that has to include their key person, and familiar practitioners in a nursery setting.

- Children need direct experience of how responsible adults behave and what is affectionate and respectful touch.

- If important adults restrict cuddling, young children can only make sense of this loss by taking it personally. Under fives and even more so under threes, conclude 'she (or he) doesn't like me' or 'Nobody cares about how I feel' (and the feeling could be 'excited' as well as 'upset').

- Children who are persistently deprived of affection can be emotionally at risk. The need for affection does not go away, so children are vulnerable to anyone who offers personal attention. They are then doubly at risk because children have not learned how safe adults should behave.

Discuss, with the support of your tutor in a student group, how meeting the emotional needs of young children must be a priority and can be compatible with good practice in child protection.

For further information see Lindon (2003).

The need for nurturing

As an educational psychologist working in London during the 1970s, Marjorie Boxall had many referrals from teachers who struggled with the behaviour of children who seemed unable to cope with the demands of a classroom. Boxall's observations led her to develop small nurture groups, in which she and her colleagues steadily built up children's social and self-care skills. A revival of interest in the 1990s, with a growing proportion of children who cannot manage primary classroom life, has led to the re-emergence of nurture groups. The high adult–child ratio is more expensive than the usual Reception or Year 1 ratio, but, in the long term, the cost is much less than the full social cost of letting children fail at school.

WHAT DOES IT MEAN?

Nurture groups: special groups established in primary schools to support those children whose early experiences have not prepared them to cope with the demands of classroom life.

In the nurture groups, children of five, six years and older are enabled to experience learning activities that they have missed in their early years. The objective is to combine a nurturing approach, through adult behaviour, with a supportive daily routine. Children are then enabled to learn skills crucial to group life, such as waiting for a short while, taking turns, making choices and seeing an activity through to completion. The children also need to develop a trust in adults and see them as a useful resource.

MAKE THE CONNECTION ... WITH YOUR PRACTICE

The work with nurture groups highlights the ways in which disruptive early experiences of different kinds can mean that children have not built their understanding of a predictable social world. The children's struggles also highlight what is demanded of children in most primary school environments. Practitioners need to be responsive towards those children who have persistent difficulties. But we should also be impressed by the way that many children, who are still young in years, do manage to cope.

- Follow up some of the information about nurture groups (page 111).

- Consider what kind of experiences the children may have missed.

- What may happen to more children in early years settings if practitioners feel harassed to push them through educational targets and continually 'get them ready ...' for the next stage?

EMOTIONAL LITERACY

The word 'literacy' has usually been applied to written language. But there is also a pattern of verbal and non-verbal communication about feelings – an emotional vocabulary. Children, and adults, can be more or less skilled in this area of learning and children are influenced by adult behaviour and attitudes. Adults, in their turn, have been shaped by their own childhood, their social and cultural background. The concept of emotional literacy and its application is linked with the idea of emotional intelligence.

Emotional intelligence

Daniel Goleman developed the idea of emotional intelligence as a balance to excessively intellectual definitions of skills and abilities. He wrote about adult development and focused on five broad strands:

1   *Knowing your own emotions* – the self-awareness of recognising a feeling as it happens to you, being honest with yourself about how you feel.

2   *Managing emotions* – handling feelings so that they are appropriate for the situation is an ability that builds upon self-awareness.

3   *Motivating yourself* – dealing with emotions to be able to concentrate, direct and focus your feelings in a productive way.

4   *Recognising emotions in others* – the ability of empathy includes being able to notice the social signals and tune into the emotions of other people.

5   *Handling relationships* – social relationships depend on using empathy to support other people and help to manage the emotional content.

Goleman developed a set of ideas applied to adult behaviour and reactions. Children are in the process of learning these skills – or not, depending on their experiences. To support young children, early years practitioners and parents need to have a clear view of how emotional development unfolds and be willing to reflect on their own emotional intelligence. Awareness of emotions can undoubtedly be used to manipulate and undermine others. Practical applications of concepts of emotional intelligence and emotional literacy are underpinned by pro-social values.

WHAT DOES IT MEAN?

Emotional intelligence: awareness of your own and others' emotions, the ability to harness feelings to motivate yourself and to develop relationships.

Emotional literacy: ability to express your own feelings and to recognise and understand the emotions of other people.

Empathy: sensitivity to the feelings of other people and ability to tune in to their emotions – the sense of 'feeling with' and not pity or 'feeling sorry for . . .'.

Understanding emotions

Throughout the early years, children are learning about their own and others' feelings. Undoubtedly, adults need to be open-minded in how the ideas of emotional literacy are put into practice and need to ensure that it does not become culture-specific. Aware adults need to recognise that their own feelings are involved, as well as to be realistic in expectations of children:

- Within their first year, babies show a range of emotions that are only partly provoked by their internal physical needs. Babies cry, but they also express contentment, surprise, uncertainty.

- Toddlers show their emotions through facial expression and their whole body movements. They may be uneasy about strong emotions such as anger or fear. They start to show embarrassment or pride in achievements.

- From about two years onwards, young children learn some words to express their feelings. A lot depends on their experience. For example, Judy Dunn noted that two-year-olds who had an emotional vocabulary, had mothers who had commented on emotions when children were younger.

- Three- and four-year-olds start to understand that other people have feelings as well. Even younger children can show pro-social behaviour (page 208).

LOOK, LISTEN, NOTE, LEARN

Supportive and affectionate adults can help young children as they:

- Become clearer about their own feelings.

- Are more able to name those feelings and talk about them.

- Recognise the source of strong feelings, felt by themselves or others.

- Find ways to express feelings in assertive rather than aggressive ways.

How do you use opportunities to help children in these ways? Gather some examples of individual interaction and conversations – not planned group or circle times.

Be aware that children with disabilities in the autistic spectrum struggle to understand these subtle clues, for emotional communication and many aspects for interaction in play (see, for example, Beyer and Gammeltoft, 2000).

Control of emotions

Two- and three-year-olds tend to express immediately whatever emotion they are feeling. If they are happy, it shows in their face and whole body posture. If they are distressed, the tears will come. Between four and six years of age, children show an increasing ability to inhibit temporarily the expression of strong feelings, when they judge it is not the time or place. You may especially notice children holding back their emotions when they are upset. They sense the situation is inappropriate or they do not want to show someone their distress (the idea of 'being brave'). Young children develop some level of impulse control. Nancy Eisenberg proposed that what she calls emotional regulation is the basis for a child's repertoire of social skills. Happy social interaction usually requires children to be willing to hold back sometimes on what they want and find ways to express emotions that do not alienate their friends.

WHAT DOES IT MEAN?

Impulse control: ability to hold back on inclinations or expression of feelings.

Emotional regulation: children's ability to direct or re-direct feelings.

LOOK, LISTEN, NOTE, LEARN

In early years settings, you will observe children who are trying hard not to cry, although they are distressed. Parents have many experiences of getting home with children and facing the flood of distress that the children have managed to control in nursery or school.

A growing awareness of social and cultural expectations is also part of children's learning whether and how to express strong emotions. Cultures around the world vary in social rules about expression of feelings, some being more demonstrative than others.

- What do you observe of young children and how they deal with feelings?

- Does it seem likely that some young children are already aware that some emotions are more acceptable to adults?

> ## MAKE THE CONNECTION WITH ... FAMILY LIFE
>
> ▧ Of course, adults may struggle with emotions that seem inappropriate to express, or even to feel. Robin Skynner and John Cleese (1997) discuss how all families may have one particular emotion that is hard to face. For example, the emotion of jealousy may be tough to resolve, so parents – probably re-working their own childhood – say, 'We have no jealousy in our family'.

Adult emotional literacy

> ## MAKE THE CONNECTION WITH ... HOW DOES IT FEEL WHEN ...?
>
> Tuning in to young children is well supported when adults can access a parallel experience of their own – whether from their own childhood or a carefully organised exercise experienced as an adult.
>
> Elinor Goldschmied describes how she organised two different lunchtime experiences for senior day nursery staff to provoke empathy with children's experience. Lunch on the first day was relaxed, with appetising food on tables set attractively and with plenty of social conversation. On the second lunchtime, the course delegates were told to go into lunch without warning, made to wait for their food, which was good in quality but unappetising in appearance. There were many demands from the early years advisors, whom Elinor had briefed, that delegates had to say 'thank you', everyone had to wait for the slow eaters before getting their pudding. You get the idea! The direct experience was very supportive in enabling these senior staff to reflect on how mealtime was run in their own nursery. (You will find more detail on pages 165–66 of Goldschmied and Jackson, 2004).
>
> I have heard equally creative ideas from college tutors and nursery team managers. For example, practitioners who are keen on a conveyer belt approach to so-called creative activities may be provoked to reflect if they have to endure a very directive craft session. Alternatively, how does it feel if people ruffle your hair or adjust your clothing without so much as a word? How does it feel if a trainer or tutor has asked everyone to bring a significant item from their childhood and the items are just put to one side?
>
> You need to know the group before you would try some reflective exercises. There must always be time for debriefing and discussion, with questions such as, 'How did you feel about ...', 'What were you thinking when ...' and 'What does this tell you about how children may feel when ...?'.

If you look back over the previous section, you will realise that much of what you could observe in young children's emotional behaviour will already have been shaped by messages from important adults. In order to support the development of emotional literacy and tune into children, adults have to become aware of their own emotional reactions.

Young children of three or four years of age start to appreciate that adults have feelings too. Children can be puzzled, partly because the adult world is different from the social world of children, but also because adults themselves are sometimes confused, or less than honest. For instance, an adult who is scared because a child has nearly walked into the road may shout at the child, who hears the anger and cannot read the adult's mind to understand, 'I was scared you might hurt yourself'.

Emotion coaching

John Gottman undertook longitudinal research in the USA with parents on how they dealt with emotions within family life and relationships with children. He interpreted his findings about the psychological and physical well-being of children through making sense of the different parental styles of handling the 'negative' emotions of anger, sadness, envy and so on.

He distinguished four styles in parents' overall approach, which are equally applicable to any adults responsible for children:

1   A dismissive approach was taken by some parents. They ignored or trivialised children's negative emotions. Children took the message that their parents did not notice their feelings or that such feelings were silly and unimportant compared with proper adult concerns.

2   Some parents were actively disapproving of children showing negative emotions. They criticised and punished them.

3   Another style was a laissez-faire approach by parents who were accepting of their children's negative emotions but failed to guide their children in the expression of strong feelings and did not set limits to behaviour.

4   A fourth group of parents accepted their children's expression of strong or negative feelings and let the children know that their emotions were heard and understood.

Gottman described the fourth option as emotion coaching. He explained that, unlike the laissez-faire approach, parents who took an active role with their children's strong emotions also explored what children might do about the situation. Parents acknowledged the emotion, yet guided children towards expression in ways that were less harmful to others.

WHAT DOES IT MEAN?

Emotion coaching: an approach when adults deliberately support children to understand and control their own feelings and to have empathy with other people.

MAKE THE CONNECTION WITH ... ADULTS' OWN FEELINGS

Some adults – parents as well as practitioners – resist accepting that young children have strong feelings, especially that they can be very sad or emotionally hurt. It can then feel more appropriate to try to jolly children out of sadness with, 'Let's go and do a picture'. Yet, the best approach, and an emotionally literate one, is to say, 'You look sad' or 'I know you miss Daddy' and offer the child a cuddle or other physical comfort.

Why do you think some adults take the 'jollying' approach?

- Is it easier to believe that young children 'get over' upsets quickly? Maybe also that adults struggle with their own distress at seeing an upset child?

- Some practitioners may learn the 'jollying' approach from apparently more experienced colleagues. It just seems to be the right thing to do.

- Some adults are concerned that acknowledging a child's upset will make them more distressed. The opposite is usually the case; acknowledged children tend to calm. Children get very confused if they are sure they look upset and nobody seems to notice at all!

- Do some practitioners feel that distress in a child is an implicit criticism of their professional skills: they should be able to bring a child round swiftly?

What do you think? And what can be done to support early years practitioners in taking more of an emotion coaching, or emotionally literate, approach?

Also, look back at the research of James and Joyce Robertson (page 77). Why do you think that medical staff preferred to believe that children in hospital were not really upset?

Self-esteem

The term 'self-esteem' has become familiar within supporting children's emotional development. It has some ground in common with emotional literacy but is not quite the same. There are several aspects to what is usually meant by the term:

- In the broadest sense, your self-esteem emerges from an overall evaluation of your own self-worth.

- Your level of self-esteem is created by the gap you perceive between what you wish to be and what you believe you are. So a person's self-esteem could be anywhere between very high and extremely low.

However, the judgements are subjective. Individuals vary in the standards they apply and the areas of their life in which they feel achievement is important. One person might feel that musical talent is very significant, yet their close friend might be desperate to experience success in sports.

Children's potential development of a sense of self-esteem progresses hand in hand with the rest of their development. Their abilities of communication support close relationships and friendships. Thinking and reasoning abilities help them to make sense of what they experience, sometimes reaching very different conclusions from the adults who are involved in the same situation.

- By about seven years of age, children's experience builds towards their personal internal judgements that create a sense of self-esteem. By then, they have a sense of the gap between 'what I am' and 'what I ought to be'.

- The level of a child's self-esteem, and the room for positive or negative shift, is affected by the support they experience from family and friends. However, individual children vary in temperament: how harshly they judge themselves and how resilient they are to criticism from others.

- Children have learned to focus on those areas of their life that they believe are important for success, mainly because other people have indicated these areas are to be valued and others to be dismissed.

- Children's level of self-esteem is affected by the extent to which they feel accepted for what they are and treated as people who can continue to learn.

LOOK, LISTEN, NOTE, LEARN

The psychological literature on self-esteem suggests that a healthy level is built through five broad areas:

1 Feelings of competence or lack of ability in learning: can I do it? what about my mistakes?

2 Confidence in physical skills and abilities.

3 Social acceptance: having friends, people who want to be with me.

4 How I behave – am I acceptable, what if I do something wrong?

5 Physical appearance – how do I look and is that fine?

Take each of these in turn. Reflect and observe in what ways you support children in each area, while helping them to have realistic expectations for what they can manage. You can also look at constructive feedback (page 110).

DISPOSITIONS – WHERE FEELING MEETS THINKING

Learning is not all intellectual or rational; feelings are equally involved. It is important that children develop in confidence that they can learn. Part of healthy personal development for young children, including self-esteem, is a growing sense that they are competent individuals. By three or four years of age, and certainly within the early years of school, it dawns on children that there is a great deal that they do not yet know. Children can feel overwhelmed by this prospect, unless they have already developed confidence that they are learners and that it is not all their responsibility, because adults are supposed to help.

TAKE ANOTHER PERSPECTIVE

- Apparently Albert Einstein said, 'I am neither especially clever nor especially gifted. I am only very very curious' (quoted in Wiseman, 2004: 85).

- What are the advantages for children's learning if they develop lively curiosity?

The positive disposition to learn

Lillian Katz developed the concept of dispositions: habits of mind and a pattern of behaviour that is directed towards a broad goal. She suggested that adults often wish children to develop curiosity, creativity, independence and other dispositions. Of course parents and practitioners can vary about the exact form such dispositions take in practice and what is regarded as positive in their socio-cultural group.

Margaret Carr developed these ideas and was part of a team that made positive dispositions a strong theme in Te Whāriki, the bicultural early years curriculum for New Zealand. Knowledge, skills and attitudes are seen to combine as dispositions, such as the habit of mind to be curious. Dispositions are encouraged by adults, rather than taught and the task of supportive practitioners is to create a learning environment that enables them to promote positive dispositions in children. Young children may be able to kick or catch a ball, but that ability does not mean that they will be disposed to play at ball games. If children have been teased about their lack of skill, they may be disinclined to practise. On the other hand, if the children have been encouraged, they are likely to have a positive disposition to learning, not only ball games but probably other skills.

Enjoyable spaces can help children to focus

WHAT DOES IT MEAN?

Positive dispositions to learn: an outlook, attitudes and pattern of behaviour that will support children to be, and want to be, learners.

Margaret Carr described five broad domains of learning dispositions:

1 Taking an interest.

2 Being involved.

3 Persisting with difficulty or uncertainty.

4 Communicating with others.

5 Taking responsibility.

She then considered each domain in three parts:

1 *Being ready*: that children see themselves as someone who can participate in the learning. This outlook needs to be supported by the second part.

2 *Being willing*: children feel their environment has opportunities and, from their perspective, is safe for learning.

3 *Being able*: children have or are developing the knowledge and abilities that support their inclination. Feelings of competence can support being ready and willing.

LOOK, LISTEN, NOTE, LEARN

Children's positive disposition to learn includes:

■ Curiosity and the wish to find out and explore.

■ A desire to become competent, to be able to do or say something.

■ Motivation to keep trying, even if something is difficult or confusing.

■ A sense of satisfaction for children when they manage a new skill or idea.

This positive outlook can develop over time with adult support. Reflect on your own practice – in what ways are you promoting this positive disposition?

■ What is done to support children – from adult behaviour or the way that the learning environment is organised?

Alternatively children may learn from negative experiences because adults highlight mistakes – there is no point in trying.

■ Be honest, are there aspects of your practice, or that of your colleagues that you need to raise diplomatically, to turn back from this situation?

We need to hold developmentally appropriate expectations. You could make short observations to show how curiosity or perseverance could appear with:

■ Toddlers, younger than two years.

■ A four-year-old.

■ A six- or seven-year-old.

■ Perhaps also an adult like yourself.

Engagement and involvement

Ferre Laevers, working in Belgium at the Centre for Experiential Education in Leuven, has developed concepts and measurement around young children's level of engagement and involvement in their nursery or school experience.

Laevers was interested in the links between learning and children's sense of well-being. He observed that you could conclude that children felt at ease, and therefore were in a positive emotional state for learning, when they felt able to act spontaneously in their nursery, expressed their feelings, exuded vitality and looked as if they were enjoying themselves. A sense of well-being eased deep involvement in learning but did not ensure it. Laevers was concerned, like other early years researchers, that the layout of the learning environment was crucial, including use of space and sufficient, but not too many, play resources. He stressed the need for children to be able to make genuine choices and that adult support should follow the child.

Laevers made the point that when children are impressed with materials they are keen to get involved, they do not need to be pushed. He suggested that children's involvement in learning was encouraged by challenges that were neither too easy nor excessively hard. The challenge should be at the edge of the children's current competence – a link with Vygotsky's zone of proximal development (page 178).

Christine Pascal and Tony Bertram developed Ferre Laevers' ideas in their Effective Early Learning (EEL) project, run from Worcester College. This research with early years settings has focused on a range of adult behaviours summed up as 'engagement'. They define this term as a set of personal qualities of the adults involved in supporting children's learning. The EEL observational research has worked to ground these qualities in what adults actually do and in differences between adults who work with children.

Pascal and Bertram have identified that the key features of more, or less, constructive behaviour with children are:

- *Sensitivity* – of the adult to the feelings and emotional well-being of children. The term also refers to empathy and genuineness on the part of the adult. Sensitive actions acknowledge children's sense of insecurity and offer encouragement.

- *Stimulation* – the way that an adult intervenes in the learning process. Pascal and Bertram have observed how adults introduce or offer an activity. Adults can be more, or less, stimulating in the ways they offer information or join an ongoing activity to promote thinking or communication.

- *Autonomy* – describes the degree of freedom given to the child to experiment. Effective adults support children to make judgements, choose activities and express ideas. The dimension of autonomy includes how adults deal with conflicts, rules and other behavioural issues. A positive approach includes the participation of children in rule-making.

Mastery or learned helplessness

Kathy Sylva reviewed the research into the effect of the well-funded, carefully planned early educational intervention programmes. Long-term tracking of the children has pointed to the great importance of how adults encourage children to view learning. The results are equally relevant whatever your setting or your professional background, because the research did not suggest simple answers that a particular kind of setting or specifically trained adult was inevitably best for children. What mattered most was the impact that different adult styles exert on children's outlook, their dispositions towards learning and themselves as potential learners.

Kathy Sylva draws on the concept of mastery behaviour in children, developed through research undertaken in the USA by Carol Dweck and her colleagues. In her studies of children and learning, Dweck interpreted important differences by describing whether children had developed an orientation of mastery or learned helplessness. Children with a mastery approach saw new learning tasks as a challenge rather than a threat. Their outlook, when faced with a difficult problem or one at which they initially failed, was to look carefully at their strategy and try another approach. In interviews with the researchers, children with a mastery orientation showed that they believed effort usually paid off. They did not think that difficulties arose because they were stupid. The children valued persistence, took a problem-solving approach and felt good about themselves and their capacity to learn.

WHAT DOES IT MEAN?

A mastery orientation: a positive outlook that assumes problems can be resolved and that it is worth persevering.

Learned helplessness: when children give up easily, feeling that they are incompetent and cannot deal with new challenges.

In contrast, children who had learned what Carol Dweck called a sense of helplessness were far more likely to view new or difficult tasks as threats to be avoided. This group did not persevere or try alternative strategies when the experimental tasks became difficult or children experienced initial failure. They started to chat or engage in other kinds of off-task behaviour. In interviews, these children expressed beliefs that failure showed you were 'no good' at something. They felt negative about themselves and so wanted to get out of the situation. The children had taken on an idea of innate ability: that people are either naturally good at something or useless, and practice will not help.

MAKE THE CONNECTION WITH . . . YOUR PRACTICE

Mastery and learned helplessness are not absolutes. Children (and adults) show greater or lesser degrees of their orientation. Neither orientation is linked with measurable intelligence. A child could be potentially very able, yet feel helpless and hopeless. The outlook may be influenced by temperament (page 195) but mainly depends on children's learning experiences.

- Carol Dweck and her team do not propose that children are made unrealistically optimistic about their capacities. An honest awareness of current strengths can go hand-in-hand with a desire to learn more.

- The research suggests that children are helped to develop a mastery orientation when adults encourage them in the satisfaction of learning a skill or gaining more knowledge.

- When adults organise children's learning towards success on particular tasks, children may learn to focus more on what they can or cannot do currently, with less sense of continuing to learn.

What can you do in your practice to promote a mastery orientation with children? In what ways do you set a good example and model to children when you approach something new or react when something goes wrong? Reflect on what kind of adult behaviour could push children towards learned helplessness?

Constructive feedback

The idea of how to give useful, accurate and supportive feedback has been explored largely within organisational psychology and with application to adults in the work setting. Yet much of this area is equally relevant to children, with some minor adjustments of language. Constructive feedback, given to children at the time, was identified as important in the EPPE project and the detailed observation of the most effective centres taken on by the REPEY (Researching Effective Pedagogy in Early Years) follow-up research (page 175).

Children can be resentful when adults mainly criticise, but it is not helpful to hear an undiscriminating stream of positives. If adults always say 'That's lovely' or 'wonderful drawing!', children do not feel that the praise is genuine. The same phrase or level of emotion is expressed, whatever the child has done. Also there will be many times when children have not grasped an idea or could manage better with a different technique. Children do not fall apart if their mistakes or misunderstandings are pointed out with warmth and respect. The problem comes when adult intervention is dismissive and fails to be balanced by recognition of what has gone well.

TAKE ANOTHER PERSPECTIVE

- Children become disheartened when adults find fault or only notice the mistakes.

- Parents or early years practitioners may genuinely believe they are being helpful. Perhaps their own childhood has left them thinking, 'children have to know what's wrong – how else will they learn?'.

- How may adults who struggle to be encouraging turn their own style around to support young children?

Useful, constructive feedback for children addresses feelings as well as facts:

- Positive feelings can be expressed in words of encouragement to children along with positive body language and smiles.

- Negative feelings, if appropriate, should be worded very carefully. There may be times to say, 'I'm disappointed by . . .' but what follows has to be constructive and avoid blunt criticism. Concerns should be expressed factually. Adults should, however, acknowledge and deal sympathetically with children's negative feelings about their abilities.

- Positive factual feedback is useful for children: what has gone well and why or how a child's perseverance has paid off.

- What could be negative factual feedback can be valuable if given in a constructive way – covering what has gone well and what has gone awry – and a genuine help to children to learn from mistakes.

MAKE THE CONNECTION WITH . . . YOUR PRACTICE

- Watch and listen for examples of constructive feedback: from adults.

- Reflect on your practice and how you might catch an opportunity for constructive feedback next time.

Here are some suggestions to consider in your own work. Of course, you need to find a form of words that sits comfortably with your personal style. But make sure, by watching a child's face and listening to any words in reply, that the overall impact is constructive and encouraging.

- Knowing a child well can help adults to boost children's confidence. Perhaps you can remind a child how 'you told me you'd never ever be

---

able to do up your buttons. And look at you now. Don't worry, we'll work out this problem with the water and the guttering'.

▦ So long as adults help, children can learn from mistakes and frustrations. Some children need a great deal of reassurance along the lines of 'I can hear you're having trouble with the scissors. Show me how you're doing it'. Careful observation helps you pitch the level of your help.

▦ Invite other children to help with, 'I think Chris worked out how to ...' or 'I'm sure Tanya knows a lot about ...'.

You may also like to look at the section on modelling on page 203 and using encouragement from page 201.

LOOK, LISTEN, NOTE, LEARN

■ In a family home or an early years setting, where constructive feedback has been established, you will find that the children treat each other this way as well. Perhaps one child tells another 'Well done' or a genuine 'Thank you for helping me' or pays the compliment of 'I like your picture'.

■ Listen for any examples of this kind in your own setting. If you hear none or very few, then reflect on whether children can imitate your model.

If you want to find out more:

☆ **Bowlby, John** 1965 *Child care and the growth of love*. Harmondsworth: Penguin.

A summary of the ideas of maternal deprivation and gives a window onto the social values and assumptions of the time.

☆ **Boxall, Marjorie** 2002 *Nurture groups in school: principles and practice*. London: Paul Chapman Publishing.

Explanation and description of nurture groups and how they can support children. See also http://www.nurturegroups.org

☆ **Carr, Margaret** 2001 *Assessment in early childhood settings*. London: Paul Chapman Publishing.

Discussion of dispositions but also an approach to children's learning through how it is embedded in the situation and ways to enable participation.

★ **Dunn, Judy** 1993 *Young children's close relationships beyond attachment.* London: Sage.

Discussion of research into children's relationships, useful because it relates social development with children's cognitive and language development.

★ **Edwards, Anna Gillespie** 2002 *Relationships and learning: caring for children from birth to three.* London: National Children's Bureau.

Report and commentary on the detailed observational research undertaken by Peter Elfer and Dorothy Selleck.

★ **Eisenberg, Nancy** 1992 *The caring child.* Cambridge MA: Harvard University Press.

Discussion of ideas about pro-social behaviour and emotional development.

★ **Elfer, Peter; Goldschmied, Elinor** and **Selleck, Dorothy** 2003 *Key persons in the nursery: building relationships for quality provision.* London: David Fulton.

Full discussion of the ideas behind the key person system. The authors also address common reservations about this way of organising a nursery.

★ **Goleman, Daniel** 1996 *Emotional intelligence – why it can matter more than IQ.* London: Bloomsbury.

Explanation of the ideas of emotional intelligence.

★ **Gottman, John** and **Declaire, Joan** 1997 *The heart of parenting: how to raise an emotionally intelligent child.* London: Bloomsbury.

Research and practical suggestions for supporting children's emotional development. Written for parents but just as relevant for practitioners.

★ **Healy, Jane** 1994 *Your child's growing mind: a practical guide to brain development and learning from birth to adolescence.* New York: Doubleday.

Accessible summary about research into brain development and applications to support children.

☆ **Henry, Margaret** 1996 *Young children, parents and professionals: enhancing the links in early childhood*. London: Routledge.

A positive emphasis on how practice in early years settings has much to learn from family life with babies and toddlers.

☆ **Learning and Teaching Scotland** *Birth to Three: supporting our youngest children* 2005. Download from www.ltscotland.org.uk/earlyyears/birthtothree.asp

Good practice guidance for early years practitioners in Scotland. More supporting materials available on the website.

☆ **Pascal, Christine** and **Bertram, Tony** 1997 (eds) *Effective early learning: case studies in improvement*. London: Hodder and Stoughton.

Descriptive reports of the effective early learning (EEL) project and the ideas behind the approach.

☆ **Rutter, Michael** 1972 *Maternal deprivation re assessed*. London: Penguin.

Review of the research and interpretation. (Second edition published in 1981.)

☆ **Rutter, Michael** 1999 'English and Romanian adoptees study (ERA)'. In Ceci, Stephen and Williams, Wendy (eds) *The nature–nurture debate*. Malden MA: Blackwell.

One report of this longitudinal study of children adopted into English families from the Romanian orphanages compared with English adopted children.

☆ **Schaffer, H. Rudolf** 1998 *Making decisions about children: psychological questions and answers*. Oxford: Blackwell Publishing.

Summary of some research about early experience and long-term effects.

☆ **Shore, Rima** 1997 *Rethinking the brain: new insights into early development*. New York: Families and Work Institute.

Well-described and -illustrated book about early brain development and implications for good practice.

☆ **Sure Start/DfES** 2002 *Birth to three matters: a framework to support children in their earliest years*. Free pack with video, tel: 0845 6022 260.

There is a substantial research review on the CD Rom, also sold as a booklet.

☆ **Sylva, Kathy** 1994 'The impact of early learning on children's later development'. In Ball, Christopher (ed.) *Start right: the importance of early learning*. London: Royal Society of the Arts.

A detailed review of the relevant research and the implications for practice.

☆ **Tizard, Barbara** 1986 *The care of young children: implications of recent research*. London: Thomas Coram Research Unit: Working and Occasional Papers No. 1.

A valuable re-think of ideas in the mid-1980s. Unfortunately no longer in print – you might find a copy in a university library.

☆ **Trevarthen, Colwyn; Barr, Ian; Dunlop, Aline-Wendy; Gjersoe, Nathalia; Marwick, Helen** and **Stephen, Christine** 2003 *Meeting the needs of children from birth to three*. Summary on http://www.scotland.gov.uk/library5/social/ins6-00.asp. Download full research review from http://www.scotland.gov.uk/about/ED/IAC/00014478/page705680189.pdf

Substantial research review with practical applications to day care.

Theory and research within developmental psyc[h]
disciplines has given limited attention to physic[
]Gesell and his team documented physical skills
development, as part of establishing norms for [
]18). Otherwise, theorists and researchers have [
]interested in cognitive development and com[
]because these skill areas distinguish humans [
]mammals.

Whatever the exact reason, developmental psychology has tended to describe physical growth and change in skills and then has moved on, without much theoretical speculation about what such changes mean for children. There are sound developmental reasons why we should not take physical development for granted. The main sections in this chapter are:

* Physical development and children's experience.

* Learning through the senses.

* The importance of outdoor learning.

PHYSICAL DEVELOPMENT AND CHILDREN'S EXPERIENCE

Children's physical development is important for their all-round development and well-being:

* Children's physical growth makes new behaviours possible. Young toddlers take time to be able to gain the balance to walk with confidence and carry something at the same time. Young children love playing with a ball, but even six- and seven-year-olds struggle to hit a ball with a bat.

* Children's growth determines their potential experiences within their everyday life. A crawling or walking toddler can take independent action to cross the room to something of interest. Three-year-olds, able to manage their clothes in the toilet, can take more control of personal routines.

* Confident physical skills support co-operative play between children and enable them to take pleasure in organising themselves in construction, gardening or pretend play projects.

* Children's growth affects the responses of other people. Children who are smaller or larger than average, compared with their peers, are often treated differently by children and adults.

* A sense of physical competence, or incompetence, affects a child's sense of

Taking a video apart – happy use of fine physical skills

self-esteem. All children need to learn the skills of co-ordination but some feel 'clumsy', compared with their peers.

■ Children need to be active in childhood, because regular and lively physical activity builds muscle strength, lung capacity and bone density. Basic physical fitness is laid down in childhood and there are limits to how far you can repair the deficiencies later. Insufficient physical activity, especially accompanied by unhealthy eating habits, increases all the serious health risks associated with obesity.

■ Physical confidence, through plenty of practice in large and fine physical movements, is crucial for children to manage the bodily control necessary later for writing and reading.

LOOK, LISTEN, NOTE, LEARN

Watch and listen to children of different ages. How do their current physical skills open up possibilities or currently place a limit on what the child can do without help?

Find an example of some or all of the following ideas:

■ How the development of physical skills affects the response of other people to a baby or child. For instance, a crawling child can reach things that were previously safe. Do carers start to say 'no' or move things out of reach?

■ How is a child's world affected when disability means that independent mobility is postponed or will always be difficult?

■ The physical development of successful toilet training means people are not impressed with dry pants any more. How do children feel if perhaps the appreciation tails off too quickly?

■ Does sheer size affect social interaction? What tends to happen if children are larger or smaller than average for their age?

■ How do children feel if they are physically less confident than their friends?

Physical growth changes a child's social world

Contrast your mental picture of a newborn baby with a mobile and active seven- or eight-year-old. Human newborn babies are helpless, especially compared with other young mammals who struggle to their feet and start to follow their mother within an hour of birth. Our babies have reflex actions at birth but they are scarcely able to make deliberate physical actions. If all has gone well, a child of seven or eight years is physically co-ordinated, able to choose from a wide range of large physical movements and fine skills to achieve different purposes. It is an impressive achievement.

Getting the hands free

Young children's physical development underpins many of the other learning tasks that they face, because the growth of physical skills is not simply more of the same. The development of skills changes the qualities of experience for a young child. Elinor Goldschmied pointed out that until babies are independently mobile, they are dependent on their carers to bring things of interest to them and often to hold the item steady for the baby. Her idea of the treasure basket was a resource for babies who could manage to sit securely. This new skill gave the babies 'time on their hands'.

LOOK, LISTEN, NOTE, LEARN

- The physical skill of being able to point with hand and/or fingers opens up another perspective for young children, linked with communication.

- Pointing is a way for older babies to communicate to adults or helpful older children what it is that they want.

- But pointing is also a social skill, it enables the older baby to indicate something of shared interest. I watched a baby of about one year of age entranced as he was able to direct his father's attention to one thing after another on our local street.

- Gather examples of how older babies use their power of pointing. When does this skill first emerge?

Independent mobility

Observation of babies demonstrates their powerful drive for physical control. Before they become mobile, babies spend a lot of their waking time using their current physical skills. Their ability to control their body moves steadily downwards, with control of the head being the first task. If you watch babies under one year old, it is very noticeable how much effort they put into moving their limbs, getting hold of objects and attempting to move themselves by whatever method they can manage. Mobility becomes a key issue for them and for their carers, since an immobile baby is very dependent on what adults, or other children, bring to them or take them towards.

Young children develop their ability to use and learn further physical skills, yet physical development is not separate from everything else that they are learning. Annette Karmiloff-Smith shows how careful watching of babies' and toddlers' physical abilities can often highlight other, less obvious, aspects to their development. You will see their persistence, creative attempts to solve problems – 'how do I get hold of this?' and 'how do I make that work?' – and their delight with achievements. The boxed example from my own family diary illustrates how Drew's developing physical skills opened the door for a great deal of learning within other aspects of his development.

MAKE THE CONNECTION WITH ... HOLISTIC DEVELOPMENT

These are some highlights from the diary I kept of my son, Drew. When these events happened he was a toddler of 16–17 months.

- Drew will go and find Lance when I suggest 'Go and show Daddy' even if that means going upstairs.

- Drew makes us laugh by standing on tip-toe or walking backwards. He falls over deliberately sometimes and gives his loud 'stage' laugh.

- Lance has started a game with Drew where Lance says 'One, two, three go!', and Drew runs and throws himself into Lance's arms. Drew now makes sounds in the same rhythm when he jumps on his own or throws himself onto the floor cushions with a 'Da, do, da, dah!'.

- Drew is safe to let walk into the garden from the back door. He has his little watering can and wants to water the flowers as well as smell them.

- He wants to use the J-cloth to wipe up his highchair tray, as he sees me do. He likes putting objects into containers so he is happy sometimes to help in tidying up his toys.

- He can get out the books he wants from the shelf and has learned to work the pulls in the books with moveable parts.

- He is so pleased with himself when he makes something work. He can get all the cones onto his rod and, if one of us engages the mechanism, Drew can press the lever and shoot them into the air. He stamps his feet in appreciation or applauds himself by holding one hand steady and clapping the other against it.

Questions

- The highlights are all led through physical development, but what other skills are shown in these examples?

- Make an observation of a toddler of a similar age. What can he or she manage in terms of physical skills? Then look for how these skills open up other areas of development.

Practice in physical skills is crucial for learning

The research into brain development in very early childhood has confirmed that babies and toddlers need to be able to move. They need plenty of hands-on learning, and safe feet-on and mouth-on contact to learn through their senses. The enjoyable practice of crawling, grasping and handling objects builds vital neural connections in young brains. Babies and children need to repeat and practise in order to firm up those connections. The neuroscientists express it as 'the cells that fire together wire together'. This need for happy practice is not restricted to physical development, but so much of early learning is led through the drive to move. Continued experience in any area of development firms up neural connections, until they form the complex neural pathways on which babies build more learning. Those connections that are not strengthened by repeated experience are less strong and may fade away.

LOOK, LISTEN, NOTE, LEARN

Observe one or more babies over the time that they learn to crawl. (Not all babies crawl; some move by bottom shuffling.) You will see the external version of what is being built in the baby's brain.

- Babies who are ready will have built the muscle strength to be on all fours, but the problem is 'how do you move?'. Babies often rock to and fro, looking up perplexed because, despite all the vigorous movement, they have not actually travelled at all.

- Then, quite often babies manage to move but, because the top half of their body is currently the stronger, they go backwards. They sit on their bottom, look around expectantly and their face often crumples in disappointment.

- But babies keep trying and are soon rewarded with forward motion, that they practise enthusiastically over the days. You will see the gleam in their eye, as they spot something of interest, move from sitting to crawling, reach their destination, sit back on their bottom and reach out their hands.

- You have seen in action the development from an immature set of neural connections to a fully functioning neural pathway, that is linked also to baby thinking and forward planning.

Sally Goddard Blythe has pointed out the dangers of failing to appreciate what babies and toddlers learn through movement and the long-term consequences of undervaluing the importance of physical development. In one sense, Sally Goddard Blythe travelled backwards from her work with older children who had co-ordination difficulties. She also explored when physical factors seem to underpin dyslexia and Attention Deficit Hyperactivity Disorder.

Goddard Blythe talks about 'the first ABC': that attention, balance and co-ordination are the crucial building blocks for later learning. She stresses that:

- Children need confidence and competence in large movements as well as fine co-ordinations. Pushing young children into writing exercises does not help them to learn to write at an earlier age. Such pressure creates unsuitable physical habits for handwriting and gives children negative experiences of early writing.

- Babies and children should not be rushed through their physical skills. For example, the actions of crawling help babies and toddlers to establish their sense of balance and are often the first experience of synchronising the left and right sides of the body. The necessary co-ordination of moving hands and vision in crawling is undertaken at the same distance that children will use some years later in reading and writing.

- Children need plenty of relaxed opportunities to move in order to understand the messages from their body. This physical feedback about touch, grasp and balance is called proprioception.

- From her research, Sally Goddard Blythe agrees with other observers of early years practice, such as researchers concerned with outdoor play (page 130), that young school-age children, let alone of nursery age, cannot be expected to sit and concentrate for long periods without physical breaks.

LOOK, LISTEN, NOTE, LEARN

- Sally Goddard Blythe observes that the most advanced level of movement is the ability to stay totally still. You may recall that dilemma from learning to ride a two-wheeled bicycle. But, toddlers who are mastering the skills of walking, have to keep moving to maintain balance.

- Watch them and you will see that toddlers wobble when they come to a stop and plump down on their bottoms. It is only after plenty of practice that confident walkers are then able to stand still.

- Observe, or recall, how the most difficult part of learning to ride a two-wheeled bike is the slow moving part between being still and getting enough speed to hold the momentum.

WHAT DOES IT MEAN?

Proprioception: the ability to recognise and use the physical sensations from the body that give feedback on balance and the position of our limbs.

LEARNING THROUGH THE SENSES

Young children learn a very great deal through direct contact. They need the reassurance of touch, cuddling and being rocked (page 92). Also they learn about the world through their senses. Researchers concerned to bring back awareness of the outdoors often highlight the power of learning through the senses and the opportunities of the natural world. The delights of a sensory room or a sensory indoor corner have, in some cases, reached early year settings through an awareness of the needs of children with disabilities. However, such resources are truly inclusive.

TAKE ANOTHER PERSPECTIVE

- The focus on learning through the senses highlights the experiences of children who have reduced use of one of their senses, for example vision or hearing. Parents and early years practitioners need to reflect carefully about what needs to be adjusted and what does not.

- Look at some of the practical ideas offered by the National Deaf Children's Society http://www.ndcs.org.uk and the Royal National Institute for the Blind (RNIB) on http://www.rnib.org.uk

The importance of hands-on learning

Elinor Goldschmied worked with day nurseries in England and in Italy and was influential in bringing the importance of learning through the senses back to early years practice. By the late 1970s Goldschmied was very concerned about over-reliance in family homes and nurseries on commercially made plastic toys. (The situation has definitely worsened since that time.) Elinor Goldschmied developed the treasure basket to promote relaxed exploratory play that enabled babies to discover for themselves. She stressed the importance of materials that support all of children's five senses: hearing, vision, touch, smell and taste. She also identified a 'sixth sense' in children's sensitivity to their own bodily movement and recognition of what physical skills feel like when they are used. This idea is very similar to that of proprioception (page 121).

Toddlers often still enjoy playing with the treasure basket or with collections of similar kinds of materials. This activity extended naturally into discovery or heuristic play that Elinor Goldschmied developed for day nurseries. (The term 'heuristic' was taken from the Greek word eurisko, meaning 'serves to discover'.) A heuristic play session is a special time when mobile toddlers and young children have access to a rich resource of recycled materials, none of which are conventional toys. As with the treasure basket, the aim is that toddlers play as they wish and adults watch with interest. Adults help if asked, or offer help as appropriate, but do not direct children's play by actions or words.

WHAT DOES IT MEAN?

Treasure basket: a play resource developed by Elinor Goldschmied for babies who can sit unassisted. The low basket contains a range of safe and interesting objects that are not conventional toys.

Heuristic play: an exploratory play resource for toddlers and young children, also developed by Elinor Goldschmied and using a wide range of ordinary objects and recycled materials for children to play with as they choose.

LOOK, LISTEN, NOTE, LEARN

Gather observations of sitting babies who are able to enjoy the treasure basket on different occasions.

- How do individual babies approach the choice in the basket? What do they like and what do they do with items? Do some babies return to the same item over time?

- Two babies can sit with the same basket. Do they have different styles of exploration? Does one baby offer any items to the other?

Gather observations also of a heuristic play session:

- What interests individual children? What do they want to explore? Do they watch each other or hand over items?

- In what ways do children invite your help or interest?

- What have you learned about the skills, interests and preferred ways of exploration of the babies or the toddlers?

Learning through schemas

Chris Athey developed Piaget's idea of schemas as part of a series of early educational intervention projects based at the Froebel Institute in the Roehampton area of south London through the 1970s. The objective was to support children from less socially advantaged homes and the project aimed to work in partnership with the children's parents. The approach through schemas was a deliberate attempt to create common ground between the teachers and parents, mainly mothers.

Chris Athey described schemas as 'cognitive constants'. They are often a repeated sequence of similar physical actions that show a combination of young thinking and exploring. Schemas are patterns of behaviour that are linked through a child's current interest and which form the basis of exploration and play for young children. For example, the play behaviour of one child may be described through a fascination with a schema of 'enveloping'. Perhaps this child explores many different ways of covering herself or objects, or investigates the possibilities through craft activities that include wrapping.

Chris Athey developed the concept of schemas far beyond Piaget's academic interest in children's cognitive development. Use of the schema approach in nurseries has been a positive means to help practitioners and parents to respect toddlers' play explorations, when it might seem like 'just messing about' or not 'proper playing' to adults. For instance, a child who is thoroughly absorbed in his exploration of an 'inside–outside' schema may move objects from place to place and may put items inside others. Unreflective adults may become annoyed that the child wants to put play materials or other objects where they do not belong. The child may also be much more interested in nesting various containers and items than making the model that a practitioner has on her list for today.

MAKE THE CONNECTION WITH ... PHYSICAL DEVELOPMENT

Arnold Gesell, who focused on the maturational approach (page 18) nevertheless saw the connection when he said that a two-year-old 'thinks with his muscles' (1954).

WHAT DOES IT MEAN?

Schemas: patterns of behaviour that are linked through a child-chosen theme of interest and from which a child explores in different situations.

Tanith busy transporting

The interest in schemas has continued and the use of this concept as part of partnership is strongly shown in the work of the Pen Green Centre in Corby. Cath Arnold describes ways of using the concept of schemas through the early development of individual children. For example, at one point Harry is very interested in connection and disconnection. Georgia spent several months exploring a schema of enveloping that first appeared to arise from her concern that the rabbits would get wet without a protective covering.

Carmel Brennan describes examples, in words and photographs, of how young children organise their own play exploration through their current schema. Ali is a girl who likes to envelop: she is busy wrapping up her doll in the visual example, but Ali also likes to wrap presents for her friends and to make her baby dolls cosy. Martin is very absorbed in filling bags and moving materials around his playgroup. Sometimes he is being a customer in the shop corner, but his interest in filling and transporting is more extensive than this role play.

LOOK, LISTEN, NOTE, LEARN

When my daughter was 18 months old she liked moving bricks and dolls around in her wooden trolley indoors, anything in the small wheelbarrow out of doors and her older brother in his buggy when we went on walks. Tanith had a big bag, in which she carried around a range of objects that were important to her. However, she also added objects that were important to us, such as her father's watch and the remote control for the television. It was crucial that we did not get cross with Tanith: she had not stolen these objects and she kept them safe. So, as well as explaining that Daddy's watch should be left where she found it, we also got used to asking Tanith to open her bag when we could not find something.

One way of making sense of Tanith's behaviour is to say she was exploring a 'transporting' schema. It was not her only way of exploring at 18 months, but it was a strong theme in how she worked with and on her environment in the latter half of her second year.

Think about and observe children you know. Can you see the pattern of a schema in their play? For instance, you could look for:

- *Rotation*: an interest in things that turn like wheels, objects that roll or a child's physical exploration of spinning around herself or waving her limbs in a circular motion.

- *Orientation*: a fascination with how things seem from another angle, explored by turning objects around or the child twisting or hanging upside down.

- *Connection*: how things are or could be joined together. A child might explore this in crafts, in stringing together toys or showing connections in a drawing. The opposite schema of separation can lead to havoc when children have the physical skills to disassemble objects that adults would rather they did not!

Make notes and compare your observations with a colleague.

Brain-based learning

Advances in computer imaging have greatly extended understanding of how human brains work and of early brain development. Reviews, such as that of Jane Healy, show that many insights give strong support for existing good early years practice that tunes in to what and how young children learn. Thorough knowledge of child development, linked with the brain research, can make daily interactions with young children more supportive of their learning.

TAKE ANOTHER PERSPECTIVE

It is important to note two key issues.

1 There is still a very great deal that is not known about the brain and how it works.

2 Practitioners, and parents, need to be wary of commercial interests that have seized the research as a way to sell toys, videos and kits for parents.

You will find many claims for products that will 'boost your child's brain power'. Some materials may be useful, even though the promises are overblown. However, you can support young brain development through using simple play resources with your attention and a warm relationship.

For example, singing and music is beneficial for young children. But an entire industry has grown around the claim that listening to Mozart will boost measures of intelligence. The original research was on college students, the effect was short lived and the experiment has not been successfully repeated. Look at http://www.skepdic.com for discussion of the so-called Mozart Effect, as well as other claims based very loosely on research.

Prior to advances in neuroscience, research and theory about the process of learning highlighted four general stages in awareness:

1 *Unconscious incompetence* – you are unaware of an area of knowledge or skill; you do not know that you do not know.

2 *Conscious incompetence* – you are only too aware that you do not know, cannot understand or manage a skill, but you want or need this ability.

3 *Conscious competence* – when you are able to use knowledge or manage a skill, but you have to attend carefully while you do it.

4 *Unconscious competence* – when you have practised enough that this area seems automatic, ideas are obvious and you do not have to concentrate.

(These ideas have been around for years. I have been unable to track who originally laid out this cycle – information gratefully received!)

LOOK, LISTEN, NOTE, LEARN

- Adults already have a great deal of learning experience. You may be aware of stress or discomfort when you need to learn something new. Use the four stages to reflect on a skill that you learned as an adult, such as driving a car.

- Now, look at the process of learning from children's perspective. Skills that seem easy to you are less than obvious to children; ideas that are crystal clear to you may be a mystery to them. (See also 'Are we talking about the same thing?' on page 187.) An awareness of the cycle of learning fits well with the practical ideas around the concept of brain-based learning.

Awareness of how young brains operate has been brought together into an approach that is called 'brain-based learning', for example as shown by Nicola Call and Sally Featherstone for early years and Sara Shaw and Trevor Hawes for primary school. This approach links with a holistic, whole child framework (page 9).

Physical movement and well-being

The brain-based learning approach emphasises the importance of physical activity to support and promote learning.

- The opportunity to move is linked with mental alertness and emotional well-being. Increased physical activity actually increases the blood flow to the brain and promotes the neural connections of learning.

- Applications to primary school practice include the idea of 'brain breaks': that children need active interludes to aid concentration. Flexible early years practice should mean that young children provide their own brain breaks, through ease of movement and free flow between indoors and the outside resources.

- The ideas of 'brain gym' draw on the value of regular movement and exercise. The general principles are sound, although some programmes make hard-to-substantiate claims about links to the brain research. Sally Goddard Blythe also describes how regular movement sessions can help children focus and manage both the active movement and the relaxation.

- Children cannot learn if they are hungry or dehydrated. Brain-based approaches often stress that children should have easy access to drinking water. Some holistic approaches are also linked with healthy eating, such as a good breakfast and nutritious snacks and meals.

Using the senses – VAK

This approach highlights that children, and adults too, learn in different ways. A well-rounded approach to learning draws on the senses, especially visual, auditory and kinaesthetic, know as VAK for short.

- *Visual*: use of images to show and not only tell. For example, early years settings that use photos and friendly captions to remind 'Now we wash our hands' or 'Our books are happy when they are stacked like this'. Cartoons and photographs, some with the additional interest of 'lift the flap', help young children to follow a sequence for a routine. Gestures support communication and the visual element works together with the sound of spoken words (page 145).

- *Auditory*: learning is well supported when practitioners are alert to noise levels, ease of hearing and the rhythm of sounds. Selected use of music can help children as they move from one part of the day to another routine. You need to choose carefully, since music creates or supports a mood. Avoid fast music that increases in volume if you wish children to relax. Children need to be able to distinguish pieces of music. Their brains are not 'stimulated' by non-stop background sound; children just learn to ignore it. The auditory aspect to learning is triggered when you encourage children to voice their thoughts (see also page 166) or talk through their plans before plunging into action.

LOOK, LISTEN, NOTE, LEARN

Consider the three strands of visual, auditory and kinaesthetic.

- In what ways do you use each of these possibilities to support learning?

- On reflection, does your practice tip more in one direction than another?

- Can you identify your own preferred learning style?

The VAK approach does not mean that you overlook the other two senses: smell and taste.

- Think about smells. Pleasant and unpleasant aromas can affect a learning environment.

- Taste is important for everyone, not only babies who put everything into their mouths. Good food (taste and smell) is a powerful support to young children's learning, because they feel that important adults care about them and care for their enjoyment and well-being.

Use the resources at the end of this chapter to find out more about brain-based learning. The websites have a great deal of information.

■ *Kinaesthetic*: the power of touch is used as a resource for learning when children have access to natural materials, a variety of textures (not all plastic) and comfortable furnishings and dens. They benefit from space and 'permission' to move, rather than being harassed to 'sit still and concentrate'. Gestures also add the communication of movement to meaning from spoken words.

Early years practitioners need to create a learning environment with experiences that offer a balance between the three channels. Practitioners working with older children, teenagers and adults need to realise that individuals will have developed a preference for one style of learning. Sara Shaw and Trevor Hawes describe classroom planning and practice that can provide options for the diversity in any group.

TAKE ANOTHER PERSPECTIVE

Are you part of a team that plans through topics or themes?

■ Nicola Call and Sally Featherstone (2003a) provide the idea of creating a visual map with children for a topic that has been planned by practitioners.

■ The adult starts with a short explanation of the topic, some key words on paper and maybe a simple picture. But then the children take over with their ideas, fetch items and draw pictures to illustrate what will be included. String or wool is used to connect together the visual ideas.

■ There is good reason to argue that, if you cannot easily engage children in this kind of visual mapping, then the topic you have planned probably does not connect well with their current knowledge and understanding of the world. It is a step too far in terms of their zone of proximal development (page 178)

THE IMPORTANCE OF OUTDOOR LEARNING

Early years practice in the UK developed in the first half of the twentieth century with a strong emphasis on the value of the outdoor environment. Yet, changes in practice over the last quarter of that century steadily undermined outdoor learning. There is good reason for optimism that the importance of the outdoors is once again being recognised, supported by the work of Helen Bilton, Marjorie Ouvry and Margaret Edgington. However, it is important to recognise the blocks that can still undermine a full view of children's learning.

WHAT DOES IT MEAN?

Outdoor play: opportunities for children to learn in the outdoors, in a garden or other open air space.

Physical play: activities and opportunities that especially help children to use, practise and apply the full range of their physical skills.

The outdoor curriculum: focus on the value of outdoor learning and flexible planning that enables children to progress on all aspects of their development while being outdoors.

How did outdoor learning become devalued?

Nursery schools were established in the UK with a strong emphasis on children being outside and physically active. Pioneers such as Margaret McMillan built their early years curriculum upon the value of outdoor experience and play for young children. The first nursery schools were set up largely for children who could be at a social disadvantage. But, an equally strong concern was that the traditional primary school model was inappropriate for younger children. The generous nursery garden was never envisaged as a school playground, so it was not an area to be used only for short 'break times'.

MAKE THE CONNECTION WITH ... TOP-DOWN PRESSURES

- The loss of outdoor learning is symbolic of the whole top-down pressure that has unbalanced much of early years practice.

- Look through this section and find your own connections with imposition of a school model (see also page 239), the whole concept of 'pre-school' (page 230) and 'getting children ready ...' for the next stage.

Respect for the outdoors continued for many years until an alternative model of early learning developed through the last decades of the twentieth century. Several strands came together that pushed outdoor play and related physical play to the sidelines for early years settings, back to more like school break time.

▨ Over the 1970s the whole concept of early education as compensatory shifted to a much stronger focus on cognitive development. A wide range of pre-school compensation programmes were launched and tracked for measurable changes in children's development (page 107). The more valued learning was now believed to happen indoors, not out in the garden.

▨ The task of early years settings in the UK came to be defined as preparing children for school, and more specifically not to fail in school. In contrast, many European early years systems see their task as contributing to the raising of the next generation, preparing children for life in society, not exclusively to fit the role of school pupil.

▨ A top-down school model affected early years teams through the 1970s and 1980s and many accepted a working definition of 'learning' and 'concentration' as something that happened when children were sitting still at indoor activities. The outdoors became the place where 'children let off steam'. Marjorie Ouvry adds that early years settings linked with a primary school also risked taking on the view that physical activity was the same as PE, traditionally a low priority subject in the school curriculum.

▨ By the late 1980s and 1990s discussion about early learning in different settings had become very focused on intellectual development. Anxieties about children's later achievement in school, and pressures about inspection,

Plenty of learning outdoors

made matters worse, especially if early years teams lacked confidence to promote children's all-round learning.

Sufficient time to play and learn outdoors

Marjorie Ouvry describes the need to challenge the circular logic that develops when outdoor learning is dismissed. Adults find excuses from the weather, how long it takes to set up outdoor equipment or that children get too noisy. Any excuse is found to limit time outside with the consequence that children do not have an enjoyable time, so there is the proof that outdoors is a waste of effort. Over-anxiety about safety outside can be another reason to limit time and activities, rather than engage in problem-solving with the children. I explore this practical issue in my book *Too safe for their own good?* (Lindon, 2003b).

Over several decades, the image of nursery life became closer to that of a school day and a classroom, with the garden as break time. Even the key concept of 'learning through play' (page 236) became much more defined as activities planned by adults for their educational purposes. Free play became too often something that happened as a reward: 'when you've done your work, then you can go and play'. Yet this inappropriate practice can be challenged. Margaret Edgington and other researchers in this area describe how the entire early years curriculum can be experienced outside to the benefit of all children, but especially for those boys and girls who really need to move.

Jane Devereux and Ann Bridges (2004) describe the many ways in which children learned through being directly involved in the development of their nursery garden. They recount how an unexpected event was converted by the children into an absorbing and exciting afternoon.

> Over 100 large sacks of bark chips had been delivered for the nursery, but just dumped on the pavement outside the school. Far from being daunted, the children were keen to tackle this irritation as a problem to be solved. The adults were willing assistants, but observed with pleasure as the children used communication and mathematical skills to consider and test possibilities. Team work flourished as they organised their wheeled trolleys and the transport routes. Social skills of cooperation oiled the process as the entire delivery was moved through and into the nursery by the children and left ready for use in the next stage of garden development.

Helen Bilton identified how problems outdoors can be created because practitioners have timetabled outdoor play. Children sometimes start 'queuing' at the door and, when the garden is made accessible, they may drop what they are doing and rush outside. Vivian Paley noted the change when she increased the amount of free and outdoor playtime and spread it over a longer period in the day. The boys in particular became more willing to use table-top activities. Many UK early years settings have enabled free movement between indoors and the garden and blurred any difference between indoor and outdoor resources.

MAKE THE CONNECTION WITH ... YOUR OWN PRACTICE

Helen Bilton undertook an action research study of outdoor time in 1993. She observed the changes in children's behaviour when a 15-minute timetabled outdoor session was changed to free flow between indoors and the garden. The 'mad dash' to the outside stopped, because children keen to play in the garden realised there was no time limit. The play outside became less manic and more sustained; children were no longer trying to pack all their favourites into 15 minutes. On reflection, Helen Bilton and the nursery team realised that the very short outdoor period had been a self-fulfilling prophecy.

- **Reflect on your own practice, or different patterns of organisation that you have observed in settings.**

- **What tends to happen for children when there is limited outdoor time?**

- **How do adults interpret children's behaviour? Do they allow for the consequences of their own, adult choices?**

- **Is outdoor time seen as a source of problems rather than opportunities?**

Positive moves to re-establish the potential of outdoor learning are helped by initiatives such as the Forest School movement and outdoor action research such as the Rising Sun Woodland Project (page 269). Children flourish when they are given experience to connect themselves to the outdoors, nature and the natural world. This emphasis on the outdoors is not only an issue for urban children. For instance, the Bridgwater Forest School project in Somerset is situated in what looks to a city visitor like a more rural area. But the team working with four-year-olds in the woodland resource realised than some children had scarcely visited the countryside that surrounds their town.

LOOK, LISTEN, NOTE, LEARN

- Practitioners can best support outdoor learning when you tune in to how the outdoors is experienced by children.

- On your own, or with colleagues, stand close to the edge of a flower bed or other planted area in your garden. Stand still for a short while and take in what you can see and hear.

- Then bend at the knees and go straight down vertically. What can you see now, what is the child's eye view on this bit of outdoors?

If you want to find out more:

✶ **Arnold, Cath** 1999 *Child development and learning 2–5 years: Georgia's story*. London: Paul Chapman Publishing.

✶ **Arnold, Cath** 2003 *Observing Harry: child development and learning 0–5*. Maidenhead: Open University Press.

Each book offers a full description of an individual child and links development with theory in an accessible way, including the concept of schemas.

✶ **Athey, Chris** 1990 *Extending thought in young children: a parent–teacher partnership*. London: Paul Chapman.

The theory behind the concept of schemas in children's thinking and learning. Some examples, but the stories of Georgia and of Harry bring the ideas alive.

✶ **Bilton, Helen** 2002 *Outdoor play in the early years: management and innovation*. London: David Fulton.

Theory underpinning the importance of outdoor experience and practical suggestions to support learning.

✶ **Bilton, Helen** 2004 *Playing outside: activities, ideas and inspiration for the Early Years*. London: David Fulton.

Concepts, but also many practical suggestions and plenty of inspiring photos.

✩ **Blythe, Sally Goddard** 2004 *The well balanced child: movement and early learning*. Stroud: Hawthorn Press.

Explanation of why babies and young children need to be able to move. More details on the website http://www.inpp.org.uk

✩ **Brennan, Carmel** (ed.) 2004 *The power of play: a play curriculum in action*. Dublin: IPPA.

Helpful description of concepts into practice, well supported with photographs and children's learning stories.

✩ **Call, Nicola** and **Featherstone, Sally** 2003a *The thinking child: brain-based learning for the foundation stage* and 2003b *The thinking child resource book*. Stafford: Network Educational Press, tel: 01785 225515 or from Featherstone Education, tel: 0185 888 1212; http://www.featherstone.uk.com

Concepts behind the ideas of brain-based learning and practical suggestions. More on http://www.acceleratedlearning.co.uk and links to other sites.

✩ **Devereux, Jane** and **Bridges, Ann** 2004 'Knowledge and understanding of the world developed through a garden project'. In Miller, Linda and Devereux, Jane (eds) *Supporting children's learning in the early years*. London: David Fulton.

Chapter 17 provides an encouraging description of how much learning can happen when children are engaged in outdoor play and projects.

✩ **Edgington, Margaret** 2002 *The great outdoors: developing children's learning through outdoor provision*. London: Early Education.

Ideas and practical suggestions.

✩ **Goldschmied, Elinor** and **Jackson, Sonia** 2004 *People under three: young children in day care*. London: Routledge.

Good practical descriptions, but less strong on new developments since the first edition, e.g., no mention of any UK writers in the outdoor play section.

★ **Healy, Jane** 1994 *Your child's growing mind: a practical guide to brain development and learning from birth to adolescence.* New York: Doubleday.

Information about brain development and the real practical applications for supporting children.

★ **Karmiloff-Smith, Annette** 1994 *Baby it's you: a unique insight into the first three years of the developing baby.* London: Ebury Press.

Research and observations of early childhood. From a Channel 4 series in 1994, also a video (see page 269).

★ **Lindon, Jennie** 2001 *Understanding children's play.* Cheltenham: Nelson Thornes.

Ideas and research about play, not only the outdoors.

★ **Lindon, Jennie** 2003b *Too safe for their own good? Helping children learn about risk and lifeskills.* London: National Children's Bureau.

Concepts and practical approaches around risk, not only about physical activity and the outdoors.

★ **Ouvry, Marjorie** 2000 *Exercising muscles and minds: outdoor play and the early years curriculum.* London: National Children's Bureau.

Practical booklet about outdoor play, including dealing with practitioner beliefs that reduce or devalue the outdoors.

★ **Ouvry, Marjorie** 2004 *Sounds like playing: music and the early years curriculum.* London: Early Education.

Practical book about using music and how this experience supports young children.

★ **Paley, Vivian Gussin** 1984 *Boys and girls: superheroes in the doll corner.* Chicago: University of Chicago Press.

One of Vivian Gussin Paley's thoughtful descriptions of a kindergarten year. This book focuses on the value of boys' lively pretend play.

★ **Play Scotland** 2003 *School Grounds Literature Review.* Contact theresacasey@playforlife.fsnet.co.uk or the website http://www.playscotland.org

Substantial review of research and projects.

☆ **Shaw, Sara** and **Hawes, Trevor** 1998 *Effective teaching and learning in the classroom*. Leicester: Optimal Learning. Tel: 0116 2717217; http://www.optimal-learning.net

Application of the research about brain development and functioning to primary school practice.

☆ *Zero to Three*. Part of the Center for Infants, Toddlers and Families in the USA: http://www.zerotothree.org

Wide range of information to download, including practical ideas from research into early brain development.

7 Understanding and supporting children's communication

The majority of young children learn to speak, and many around the world learn more than one language, within their early years. Unlike some of the developments in thinking, you can directly observe and note down the ways in which children's power of speech extends over the months and years. Spoken language is only part of full communication. Children and adults also communicate by the many ways in which tone of voice, volume and different patterns of emphasis are used in speech. Non-verbal communication co-exists with the words, with messages expressed through facial expression, gestures and whole body movements.

The main sections in this chapter are:

- How do children learn spoken language?

- Early social interaction.

- Developmentally appropriate early literacy.

HOW DO CHILDREN LEARN SPOKEN LANGUAGE?

There can be no disagreement over the fact that most children manage what, from the outside, looks like a very tough task. Arguments have arisen among psychologists and linguists over how to explain satisfactorily that which very young children just get on and do. There have been several main theoretical approaches to the impressive reality of learning to speak.

Learning through imitation and reinforcement

The first attempts to explain children's acquisition of language were through basic principles of behaviourism. B. F. Skinner proposed that young children learn to speak because their parents systematically reward correct versions of the language and do not reward mistakes. Young children seem to flourish with positive feedback for their early attempts at language. They also become daunted if parents or practitioners unkindly highlight mistakes. However, most adults are considerably more flexible than a reinforcement explanation would predict. Parents and carers respond meaningfully to a wide range of grammatical constructions and pronunciations from toddlers. Correcting all or most of children's mistakes seems to inhibit communication rather than encourage it.

The ability to imitate explains partly how babies' sound-making moves towards the language that they are hearing and that children's accents become those of the people they hear around them. Yet, simple imitation cannot work as a complete explanation. Toddlers soon produce word combinations that they have not previously heard. Their logical mistakes in grammar, such as 'I goed' rather than 'I went', demonstrate the results of over-applying a rule system: of thinking, not just copying. Speech and language therapists are alert to those children whose mistakes do not follow the usual pattern of cracking the language code. Young children need to hear spoken language, so imitation is significant, but children are soon very creative in using their experience of spoken language around them.

LOOK, LISTEN, NOTE, LEARN

Children reach sensible conclusions from what they have heard. These examples are from the diary I kept of my own children.

- At 18 months Drew used the word 'more' for water. This puzzled me, until I heard myself saying, as he waved his empty watering can at me, 'Do you want some more?'.

- At 23 months Tanith used two words 'helpme' and 'helpit', which communicated different messages. 'Helpme' was said with a questioning tone and was an offer to help an adult, whereas 'helpit' was said with a pleading tone and used when she could not manage something. I traced these special words to my own phrases of 'Do you want to help me?' – often said when we were in the kitchen – and 'Do you want some help with it?', used when Tanith looked stuck with dressing or in play.

Helen Bee gives an example of logical mistakes in using grammatical rules. She quotes from a friend who heard this conversation in her family. The six- and three-year-old daughters disagreed about the dangers of forgetting to feed their goldfish compared with the dangers of overfeeding them. The conversation went this way – one imagines, with increasing volume:

- Six-year-old: It's worse to forget to feed them.

- Three-year-old: No, it's badder to feed them too much.

- Six-year-old: You don't say badder, you say worser.

- Three-year-old: But it's baddest to give them too much food.

- Six-year-old: No it's not. It's worsest to forget to feed them.
  (Bee, 1997: 217)

Listen for examples of logical mistakes in words or grammar from young children familiar to you.

- Note down what the children say and the context.

- Observe and reflect on the words or phrases. Can you track the source of the logical mistake?

- Discuss your observations and ideas with children's parents.

Children who have experienced a severely deprived childhood, with very limited human contact or care, do not learn to speak in isolation. It is a skill that needs appropriate experience, although babies and young children are flexible about the topics of conversation.

Children who hear plenty of language seem to develop their vocabulary slightly faster than those whose experience of language is limited. Babies and toddlers who have experience of infant-directed speech (page 149) also seem to develop some facets of their language slightly faster. Young children also seem to be helped by friendly extension of their short phrases, or slightly recasting what they say. For instance, the child says, 'Moggle village – little houses, little mans, little boats'. Her parent expands and gently corrects with, 'Yes, we went to the model village, didn't we? And everything was so little. There were little people and even the little boats. And the little train, do you remember the little train?'.

Biological programming

Language development is not fully explained through the details of individual children's experience. So, some theorists proposed that an innate biological system must be involved: a process within the brain that is present when a baby is born.

Working from the 1960s, Noam Chomsky first proposed that language is not learned, but emerges as part of the process of maturation: the unfolding of characteristics programmed by a genetic code. This nativist theory argued that children need to hear language spoken to trigger the system. Such an innate readiness has to be for language in general, not a specific language. Dan Slobin expanded the idea that every child has a basic language-making capacity, sometimes called a 'language acquisition device'. He proposed that the system works through a set of operating principles which programme infants to listen into sounds and rhythm, to the beginnings and ends of sound sequences and to how sounds are stressed. Steven Pinker has continued the emphasis on an inborn linguistic structure that functions to guide children's language learning.

Babies are born potentially able to produce all the possible sounds and sound combinations. But, by one year of age, they have lost the ability to discriminate sounds that are not in the language spoken around them. Also their tuneful babbling has taken on the sound patterns of the language that they hear. The concept of an innate language device overcomes the difficulties of explaining how infants home in on language so successfully. Toddlers appear to receive insufficient feedback on their early attempts to support a learning theory explanation. Nativist theory would predict that the pattern of learning language would be very similar from one language to another. When this approach was first proposed, it looked as if children learning different world languages did follow very similar patterns. However, more recent and detailed research has also found many differences.

Neuroscience supports a brain-based innate theory. Part of this explanation for language development is that human infants are born pre-disposed to tune into spoken language. The part of the brain attuned to hearing, and vision, can be observed to work before birth. Brain activity gives off small electrical discharges that can be tracked by computer imaging. Their pre-birth listening enables babies to show recognition of their mother's voice and, in some cases, familiarity with music or songs that they will have heard from the womb. However, there is no basis for enthusiastic commercial claims that parents can boost their unborn baby's brain power by playing various robustly priced tapes.

Human infants appear to be designed to be social and to pay attention to the human voice. Lynne Murray and Liz Andrews show that even very young babies are already alert, imitating and using all their senses in interaction with their social world. Parents notice when infants are unresponsive and their concerns are often the first sign that some kind of disability is affecting infant social skills. For instance, blind babies may respond only to the sound of a parent's voice and deaf babies wait for the familiar face before a smile spreads over their own face.

Language linked with thinking

Innate models of language development allowed for the abilities of children themselves and not just the input of speaking adults. Theorists, whose interest started from cognitive development, focus more on how language is a vehicle for expressing thoughts.

Lev Vygotsky proposed that young children's use of speech started as a means to guide themselves, as the words accompanied their actions. Then language began to precede the actions, with a function of planning what the child might or would do. Language freed children's mental processes from the immediate experience. Vygotsky pointed out how children and adults might use the same words, but that did not mean that children fully understood the concept represented by that word. Concepts are not given to children ready-made with the words; development in thinking also has to take place.

The social constructivist tradition (page 52) stresses that children learn words primarily because they connect with what the young child is already thinking. Words do not introduce new meanings, but give expression to thoughts that the young child has developed pre-linguistically. One source of support for this theoretical stance is the extent to which children initiate exchanges, so long as they are confident of the interest of their parent or other key adults. Another support comes from the observation that the emergence of pretend play, a significant form of symbolism, co-exists with early spoken language.

LOOK, LISTEN, NOTE, LEARN

Observation of babies and toddlers has highlighted links between how they play and their early language. The pattern is as follows:

When children's play is	They will probably	At about this age
Exploring objects and people close at hand	Communicate with gestures and sounds	0–10 months
Relating one object with another in play	Produce many patterns of sounds	9–15 months
Simple pretend actions applied only to them	First words	11–18 months
Simple pretend actions that involve other people or toys	Two-word combinations, short phrases	12–30 months
Sequences of pretend play and other play involving other people and play materials	Three-, four-, five-word sentences	19–36 months

Make some observations that could link the play of babies and toddlers with their developing communication.

- What patterns do you observe as you watch and listen to a baby or a toddler? Note the wide variation in the ages given above.

- Do you see children whose language is developing a little later than average following the same route?

Young children, learning a wide range of world languages, tend to start slowly, adding one word at a time, specifically linked with familiar objects and people. Then, somewhere between 16 and 24 months of age toddlers launch themselves into what has been called 'the naming explosion', when they add new words at a rapid pace. It certainly looks as if they have understood that things have names and their questioning tone, sometimes before they have a question word such as 'Wassat?', shows that toddlers want some answers.

- Before the naming explosion, toddlers tend to show under-extension of their current vocabulary: they act as if the word 'cup' only applies to their familiar cup or beaker.

- After that watershed, very young children switch to over-extension: they use one word to apply to similar objects or creatures. Children's mistakes are logical, for example, 'cat' is applied to any creature that is furry and has a long tail – foxes are clearly cats by this reasoning. Any round fruit is an 'apple' or any adult male is a 'daddy'. Very young children have grasped the idea of categories, but they do not yet know where to stop.

LOOK, LISTEN, NOTE, LEARN

- Identify some young children who are at the stage before the naming explosion. Note their words and how they use them. Gather examples of under-extension.

- Keep observing the same children at regular intervals and note when the naming explosion starts. Watch out now for over-extension in use of words.

- Reflect on what you find and what it tells you about this very young child's learning journey. Share your observations with parents.

So how do they do it?

Academic books and papers about language acquisition are tough to read: full of complex sentences and new words created for the purpose of this theory or research. I find it amusing that toddlers, who would understand none of these weighty concepts, just get on with the job. All of the competing theories have some merit, but no single theory offers a full explanation of how young children make the impressive leap between what they hear and the sophisticated language they eventually produce.

Margaret Donaldson summed up the situation with, 'How this level of skill is achieved so quickly is a puzzle that has occupied many minds, especially in the last few decades of active research in developmental psycholinguistics. Yet the achievement remains essentially mysterious. We do not know in any detail how it is done' (1992: 106). Nothing has happened since Margaret Donaldson wrote that summary to suggest that one theory has emerged with all the answers.

It seems that human children make the impressive leap into spoken language because their brains are programmed ready for human communication. However, children's learning is then shaped by their experience of language, especially the communication behaviour of the key adults in their environment. But it is equally important what children do with this experience; they are active linguists, just as they are active thinkers.

MAKE THE CONNECTION WITH ... YOUR PRACTICE

The practical implications of research home in on simple actions from adults to support communication, not to complex techniques. Babies and young children respond well to friendly, personal, attention and communication linked with those children's current interests. Work your way through this chapter, and then weave in Chapter 8 about thinking. Draw out the practical applications for 'what do I do?'. Compare your ideas with colleagues and fellow students.

EARLY SOCIAL INTERACTION

A major part of how you help full communication and language development is to notice and value early social interaction that builds the foundations. Sally Ward developed her Baby Talk programme from her work as a speech and language therapist, seeing children with language difficulties but also children whose early experiences did not support the development of communication.

Babies and very young children with few words need to use non-verbal forms to convey meaning. However, fluent speakers continue to communicate non-verbally, sometimes giving a contradictory message to the spoken words. For instance, the words may say 'I believe you' but the body language shows doubt.

Meaningful gestures

Gestures are an important aspect of early communication and form part of babies' body language – sending messages long before the words have come. The ability to gesture is linked with babies' increased physical control. But gestures are also a clear sign that babies want to gain and direct the

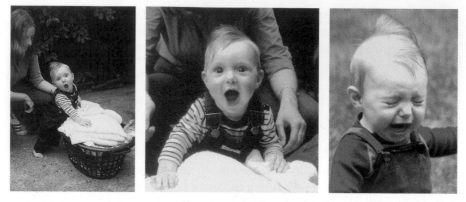

Very young children communicate clearly without words

attention of others. They use gesture to communicate a range of messages, for example:

- *Requests* – from the age of about five months, babies use hand gestures to indicate wants. A hand stretch and a look communicates, 'I want that and I can't get it'. An open and close of the hand can say 'Put it in my hand'.

- *Refusals* – babies and toddlers use a variety of limb and full body gestures to indicate reluctance or full refusal to cooperate. Then they add a firm head shake for 'No'.

- *Social contact* – gestures and sounds are used to attract and hold the attention of adults and other children. Pointing, which starts from about eight months, is a direct way of requesting adults to fetch something for a baby who is not yet mobile. Soon babies use pointing to direct attention to something interesting, to ensure an adult gazes in the same direction. Babies and toddlers often repeat patterns of gestures and sounds, such as blowing raspberries, if this behaviour has provoked a laugh.

TAKE ANOTHER PERSPECTIVE

- I call young children 'language detectives'. For example, when they understand only a few words, toddlers use the clues from familiar context. You may say, 'Please put your tissue in the bin'. They recognise 'tissue', 'bin' and your gesture towards the corner of the room. They know that tissues go in the bin (not on the floor), are pleased to follow your request and be thanked by words and smile.

- Children who are perplexed by adult questions use all the clues of your eye movements and gestures to fill the gap. In normal life, you need to be generous with those clues. If you want to check exactly what a child understands from the words alone, you need to remove the clues.

Signs as symbolic gestures

Linda Acredolo and Susan Goodwyn studied the way in which toddlers who have no words, or just a small number, use specific signs to communicate an association that they cannot say in words. The signs are a reflection of the child's personal experience, so children do not necessarily make the same signs as others. For example, Linda Acredolo's interest in signs was stimulated by realising that her young daughter made a blowing motion when she saw a fish and rubbed her hands when she saw a spider. Both these signs were the result of the toddler's alert observation: her mother used to blow on the fish mobile over Kate's cot to make it revolve and the rubbing motion was from the hand movements in 'Incey Wincey Spider'.

TAKE ANOTHER PERSPECTIVE

Attention to infant sign language can support adult interaction with babies and young children. Meaningful signs or gestures should always be used alongside simple spoken communication. Linda Acredolo and Susan Goodwyn take a naturalistic approach, encouraging parents, or early years practitioners, to use the baby's symbolic gestures as the starting point.

'Baby signing' training programmes are now a franchise in the UK. The idea came from the US research of Joseph Garcia into the development of hearing babies of deaf parents. Children seemed to benefit from the signing they learned in order to communicate with their parents. Speech and language therapists are wary (and I share their concerns) that a commercial programme can imply parents are unable to use symbolic gesturing, unless they are trained. Sign systems work well to support children with learning or communication disabilities. But there is no consistent research that suggests young children need this organised approach to promote language development in general.

Acredolo and Goodwyn found many such personal signs in the toddlers they studied. If parents took the signs seriously as communication, this approach encouraged the development of spoken language. The key was that parents responded to their toddlers' signs, and took the trouble to work out the links, talking with their toddlers about the focus of the children's interest.

WHAT DOES IT MEAN?

Infant signing: the pattern of symbolic gestures that babies develop to aid their message – a natural pattern of non-verbal communication.

Early social communication

Detailed observational research, such as that of Colwyn Trevarthen and his team in Edinburgh, has shown just how much babies are primed to interact with adult carers from the earliest weeks and months. Since the 1970s, video technology has enabled detailed analysis of communication exchanges.

For instance, when a baby or young toddler hands an object to his mother, it is not just a case of 'child stretches out hand' and 'mother takes the object'. Watched frame by frame on video, the exchange is shown to be a whole series of subtle moves by baby and mother. In this interaction, and similar ones, the moves of both baby and adult are responsive to changes in signals coming from the other. Such sensitivity is an important part of how babies make and sustain contact with caring adults and how those adults develop a communicative and affectionate relationship with the baby.

Colwyn Trevarthen and Lynne Murray looked at the reactions of babies of six to twelve weeks of age under different conditions: when mothers gave their babies full attention, when the mothers gazed without reacting and if they turned away.

- When babies had the full attention of their mothers, they reacted with smiles, coos and away-from-their-body gestures.

- When mothers gazed but did not react, the babies made similar efforts of communication. Then they became more tense, until they looked away from their mothers.

- If mothers turned away, for instance to talk with the researcher (a planned interruption in the experiment), babies looked less at their mothers, gazed at the researcher and made vocalisations and gestures that seemed to be an attempt to regain their mother's attention.

These very young babies were active in relating to their mothers and their behaviour changed in response to varied conditions. Colwyn Trevarthen has developed the concept of musicality to describe the partnership of these very early social exchanges. But the concept also refers to the alertness of babies to tuneful communication, the rhythmic flow of conversation from an adult who looks and sounds interested.

The precise and sensitive interaction was further highlighted when Trevarthen and Murray played back to the babies the video sequence of their attentive and smiling mother. This experience led to distress in the babies. Although their mother was gazing and smiling, what she did was not responsive to the babies' behaviour at the time the video was running. Babies were aware of this mis-match and their upset reaction shows how attuned they are to seeking a genuine exchange with important carers.

LOOK, LISTEN, NOTE, LEARN

Spend some time watching the communication efforts of babies of six months and younger. You may find opportunities in your place of work but there can also be chances to watch in daily life: babies with their parents on the bus, in the supermarket or in the park.

Watch out especially and make some notes (discreetly!) on:

- Those early 'conversational' exchanges when baby and adult take turns.

- How the baby reacts if the adult turns away or does not respond.

- How babies use sounds and actions to get and hold others' attention. For instance: squeals, yells, blowing raspberries or vigorous hand gestures.

- Listen and watch the adults, or older children, in the exchange. Can you observe the qualities of infant-directed speech?

Infant-directed speech

Research has established that babies respond enthusiastically to a modified version of talk that is:

- Higher pitched and said with more expressiveness than normal adult conversation.

- At a slower pace, with more pauses, when the adult looks expectant.

■ Full of simple repetitions and a circling quality to the phrases ('Hello . . . have you woken up then? . . . Have you just woken up? . . . Come on then, let's have a cuddle . . . a nice warm cuddle . . .').

Babies have been found to prefer listening to this kind of adjusted talk, even when the language spoken is not their family language. A modified form of language is also used with toddlers but often with far more links into what the adult and toddler can both see. For instance, an exchange can circle with 'Where's Asha's foot? . . . Where's your foot then? . . . Has it gone? Has it gone forever? . . . No, I can see it. I've got it now . . . I've got Asha's little foot . . .'.

Because researchers such as Colwyn Trevarthen studied mothers and their babies, this modified speech was initially called 'motherese'. However, it is more accurately called 'infant-directed speech', because this form of communication is not restricted to mothers, or even to women. Men, as fathers or carers, modify their speech in the same way and so can some children, for instance with younger siblings. Infant-directed speech seems to exert a broad effect, because adults who adjust their speech patterns for babies and toddlers are also paying attention and are physically close. Infant-directed speech has been found in a considerable number of cultures, but is not universal.

WHAT DOES IT MEAN?

Infant-directed speech: the modified version of spoken language, with lively tone and facial expression that is suited to communication with babies.

Musicality: the sensitivity of babies to tone and rhythmic flow in communication.

LOOK, LISTEN, NOTE, LEARN

■ Children as young as two years of age can adjust their language depending on the listener. You will observe that young children talk in a different way among themselves, in contrast to their words and intonation with an adult.

■ By four years of age, children usually discriminate between different forms of speech. For instance, they will simplify their language when talking to a much younger child. Five-year-olds usually explain in more detail to an unfamiliar adult than to a friend; they have grasped that adults do not necessarily know everything that they do.

> ■ I have observed children as young as three and four years of age engage babies through infant-directed speech. The children imitate an adult model and the pleased reaction of the baby is encouragement to continue.
>
> Watch and listen for examples from your own work with children. If you struggle to gather any observations, then reflect on the extent to which children are able to interact with babies, especially if you work in a setting that keeps the age groups separate. This is lost opportunity for both children and babies.

MAKE THE CONNECTION WITH . . . FAMILY SUPPORT

- Observation of very depressed mothers has shown that they are considerably less likely to use infant-directed speech. Their children still learn to speak, but the language is often not as rich or conversational.
- There is basis for concern because young children need the social context and experience of predictability in an important relationship. Family support services appropriately aim to get supportive, non-judgemental help to families where the main carer is depressed.

The intense, uninterrupted exchanges described by Colwyn Trevarthen and other researchers in this area are not typical of all interactions between adults and young babies. Outside the special observation suite, in family life and elsewhere, communication with babies is sometimes interrupted. Parents and practitioners have to share out their time and attention – a reality explored by Judy Dunn in her research. But the results from very detailed observation of mother and infant pairs are a crucial reminder for anyone involved with babies of just how much is possible.

MAKE THE CONNECTION WITH . . . YOUR PRACTICE

There are important practical messages for everyone caring for babies and young children, especially for group care, where poor practice can probably more easily lose these vital opportunities. Recall that:

- Communicative exchanges need to be sustained and not rushed. There should be a relaxed pattern of give and take, providing time for babies to respond.
- Exchanges with babies should not be interrupted regularly, as if they do not matter.
- The routines of physical care provide rich opportunities for close and sensitive communication between adult and baby.

These practical applications of the research are reflected in *Birth to Three Matters* pack in England and the guidance issued in 2005 in Scotland.

Communication between very young children

The difficulty for babies and toddlers is that their physical moves to contact another child of the same age are inevitably less subtle than those of older children. Touches may be more a poke than a pat and adults become concerned about possible hurt from toddlers' whole body clasps and semi-wrestling. However, any assumptions that toddlers are uninterested in relationships do not survive observation of the under-twos.

Elinor Goldschmied gathered observational material in England and Italy. Her videos of babies and toddlers exploring materials in her treasure basket show that gazing, touching and offering play materials are regular exchanges between young children. Toddlers and young children develop relationships with their peers that show friendly behaviour, a wish to be together and mutual enjoyment in shared activities, however simple.

LOOK, LISTEN, NOTE, LEARN

Mobile toddlers show preferences, which may persist for months, in their choice of play companion in out-of-home care, with a childminder or in a day nursery. Make your own observations over several weeks, following the preferences of a few children.

- When the young children arrive in the morning, which other children do they regularly approach?

- Given the choice, do children sit beside one or more individual children?

- Do they take play materials or books to show particular children?

A persistent myth about very young children is that they cannot play with other children, that they only play alongside them: parallel play. This belief is largely a misunderstanding of research that showed how older children spent relatively more time in co-operative play and less in parallel or solitary play than the younger ones. Research into the social and communicative abilities of very young children corrects this misunderstanding.

Carol Eckerman observed very young children in contact with each other and noticed deliberate patterns of social play, for example:

- Mobile babies establish a joint focus of interest by making physical contact with an object that another young child (or adult) is manipulating. The baby then imitates the 'play partner'. This copying action seems to signal a message of 'I like this' or 'Let's do it together'.

- In toddler interaction, imitative acts seem to open an exchange, because they often happen swiftly after the first contact. The other toddler is encouraged to imitate in return and a social connection is established.

- Reciprocal imitative games are common between toddlers, for instance, taking turns to do the same action, such as jumping off the sofa. (Adults may say furniture is not play equipment, but that does not discount toddlers' actions as real play!)

- From two to three years of age, words begin to be integrated into young children's play. Children begin to be able to co-ordinate their actions towards new play sequences in addition to familiar rituals. Verbal and non-verbal language is used to guide the interaction.

LOOK, LISTEN, NOTE, LEARN

- Look out for examples of play between toddlers in your own setting or from opportunities that arise in everyday life.

- For instance, my wait in our local health clinic was greatly enlivened by watching two young children in a double buggy. One child looked about two years old and the younger was about 18 months. They amused themselves for at least ten minutes. The older one usually started a game, but the younger one re-started a sequence, once he had played it a few times. The two of them played 'I touch your knee and then you touch mine', 'We stare into each other's faces' and 'We shake our heads hard so our hair swings about'. Pauses were filled with loud chortling, then one of the children would make the move into a game again.

Play communication between the different ages

Much play research has been undertaken by observing same-age groups of toddlers. Sometimes researchers also seem to take an inappropriately strict line over what can be defined as 'play' and what is not. Carol Eckerman's observational research challenged claims that very young children do not really play together. But another perspective is to observe mobile babies and toddlers in interaction with older children. Judy Dunn's research in families produced examples of two-year-olds who were drawn into pretend play sequences with an older sibling. When children of different ages play together, the younger ones are often assigned a role, and increasingly understand how to take a pretend role, in long sequences that they would be unlikely to manage with their peers.

Mainly friendly relations with older siblings also give the younger ones a chance sometimes to exercise some direction over the play, perhaps by clowning around and making the older ones laugh. I observed a sequence in which an 18-month-old held the attention of three older children (ranging in age from three to seven years) by running along a hallway and then sliding along on her bottom, cushioned by her nappy. The older children fell about laughing and Anna repeated her run and slide six times, delighted with the full attention of the older ones.

MAKE THE CONNECTION WITH ... REAL FAMILY LIFE

These excerpts are from my family diary. They show how an older sibling can give a lead to a younger and create games that the younger one would not develop alone or with peers. Tanith was born four days before Drew's second birthday. We involved him safely in her care and Drew gave Tanith toys from when she was able to grasp. He liked to show her how to work resources such as their bath toys. Once Tanith was a confident walker, their play became a more active interaction.

- Tanith, 13 months and Drew, 3 years 1 month: D. has started a chasing game with her. Mainly he gets her to chase him along the hall by calling her name. D. builds brick towers, says, 'What about this, Tanith?' and then she knocks them down. They both laugh loudly. Sometimes T. brings him the brick box to get him to do the game.

- Tanith, 14 months and Drew, 3 years 2 months: they still play the chasing game but sometimes T. starts it now by hovering until D. sees her. They spend time together in the playhouse we made out of a huge cardboard box, playing peep-bo through the windows. They wrestle together.

- Tanith, 15 months and Drew, 3 years 3 months: T. sits beside D. and hands him Lego for his models. They still play the chasing games and growl at each other as monsters. D. has created a rescue game. He lies down and calls out 'Tanith! Help, help!'. T. comes up, gives her hand and they walk off.

- Tanith, 18 months and Drew, 3 years 6 months: D. has invented more games for him and T. Most revolve around chase and rescue: sharks, traps and something to do with heat. They both chant, 'Hot, hot' and drag the pink bath towel around [I was puzzled by this game at the time. Tanith explained years later: it was about escaping from volcanoes]. T. copies D. a great deal in her play – how he handles the playdough, pretending to eat and drink with the tea set, counting like him and trying to jump as he does.

- Tanith is 2 years, Drew is 4 years: T. is as likely now to start their games together as D. As well as jumping about together, they spend a lot of time in the playhouse and they jointly run a pretend cafe from behind the sofa.

Drew and Tanith were not content all the time. There were days when they squabbled and I had to give them time apart for everyone's peace of mind.

You could observe play between the ages if you work in an early years setting that enables easy contact between younger and older children. Or you could talk with parents who have two or more young children.

- What do the children do together? Who leads and who follows?
- In what way is the play environment different for the second child, or third child, than for the firstborn?
- What strategies do the parents take to deal with squabbles?

DEVELOPMENTALLY APPROPRIATE EARLY LITERACY

Children have another substantial task to manage: understanding the written system of language through learning to read and to write. Cracking the written code is a challenging task for children and English is especially tough. The supportive strategy for children's learning is to build firm foundations through developmentally appropriate early experiences and for adults to understand how the skills evolve. The answer is definitely not to harass very young children to practise letter shapes or memorise flash cards.

Rich oral communication

Children need to hear, experience and use language from an early age. Conversations with young children support their learning of words and boost their motivation to make themselves understood, with ever more

A good group time is lively and interactive

complex ideas. Children benefit from enjoyable experience of playing with the sounds of their own language(s). Barbara Tizard and Martin Hughes describe 'games for fun' as children gain language skill by playing with words in joking interaction with their mothers. Judy Dunn has shown some child-oriented uses of language that are not always directed at adults. Children will play with words: putting words together in a way that sounds funny to them or saying something that they know is wrong and laughing. I call this 'nonsense talk' and it is often between children, but may be shared with adults who show a capacity to have fun.

LOOK, LISTEN, NOTE, LEARN

- Look at Robin Campbell's detailed account of how Alice steadily learned the skills to support literacy. Identify similar examples for children that you know.

- Reflect on your practice – are you creating a learning environment in which young children can be enthused about different kinds of books and story telling?

Cathy Nutbrown explains the importance of oral language as a crucial building block to literacy. She highlights that children need enjoyable ways to recognise and practise the sounds of language: how different words can have the same beginning sound (onset) or the same end sound (rime). Words with the same onset alliterate (string, strap, struggle) and words with the same rime rhyme (walk, talk, chalk). Sharing nursery rhymes and chants is an effective way of alerting children to slight differences in sound patterns and encourages them to play with language.

Equally important parts of oral language are experience and enthusiasm for stories and story telling – a link with rich pretend play for children. Children also benefit from enjoyable conversation that Cathy Nutbrown called 'literacy talk': expressing opinions about books and stories and having the words to talk about what happens, how a story makes the reader feel and effectiveness of the characters.

TAKE ANOTHER PERSPECTIVE

- Children need confidence in language for thinking out loud and developing ideas for what and how they will write. Writing is partly the technical skill of handwriting, which is itself a combination of physical skills and cracking the code of letters and how they link to sounds.

■ But writing is also content and realising that different kinds of writing fit a range of purposes. Without the broader base, children may learn to write words. But they are ill-equipped to reflect on what they want to write and to plan the details, whether it is a fictional story, an account of a real event, a letter or set of written instructions – any good reason to write.

How can conversation get lost?

Many research projects conclude that young children learn best through relaxed, social conversation. Yet research also raises the concern that time and space is not necessarily given to this learning opportunity, even in some early years settings that claim to be promoting 'early education'. So, how does conversation get lost? There seem to be several interlinking explanations.

Sometimes practitioners fail to trust the play-based curriculum. Joy Roberts undertook research into learning through play in Reception classes. She recounts what she learned by reflecting on her own experience as a Reception teacher. On one occasion, she had spent time getting children to colour in an activity sheet of a road with cars in a line and had then questioned them about the relative position of the cars. Children had willingly completed this paper task. Then, later in the same session, Joy Roberts observed some of the same children playing with a variety of vehicles. They were spontaneously using positional language, talking confidently about cars that were 'in front of', 'between', 'behind'; cars that were 'first', 'last', cars that were 'fast' and 'slow', cars that were 'turquoise' and 'silver'. They were using language to compare sizes, shape and quantity too. As Joy Roberts noted, all she had to do was watch, listen and trust the learning environment that the children were well able to use.

Jacqui Cousins drew on her years of research, and experience as an Ofsted inspector, when she became concerned about disruption to children's learning, even in settings that claimed to value 'learning through play'. She observed that practitioners had come to value the paper evidence of worksheets more than the potential of oral language. Jacqui Cousins described that conversation was often 'dismissed by the adults as "nattering or chattering". In most settings the talk of children was seriously underestimated as a tool for thinking . . . most of the talking consisted of adults asking questions. But . . . it was in spontaneous and prolonged conversations and discussions between the children that I found most examples of the children's puzzling minds' (1999: 52).

Jacqui Cousins then observed how the children themselves had learned the priorities: 'When I was listening to a child telling me about the metamorphosis of a butterfly, a younger child interrupted him and said to me, "He's big now, got to get on with his proper work". After that I noticed how many other children interrupted each other in the middle of similar discussions' (1999: 53). Anxiety can tip the balance in use of language when adults move to many testing questions: ones to which they already know the answer (page 177). A reflective practitioner can tip the balance back again, but first you have to realise what you are doing.

A further source of disruption to oral language seems to be pressure felt by early years practitioners, especially in England, to get on with literacy goals. Ann Locke and Jane Ginsborg undertook research at the University of Sheffield that assessed the introduction of Teaching Talking, a spoken language programme, in two nursery classes in a socio-economically deprived neighbourhood. The language skills of the three- and four-year-olds did not improve as predicted in comparison with the two control nurseries. However, the value of this research project is that Locke and Ginsborg tracked what had happened. Although staff had expressed commitment to take part in the study, the programme was only partly implemented in one nursery and barely at all in the second. In the Sheffield study the practitioners were unwilling to engage in conversation with the children. They felt strong pressure to ensure children would meet targets, especially related to literacy. Many staff felt they could not waste precious time on 'just talking', when they had so many activities to be completed with children in the day.

MAKE THE CONNECTION WITH ... YOUR PRACTICE

Ann Locke and Jane Ginsborg draw on the available research to stress that children learn so much through talking: that rich oral communication is also the foundation for grasping written language. They believe that children need to express their thoughts (inside-out learning) and not only listen to adults (outside-in learning).

- Reflect on your own sense of priorities or pressure experienced in a team.

- Are you overlooking the fact that having plenty of conversations is a basis for building early literacy?

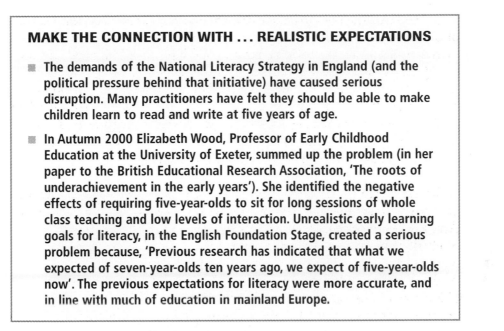

MAKE THE CONNECTION WITH ... REALISTIC EXPECTATIONS

■ The demands of the National Literacy Strategy in England (and the political pressure behind that initiative) have caused serious disruption. Many practitioners have felt they should be able to make children learn to read and write at five years of age.

■ In Autumn 2000 Elizabeth Wood, Professor of Early Childhood Education at the University of Exeter, summed up the problem (in her paper to the British Educational Research Association, 'The roots of underachievement in the early years'). She identified the negative effects of requiring five-year-olds to sit for long sessions of whole class teaching and low levels of interaction. Unrealistic early learning goals for literacy, in the English Foundation Stage, created a serious problem because, 'Previous research has indicated that what we expected of seven-year-olds ten years ago, we expect of five-year-olds now'. The previous expectations for literacy were more accurate, and in line with much of education in mainland Europe.

Do children lack conversational skills?

Speech and language teams locally and national organisations such as I CAN (http://www.ican.org.uk) have expressed concern about rising numbers of young children who seem unable to express themselves clearly or understand simple requests. The delayed or restricted language development cannot always be explained by disability; limited early language experience seems to be the main factor for much of the increase. Some commentators are swift to blame parents who fail to make time to talk with their young children and over-use of television, video or computer software.

Robin Close reviewed research on the effects of television and commented that 'Television can promote talk in young children, but this talk needs to be harnessed by an adult in creative and imaginative ways if the learning experience is to extend beyond the airing of a programme' (2004: 35). Close concluded that children who were heavy viewers of television were more likely to have delayed language development and agreed with the cautious guidance of the American Academy of Pediatrics, which advised very limited television viewing for under twos. As you might guess, it is difficult to prove exactly what is happening in this relationship between television and children's development, but part of the explanation seems to lie in all the activities that children give up if they sit in front of a screen for hours every day. Rich language development needs social interaction and television is one-way, even if there are good quality programmes for young children.

However, the research into early years practice means that children's limited conversational skills cannot be explained away by 'lazy parents and non-

Children need to feel enthused about writing as a skill you can do anywhere

stop television'. There is good reason to argue that young children are not helped in their communication by misguided early years practice. If children start in non-conversational nurseries at an early age, the responsibility lies strongly with that team.

Firm foundations for written language

Children need plenty of enjoyable conversation and other uses of spoken language. They also need adults to use developmentally appropriate methods to demystify the whole reading and writing business.

Cathy Nutbrown developed the concept of alerting young children to environmental print: the idea that writing is all around and young children learn to recognise writing-type shapes and logos. They also need to grasp the context, that writing does a job. The importance of giving children broad experience of writing is illustrated clearly by the consequences for children without this experience. Jessie Reid interviewed children who were having difficulty in learning to read or write. She discovered that most of the children were unaware of writing as a system. Children had not realised that the marks in books represented different letters, nor that there was a separate letter and number system. Their attention had not been drawn to the writing all around them, on buses, shops or street signs. So the children remained puzzled about the point of reading or writing, except that teachers seemed to want them to do it.

WHAT DOES IT MEAN?

Environmental print: writing and logos that are all around a family home, other settings and out on the street – writing that is there for a purpose of communication.

Meaningful mark-making: the range of marks that even very young children choose to make for their own purposes with any tools available.

Emergent writing: the deliberate mark-making by children that moves towards the shape and flow of the writing that they observe. Children may say now that they are writing.

TAKE ANOTHER PERSPECTIVE

Anne Hughes and Sue Ellis describe broad themes around 'becoming a writer' that are relevant to three- and four-year-olds. Young children need to understand and explore in many different ways:

- What writing looks like.

- How to make letters and symbols.

- That writing is used for a whole range of purposes in real life, for thinking and communicating.

- That people enjoy writing.

- That writing gives status and power (in a positive way) to the writer.

- That writing lets you keep ideas forever and tell others about them even when you haven't met.

Reflect on the opportunities that you provide for children to experience these six strands around 'what can writing do for me?'. Observe children in a learning environment where they can choose what and when.

Children need plenty of practice in meaningful mark-making and then their marks move towards emergent writing. Robin Campbell describes how Alice moves from drawing into deliberate shapes that look more like writing. Children imitate how an adult writer looks as well as the flow of mark-making on the page or whiteboard. Anne Hughes and Sue Ellis suggest that the major difference in literacy support between early years settings and primary school is the balance between:

- *responding* to young children when they choose to do meaningful mark-making and

- *recruiting* children into writing following a shared agenda in the group.

They describe that primary school teachers do more 'recruiting' because of the less favourable staff–child ratio and demands of the curriculum. But more direction is feasible, because the children are older, and if they have had suitable early years experiences. The balance for early years practitioners should be much more on 'responding' to exploration chosen by three- and four-year-olds and the way they want to apply their skills. Young potential writers can be undermined when early years practitioners believe they should mainly recruit three- and four-year-olds into worksheet copying and tracing of letters.

MAKE THE CONNECTION WITH . . . PARTNERSHIP WITH PARENTS

Social pressure about literacy has created a sense of anxiety for many parents. Unless they have an early years background, parents will think of literacy as 'proper' reading and writing. Early years practitioners need to be able to show, as well as tell, how children make a secure move into literacy.

Consider how you show and share appropriate early literacy through partnership with parents. You will find some useful ideas in Anne Hughes and Sue Ellis' *Writing it right?* (1998). Also Penny Tassoni, *Making their mark – children's early writing*, part of the Learning Together series of leaflets from Early Education, tel. 020 7539 5400 or download from http://www.early-education.org.uk. There are also helpful booklets from The Basic Skills Agency, tel. 0870 600 2400, http://www.basic-skills.co.uk

---

Supportive adults watch and listen in order to grasp the perspective of young children, who may still be puzzling out what exactly is this skill of reading. Penny Munn interviewed children about their understanding of reading several times during their final year before going to primary school. These four-year-olds were asked four questions: 'Can you read?', 'Who do you know who can read?', 'When will you be able to read?' and 'What will you have to do to be able to read?'.

Almost all of the sample of 56 four-year-olds were very familiar with story books. The children's behaviour towards books did not change much at all. It was their beliefs about the process of reading that altered. Most children made a significant shift over the year: from a belief that you read by turning the pages and telling a story to an understanding that reading meant decoding print in a specific way. Many children then realised that they could not read yet; it was a skill they needed to learn. When children were familiar with books, from home and not only nursery, they were less daunted by realising that they could not yet read. Children with a family background low in literacy appeared less confident and more likely to find ways to avoid the risk of 'failure'.

If you want to find out more:

☆ **Acredolo, Linda** and **Goodwyn, Susan** 2000 *Baby signs: how to talk with your baby before your baby can talk*. London: Vermilion.

Exploration of the rich communication through gesture that precedes and can support the learning of spoken language.

☆ **Campbell, Robin** 1999 *Literacy from home to school: reading with Alice*. Stoke-on-Trent: Trentham Books.

Detailed description of the author's granddaughter as she learns a love of books and stories and makes the move into early literacy.

☆ **Close, Robin** 2004 *Television and language development in the early years: a review of the literature*. For the Literacy Trust, see http://www.literacytrust.co.uk

Detailed review of research over the last three decades of the impact of television on young children's development, specifically language.

☆ **Dunn, Judy** 1993 *Young children's close relationships beyond attachment*. London: Sage.

Links children's social development and friendships with their cognitive development.

☆ **Early Childhood Unit** 2004 *Listening as a way of life*. Tel. 020 7843 6064 or download from http://www.earlychildhood.org.uk

A set of booklets about communication and consultation with young children.

✮ **Eckerman, Carol** 1993 'Imitation and toddlers' achievement of co-ordinated actions with others'. In Nadel, Jacqueline and Camaioni, Luigia (eds) *New perspectives in early communicative development.* London: Routledge.

Not an easy book to read but it is a good resource on the research concerning very young children.

✮ **Goldschmied, Elinor** 1986 *Infants at work: babies of 6–9 months exploring everyday objects.* Also with Anita Hughes 1992 *Heuristic play with objects: children of 12–20 months exploring everyday objects.* London: National Children's Bureau.

Useful video material for practical ideas within early years settings and for provoking discussion.

✮ **Hughes, Anne** and **Ellis, Sue** 1998 *Writing it right? children writing 3–8.* Dundee: Scottish Consultative Council on the Curriculum. Tel. 01382 443600, http://www.ltscotland.org.uk

Very practical book about building firm foundations for the writing side of literacy, including how children need reasons to write.

✮ **Locke, Ann** and **Ginsborg, Jane** 2003 'Spoken language in the early years: the cognitive and linguistic development of three- to five-year-old children from socio-economically deprived backgrounds'. Educational and Child Psychology 20(4), 68–79.

This research continues at the University of Sheffield and the authors are writing a book which will include the original study and follow-up research.

✮ **Munn, Penny** 1997 'What do children know about reading before they go to school?'. In Owen, Pamela and Pumfrey, Peter (eds) *Emergent and developing reading: messages for teachers.*London: Falmer Press.

An account of the research described on page 162 that brings alive the ways in which children grasp the whole business of learning to read.

✮ **Murray, Lynne** and **Andrews, Liz** 2000 *The social baby.* Also a video of the same title. Richmond: The Children's Project. Tel. 020 8546 8750.

Well-illustrated description of very early social interaction. The video uses the same footage with commentary and ideas from parents.

☆ **Murray, Lynne** and **Trevarthen, Colwyn** 1985 'Emotional regulation of interactions between two-month-olds and their mothers'. In Field, T.M. and Fox, N.A. (eds) *Social perception in infants*. Norwood: N.J. Ablex.

Account of the research described on page 148.

☆ **Nutbrown, Cathy** 1996 *REAL Project Early Literacy Education with Parents: a framework for practice*. Video from Sheffield University.

Practical video that explains the REAL project and offers helpful ideas about building early literacy in nursery and in partnership with parents.

☆ **Pinker, Steven** 1994 *The language instinct: how the mind creates language*. New York: Morrow.

One of the proponents of an innate language structure to support a maturational explanation of language development.

☆ **Reid, Jessie** 1983 'Into print: reading and language growth'. In Donaldson, Margaret, Grieve, Robert and Pratt, Chris (eds) *Early childhood development and education: readings in psychology*. Oxford: Blackwell.

Research that illuminates the difficulties of children who have not cracked the code of written language.

☆ **Tizard, Barbara** and **Hughes, Martin** 2002 *Young children learning: talking and thinking at home and at school*. Oxford: Blackwell.

Research contrasting the experiences of young children in the different settings of home and nursery. Food for thought about early years practice.

☆ **Trevarthen, Colwyn; Barr, Ian; Dunlop, Aline-Wendy; Gjersoe, Nathalia; Marwick, Helen** and **Stephen, Christine** 2003 *Meeting the needs of children from birth to three years*. http://www.scotland.gov.uk/about/ED/IAC/00014478/page705680189.pdf

Extensive research review with practical applications to quality in childcare and family support. The full report is nearly 150 pages, but you can access a practical summary on http://www.scotland.gov.uk/library5/social/ins6-00.asp

☆ **Ward, Sally** 2004 *Baby talk*. London: Arrow.

A practical programme to encourage adults, parents or practitioners, to spend time in social conversation and interaction with young children.

8 Thinking and learning

Over the last few decades there has been increasing interest in the abilities of young children. Research into very early communication has produced detailed descriptions of what babies and toddlers can manage. You will have noticed that much of the discussion in Chapter 7 about communication also shed light on children's thoughts. But are very young children thinking before they can put those thoughts into spoken words, and how can adults best support the development of thinking? The main sections of this chapter are:

- Very young thinkers.

- The sounds of the children thinking.

- Working within the zone of proximal development.

VERY YOUNG THINKERS

Young children use their spoken language to think out loud. You will hear two-year-olds guide themselves in an activity with 'No, not dat' or 'Put in there'. Older children talk themselves through a task as well as using their language in pretend play. This type of self-directing speech becomes quieter as it develops, evolving into the low mutter that older children (and some adults too) use when they are tackling a new or difficult task. Otherwise this type of self-directing language becomes silent, as internal speech.

Thinking shown through actions

Even if they do not talk, the behaviour of very young children shows evidence of thinking, planning and use of memory.

- Crawling babies and toddlers remember where their toys are kept. They can be persistent in searching out objects they are not supposed to have, a source of frustration to parents at home.

- Under twos recall and show you that personal objects belong to a particular person. Very young children demonstrate this understanding by taking a bracelet to their mother or pointing to a bag and saying 'Nana'.

- Very young children show recognition of people and places. Older babies may kick their legs in glee as they recognise the last part of the walk to reach the park or their grandparents' home.

Alison Gopnik and her colleagues show that it is possible to design simple experiments that explore how very young children are busy thinking. Toddlers were shown two bowls, one with cheese crackers and the other with florets of raw broccoli. Given a free choice, every toddler ate the crackers. Then, the researcher tasted the food and indicated by a delighted face and 'yum' that she liked one choice but, with a disgusted face and 'yuk' that she disliked the other. Then she put the bowls back near the toddler, held out her hand and said, 'Could you give me some?'. The 14-month-olds gave her their own preference, a cracker, whatever she had indicated. But toddlers who were 18-months-old gave her the broccoli, if that had been her preference. Think about it – such young children deduced an adult's choice from their own observation. They gave the researcher her choice of raw broccoli, although toddlers' personal experience suggested that she must be mad!

Researchers are people too and Alison Gopnik shares a personal example of very young thinking power. She had returned home from an extremely hard day at the university to find she had failed to defrost the dinner. It was the last straw; she sat on the sofa and burst into tears. Her son, not yet two years old, ran to the bathroom, fetched a box of plasters and proceeded to put them on her at random. Her toddler did not know what was wrong, but it clearly needed a lot of patching up, and his strategy worked because his mother stopped crying.

When you are close, you will understand what interests toddlers

Annette Karmiloff-Smith describes how even babies seem to have a very basic idea of number, long before they can count. She describes a family example from the *Baby it's you* project and an experiment. Five-month-old Sarah's parent had noticed that this young baby seemed to have a sense of how many toys should re-appear in a hiding game. Her parent dropped one of the toys by mistake and only two re-appeared on Sarah's highchair. The baby looked very puzzled. In a deliberate experiment, babies of three or four months were shown a sequence of images that appeared on a screen. The exact items varied but there were always three in total. Soon, the babies become bored and looked for a shorter time, although these were different sets of items or toys. Then the image changed and showed only two items in total. The babies suddenly looked at the screen for longer.

LOOK, LISTEN, NOTE, LEARN

Toddlers use rich non-verbal communication to say what they cannot yet express in words. At 16 months, my daughter used to fetch her outdoor shoes and wave them at me when she wanted to go out for a walk. If I was slow to react, Tanith would then get my shoes and push them at me until I co-operated.

■ What does this example tell you about toddler communication, memory and thinking?

■ Gather some examples of meaningful gestures and actions from under twos. Discuss them with your colleagues and share with children's parents to support, 'she's thinking already'.

MAKE THE CONNECTION WITH ... GENERAL KNOWLEDGE

Children are learning not only their own personal name and those of other family members, but also the cultural tradition of family names. At 2 years 2 months, our son, Drew, had grasped that Mama was also called Jennie and Daddy was also Lance. He was prepared to believe that Lance had another name, Lindon, and that he, Drew, also was Lindon. But he laughed uproariously and gave a disbelieving 'No!' when told that Mama and baby Tanith were also Lindons. He took the view there might be two people with the same name in the house, but it was clearly a joke to suggest there could possibly be four. He reacted in exactly the same way when told that he had once been a baby like Tanith.

■ Watch out for examples of the children in your care as they build a picture of themselves in relation to others.

■ Do you find that children's current knowledge leads them to conclude you are making a joke, when what you say makes no sense to them?

What happens outside the laboratory?

Alison Gopnik and Annette Karmiloff-Smith are happy to combine evidence from experiments with observations in family homes. However, experimental research, and the underlying theory, has sometimes led to firm statements about children's lack of ability that do not survive observation in natural settings. From the 1980s Judy Dunn and her team chose to watch and listen to children in their own home. Dunn challenged the reliability of conclusions about early thinking, when so much information was lost for experimental control. Judy Dunn was also convinced it was impossible to make sense of children's cognitive development, while it was treated as separate from their emotional development and key relationships.

Judy Dunn's research showed the subtleties of children's social and play behaviour with siblings in the family. Very young children are drawn into pretend play, a form of activity that is often claimed to be beyond the understanding of this age group. She quotes the example of two-year-old Rose who enters into the imaginary play of her sister Nell, who is four years of age by insisting that she (Rose) is one of Nell's imaginary friends. One can imagine the kind of argument that probably followed this sequence. This example raises the possibility that many genuine play interactions involving siblings, or young friends, could be overlooked because adults need to intervene over conflicts.

MAKE THE CONNECTION WITH ... VERY YOUNG CHILDREN AND PLAY

Judy Dunn's observations have shown how shared play sequences illustrate that very young children must be thinking, remembering and planning. Look back also at the description of Carol Eckerman's research on page 152.

Reflect on your own practice, especially with very young children.

- Are you expecting 'real' play to be longer, more complex or not resulting in tears?

- When you look through the eyes of a toddler, you may be able to re-direct play in a friendly way, without stopping an entire game.

- A positive and friendly adult approach to setting boundaries can co-exist with appreciation of the playful nature of some of children's actions.

THE SOUNDS OF THE CHILDREN THINKING

The heading of this section is taken from Vivian Gussin Paley, who was for many years a teacher of three- and four-year-olds in the USA. From the

1970s she wrote up her experiences of the kindergarten year that were published in a book. Her accounts have each revolved around a main theme, shaped by Paley's reflective comments about the children, but also what she personally learned from the group of children.

Vivian Gussin Paley explains the significant turning point in her practice with, '. . . I became a kindergarten teacher and had curriculum guides . . . [I] believed it was my job to fill the time quickly with a minimum of distractions, and the appearance of a correct answer gave me the surest feeling that I was teaching. It did not occur to me that the distractions might be the sounds of the children thinking' (Paley, 1988: 7).

Learning through social conversation

Vivian Gussin Paley is honest that she had envisaged circle time as the opportunity for her, as the teacher, to raise issues she judged to be important for the group. She listened to her tape recordings of circle time and realised that children were highly motivated to discuss issues that arose in their play. The most impassioned discussions, and arguments, arose from the children's pretend play. Following her recognition of what really enthused children, Paley started to record other parts of the nursery day and so built up her observational material on children's thinking and learning.

Vivian Gussin Paley's reflective observations are useful in many ways to support good practice with young children. One significant application is to be wary about how group time is planned and run. Young children learn most usefully from interactive, personal conversation. There is a limit to what they can manage and enjoy within group time.

Hilary Cremin undertook research in the UK to explore theory and actual practice in running circle time in primary schools. She concluded that this approach could work well when practitioners had a realistic and flexible plan for circle time and when this part of the school day was a valued part of the curriculum. However, she concluded from observations that circle time could be ineffective at best and damaging at worst when practitioners did not understand good communication skills and pushed on with the session plan regardless. She gives one example of poor practice when a teacher was asking children to share how they felt about bullying. Yet at the same time one girl in the circle was being ill-treated by other children who wiped the talking object (the object that children hold in circle time when it is their turn to talk) after she had held it 'so that they would not get her germs' (Cremin, 2002).

MAKE THE CONNECTION WITH . . . YOUR OWN PRACTICE

Bear in mind that Hilary Cremin's cautions about circle time were from observation in primary schools. Early years practitioners need to be even more careful about what can, and cannot, be done well through group time.

Reflect on your own practice and what will genuinely support young learning. Do you even 'have to get' young children into a group?

- Reflect on the words of Vivian Gussin Paley: 'It did not occur to me that the distractions might be the sounds of the children thinking'. Are you tempted verbally to pull children back onto what seems like the 'right' track for their attention or use of communication?

- Young children have a short gap between thinking something very interesting and needing to say it out loud. They cannot wait for long.

- In fact, children who regularly 'interrupt' circle times may well be the only ones who are really listening to you. Yet, unreflective practitioners can label the children as disruptive or rude.

- Look at the *Persona Dolls in Action* video (tel. 020 8446 7056), the section where a practitioner introduces Polly, who is in a wheelchair. What do the three- and four-year-olds understand, what do they want to pursue in this conversation and how does the practitioner follow their lead?

The intellectual search

In the early 1980s Barbara Tizard and Martin Hughes undertook a small-scale research project that had some large-scale repercussions. They observed the conversations of 30 four-year-old girls in half-day nursery class with their teachers and also at home with their mothers. The researchers made the observation that the girls usually had longer, more complex conversations at home than in their nursery. They also observed that the girls' nursery teachers tended to underestimate the children's language competence and how they handled many abstract ideas.

The team recognised that the adult–child ratio was different between home and nursery, although they pointed out fairly that mothers were trying to do many tasks in addition to talking with their daughters. The major point made for early years practice was that the nursery staff's view of their role for language was limiting the potential for conversations. The practitioners were focused on the questions they wanted to ask and frequently used talking time to serve an adult educational agenda.

In the mid-1970s and early 1980s good early years practice in the UK was influenced by the ideas of Joan Tough, an educational psychologist who promoted a dialogue led by adult questioning techniques. Tough built on Marion Blank's concept of cognitive demands and led a practical research project involving many nursery classes and schools (Tough, 1976). Barbara Tizard and Martin Hughes challenged the 'everybody knows' platform that such adult behaviour was best for children's learning, as well as the assumption that nursery must be a richer learning environment than a family home.

MAKE THE CONNECTION WITH ... BEING A REFLECTIVE PRACTITIONER

Barbara Tizard and Martin Hughes posed a legitimate challenge but their research provoked a defensive reaction at the time from some early years professionals and writers. However, good practice cannot be led by 'because we say so ...!' or by a belief that outsiders cannot grasp the intuitive knowledge possessed by insiders. A second edition of Tizard and Hughes' *Young children learning* was published in 2002 and the concepts are just as important to consider now as they were in the 1980s.

Wise practitioners (and trainers or writers!) take account of different kinds of evidence to guide them. There were some very positive ideas in Joan Tough's project. I still value what I learned about the different uses of language for children and adults. However, Tizard and Hughes' research was a crucial 'take a moment' turning point, and not just for me. I have spoken with early years practitioners, whose careers also encompass the 1970s, who describe how the children's reactions made them re-think their language behaviour.

One experienced nursery head, who was involved in the project led by Joan Tough, told me of her own turning point. One day a four-year-old boy had agreed that she could sit down beside him, yet said firmly, 'But you are not to ask me any questions!' – emphasised with body posture and finger waving.

Barbara Tizard and Martin Hughes developed the concept of 'a passage of intellectual search' to describe some of the conversations that they recorded. They define this kind of pattern as, 'a conversation, in which the child is actively seeking new information or explanations, or puzzling over something she does not understand, or trying to make sense of an apparent anomaly in her limited knowledge of the world' (2002: 91).

WHAT DOES IT MEAN?

Passage of intellectual search: a sustained conversation, led by the children's own questions, in which they work to make sense of an event or idea.

The typical pattern of these episodes is a sequence of questions put by the child to the adult. Children consider the adult's answer and relate it to their current knowledge. The fit or lack of fit then often leads to further questions. Careful observation of young children's intellectual search led Tizard and Hughes to the useful distinction that children's thinking develops along two equally important tracks:

1   Children need to learn details and they are hungry for information. Children whose enquiries meet with a positive adult response go on to ask other questions, when they are ready.

2   But four-year-olds are also working hard on a framework to enable them to make sense of the information. Their questions sometimes show an awareness that something does not fit, a sense of 'But that can't be right because . . .'.

LOOK, LISTEN, NOTE, LEARN

Tizard and Hughes (2002) give several examples of conversations between daughters and their mothers in which the three- or four-year-old is trying to make sense of something that puzzles her. Look at any of these examples:

- Penny, and how Father Christmas knows what you want and whether he gives birthday presents too (page 91).

- Rosy, trying to unravel the mystery of money, why and how the window cleaner gets paid (page 95).

- Beth, and the mysteries of sloping roofs (page 99).

See if you can identify what the child currently understands and what is puzzling her. How is she trying to make sense of the situation? How does or could her mother help?

The examples also show that, even if you know children well, it can still be tough to work out what they do not understand. See also the conversation on page 180 about working within the zone of proximal development.

- Collect your own examples of conversations that children themselves are using to drive a passage of intellectual search

Involved adults can be part of sustained conversation and thinking

---

MAKE THE CONNECTION WITH ... AN INDIVIDUAL LEARNING JOURNEY

The intellectual search is often not restricted to a single conversation. Children who are confident of adult attention return to the same subject days, or even weeks, later. Early years practitioners who are serious about supporting young learning, will follow children's leads. You let them determine the precise direction of adult-initiated topics and develop their own projects.

- I was able to track how my son Drew explored many issues around his knowledge and understanding of the world over the months that he was a four-year-old. Some of his questions addressed issues of bodies, death and why unhappy things happened in the world. Look at the description on page 41 of *What does it mean to be four?* (Lindon, 2003a).

- In co-operation with children's parents, you could track the absorbing interests of three- or four-year-olds over a period of months.

Sustained shared thinking

The EPPE research project identified that effective early years settings were those with practitioners who used their attention and communication skills to promote sustained shared thinking with young children. This concept has much in common with the passage of intellectual search (page 171), not least that helpful adults need to listen and be careful about over-use of questions. The REPEY team observed in more detail the work of twelve settings identified as especially effective in supporting young children to learn.

Opportunities for sustained shared thinking were unlikely to happen unless children were able to interact with adults on a one-to-one basis, or with a few of their peers in a very small group. Such a process was simply not possible in adult-led larger group time. The team linked this observation with the importance of a learning environment that enables a great deal of child-initiated and -chosen activities, rather than a balance towards adult-led. The children in Reception class were usually less able to make so many choices – part of the ongoing problem in England about making Reception class genuinely part of the Foundation Stage. Some Reception teams manage this appropriate focus. But research and informal observation suggests than many teams struggle, not least because too often there is no team but only a single practitioner with a large class of children who are still very young.

WHAT DOES IT MEAN?

Sustained shared thinking: communicative interaction between adults and individual children that support them to explore and understand events and ideas.

MAKE THE CONNECTION WITH ... HOLISTIC DEVELOPMENT

The EPPE research confirmed that the best outcomes for children were when the practitioners in their early years settings behaved as if cognitive and social development were equally important. Staff gave time and attention to interaction and emotional support. You can link this point to Judy Dunn's argument that it makes no sense to study cognitive development as if it has nothing to do with emotions.

Look at the example of Rosie and Ben's pretend play in my book *What does it mean to be four?* (2003: 54–55). What is happening between two friends who are absorbed in play and where supportive adults are close by and attentive?

LOOK, LISTEN, NOTE, LEARN

Look at examples of sustained shared thinking given in the REPEY research report (REPEY project *Researching Effective Pedagogy in Early Years: Brief No. 356*
http://www.dfes.gov.uk/research/data/uploadfiles/RB356.doc).

For instance:

■ The lively exchange between two four-year-olds about how God made us, blood and bones (page 45). Note in that sequence that the teacher sat and mainly listened as the conversation flowed to and fro. But she brought in a dog's skull and a skeleton later in the week.

■ Joining in pretend play about being a dog (page 44).

■ Participating in children's imaginative use of playdough (page 47).

In any of these examples what can you learn about:

■ What each child probably understands so far? What is confusing to any of the children at the moment?

■ The current interests of any of the children?

■ How the different practitioners come alongside the children? Can you identify any of the supportive techniques discussed in this chapter?

■ What could have happened if the practitioner in any of the examples took over the conversation or asked lots of testing questions?

Who gets to ask the questions?

All the examples in this section demonstrate that it is crucial that children can take the lead and ask the questions they want to pose right now. In a relaxed learning environment (at home just as much as in nursery), children lead their own intellectual search. In order to promote sustained shared thinking, adults have to listen and contribute to a proper conversation.

Jacqui Cousins continued this line of research with Martin Hughes and other colleagues. She heard many perceptive questions posed by four-year-olds about issues that intrigued them at that moment. Children's searching questions showed how much they wanted to make sense of new experiences, which they realise are currently outside their knowledge. For example, children expressed great interest in what 'Ofsted ladies' did and why. Some observational material was generated during Jacqui Cousins' time as an inspector. One boy wanted to know what would happen to the research observations and asked, 'Will you write all those words in your book or will you cut them into bits and give them to our mums and dads . . . like an MOT? . . . We just got one a them' (Cousins, 1999: 23).

LOOK, LISTEN, NOTE, LEARN

Reflect on your use of questions with children – either as you think about your individual practice or in team discussions. Do you consider sometimes 'Is this a genuine question that I am asking?'. Ways of checking can be to ask yourself:

- Do I really want to know the answer from the child(ren)?

- Do I already know the answer?

- Does the child have the answer and I do not?

With thanks to Saplings Nursery in South London for these points. Their development team first got me thinking around 'questions about questions'.

It is well worth considering, 'Do I ask a lot of questions?'. Or 'Do I ask a lot of testing questions, to which I know the answer, but I want to know whether the children can give the correct reply?'. Practitioners are often encouraged to focus on open-ended questions and avoid closed questions to which there can be only a one-word answer. But there is definitely a place for this kind of question, when the child has the answer and you do not.

You need to reflect on children's replies to your questions:

- Do children give me 'odd' answers? 'Wrong' answers?

- What can I learn from their replies?

- Do the children seem confused but keen to co-operate?

- Do they go silent, change the subject, wander off?

Maybe children want to co-operate, but they are confused about what you are asking. Perhaps you and the children are not actually talking about the same thing (page 187). Perhaps your question does not connect closely enough, or at all, with their current understanding. You are out of the zone of proximal development (page 178).

Jacqui Cousins also suggests valuable open-ended questions from adults: 'What made you say that?', 'Do you mean . . .?', 'I wonder what you were thinking then' and 'What made you ask that question?'.

/ou do?

s for supportive adult behaviour are straightforward. Glenda
and Gillian Williams sum up the situation for early years
practitioners with, 'While teaching is a complex, highly interactive process,
much of the teaching process involves the continuous use of very simple
and subtle verbal interactions that may only last moments' (2004: 2). These
interactions build into a sustained dialogue and children can return to an
interest. Each adult contribution is enough to help, but not so much as to
take over from a child.

MacNaughton and Williams explore a range of techniques in detail and
place adult verbal and non-verbal behaviour in context. They point out that
the apparent simplicity of positive techniques such as encouraging and
describing can mean that they are overlooked or, like questioning, are over-
used. They describe more complex interventions such as scaffolding and co-
construction. However, context is always key: 'Successful use of these
techniques relies on knowing when to use them (timing) and what can be
accomplished (or not) by using them' (2004: 2).

**MAKE THE CONNECTION WITH . . . USE OF COMMUNICATION
SKILLS**

Look back also at the section on page 170 about how adults can best use
their own skills of communication.

WORKING WITHIN THE ZONE OF PROXIMAL DEVELOPMENT

Lev Vygotsky was especially interested in how adults could best help
children to learn. He saw the adult task as a far more active role than
proposed by Piaget, not least because Vygotsky viewed intelligence partly as
the ability to benefit from instruction. Like Piaget, Vygotsky saw play
activity as a crucial means for young children to learn, but he saw adults as
important resources who would guide children and share ideas and
strategies.

Moving on from current understanding

Vygotsky's description of the zone of proximal development guides adults
to an active role to intervene wisely in children's learning. Children's zone
of proximal development is the area of possibilities that lies between what
they can manage on their own – their level of actual development – and
what they could achieve or understand with some appropriate help – their
level of potential development.

Vygotsky believed that the focused help could come from either an alert adult or from another child whose understanding or skills were slightly more mature. The size of the zone is not fixed; some children may have a larger zone of proximal development than their peers. Assistance supports children to go slightly beyond their current competence. The help builds on the child's existing ability, understanding or skill, rather than trying to introduce completely new ideas or ways of behaving. This pattern of help is sometimes called the Vygotskian Tutorial.

LOOK, LISTEN, NOTE, LEARN

Use the diagram of the zone of proximal development (Figure 8.1) to reflect on individual children whom you know well.

- What can this child do or understand with full confidence? What is she keen to manage but currently uncertain or puzzled about? How could you help, without taking over or pushing a step too far?

Look at the illustrated examples of working within the zone on pages 6–9 of Carmel Brennan (2004).

Lev Vygotsky described that children can help each other as well.

- Look out for examples where one child helps another in play in such a way that younger or less sure children extend their learning.

- How might you plan the learning environment or the routines so that opportunities are created for children to help each other in this way?

- Jacqui Cousins gives a good example of how one four-year-old, Sonnyboy, helped his friend David and other children to understand number by sharing his strategy of counting by fingers and using real items to count up to the right number (Cousins, 1999: 18).

WHAT DOES IT MEAN?

The zone of proximal development: the area of potential learning for an individual child at a given time.

The Vygotskian tutorial: the helping approach offered by an adult to a child – support that is sensitive to that child's current zone of proximal development.

Fig. 8.1   Working within the zone of proximal development

All the child's current skills, abilities and understanding

We have to start here with the children, for any flexible, adult-planned activity
or joining in their spontaneous play.
Anything we do has to make a firm connection for babies, toddlers and young
children with what they can manage now.

The child's level of actual development (now, without any help)

The zone of proximal development, in which help can be given now

All your words, actions, suggestions are a gentle extension of what the child has
already grasped – not a great leap forward.
If a child cannot manage something or looks puzzled, then helpful adults go
back to a simpler version.

The child's level of potential development (now, with help)

What is yet to come – the future in this child's development

We do not start here, with a learning goal we want young children to achieve.
What is obvious to us as adults may be far from obvious yet to the children.
If our learning intentions are way off children's current level, then we are
wasting our time and that of the children, and we may well upset them.

The zone can look like Figure 8.1. A college tutor I met also had the
creative idea that the zone could be represented as a set of three concentric
circles. I am not aware that Lev Vygotsky recorded the zone in
diagrammatic form, so use the image that best works for you, your team or
your students.

MAKE THE CONNECTION WITH . . . A REAL EVENT

When my son was five years old, his close friend moved house and we
were invited to tea at Piya's new home. I drove most of the way, then
parked to check my London A–Z. Drew and I had a conversation that
went like this:

Drew: How do you know where Piya lives?

Jennie: His Mum gave me their new address. I know it's round here somewhere. I'm just not sure of the last bit.

D: So how can we find it if you don't know?

J: I've got the map. I'm going to find it on the A–Z.

D: (looking at the map) But how can you find it on there?

J: It's okay. I know the name of the road.

D: But there's no houses or anything on it [the map]. How can you find Piya's house on that?

J: Ah, right. The map doesn't show houses and things. But it shows me the roads. Look. We're here now and Piya's road is there. The map tells me we have to turn right, go straight on a bit and then turn left.

D: But what about his house?

J: That'll be alright because I know the number. We get onto Piya's road and then we look out for number fourteen. The houses will have numbers on the door.

Drew and I talked some more and I understood more about what he needed to know from me, as well as the extent of what he knew already. Thinking afterwards, I realised that Drew had experience of two-dimensional plans that related to three-dimensional settings. For instance, he was able to follow exploded diagrams to make small Lego models. But those instructions had drawings that looked like the Lego pieces in front of him. He had a roadway for his cars, but that had the outline of buildings on it. The A–Z was a two-dimensional representation with even more detail removed. This example highlights, for one aspect of learning, the current understanding of an individual boy.

▪ Look and listen for similar examples in your work with children.

Disembedded thinking

Margaret Donaldson developed the key concept that children are increasingly required to manage disembedded thinking. By this term she meant the kind of thinking when children have to handle ideas without familiar and concrete reference points. The primary school curriculum requires this kind of abstraction, but six- or seven-year-olds are increasingly able to manage without a hands-on context. On the other hand, three-, four- and five-year-olds need to make clear connections with the knowledge and ideas that they understand so far.

Margaret Donaldson and her team showed how young children could grasp quite abstract ideas, so long as they could relate them to a conceptual

Finding out what happens when . . .

framework that made sense. Young children are busy thinking, but they can only work from their current understanding. Margaret Donaldson described that they are dealing with a great deal of information to build their knowledge, but at the same time working on a conceptual framework to make sense of new experiences or ideas.

LOOK, LISTEN, NOTE, LEARN

■ Margaret Donaldson (1978: 53) quotes a recorded exchange between a five-year-old girl and a researcher. The conversation happened shortly after the death of Donald Campbell while attempting to break the world water speed record. A few months before, a researcher, Robin Campbell, had visited the school.

■ The child asked, 'Is that Mr Campbell who came here – dead?' (with dramatic emphasis). The researcher replied in a surprised tone, 'No, I'm quite sure he isn't dead'. The child replied, 'Well there must be two Mr Campbells then, because Mr Campbell's dead under the water'.

■ Reflect on that short exchange, what does it tell you about the reasoning powers and likely current knowledge of that five-year-old?

■ What can the example also tell you about the importance of conversation and children's confidence to ask their own questions (see also page 176)?

WHAT DOES IT MEAN?

Disembedded thinking: dealing with concepts in the abstract, without an immediate reference point in direct experience.

MAKE THE CONNECTION WITH ... CHILDREN'S UNDERSTANDING

The less a situation makes sense to children through links with their existing experience, the more they are dependent on making some sense of it through what they guess the adults want them to say.

Robert Grieve and Martin Hughes explored what happened when children were asked meaningless questions by adults, such as 'Is red heavier than yellow?'. Young children worked hard to co-operate and gave answers that made as much sense as possible out of a nonsensical situation. Some children argued that red was heavier because it was darker, or they explained their answer by reference to specific red and yellow objects close to them. Children created a context to create sense, when the only existing sense was that, when adults ask children questions, they expect an answer.

▓ This perspective is very useful to bear in mind when children give you odd answers to questions that seem perfectly clear to you.

The example of number

Children can manage much better when they are able to embed a potentially confusing abstract idea in a familiar context, either by direct, hands-on exploration or by a visual image summoned up through words.

Martin Hughes has undertaken research to explore children's understanding with special application to their grasp of early mathematical concepts of number. His studies (reported in Donaldson *et al.*, 1983 and Hughes, 1986) demonstrate the impressive thinking power of four-year-olds, as well as the point at which they no longer understand the concepts being used by the adult.

In one study, Martin Hughes showed that well over half of a group of three- and four-year-olds could manage hypothetical ('what if . . .') counting, so long as the imaginary situation, described in words, made sense within children's own experience. So this age group could often give the correct answer to a question such as, 'If there were two girls in a shop and another one went in, how many girls would be in the shop now?'. The children could transform the words into a familiar visual image in their imagination. They could often produce the correct answer, although they had nothing tangible in front of them to count. Without a familiar context, adult questions about number can sound like nonsense to young children. For example, Martin Hughes asked Patrick (four years and one month) these questions:

MH: How many is two and one more?

P: Four.

MH: Well how many is two lollypops and one more?

P: Three.

MH: How many is two elephants and one more?

P: Three.

MH: How many is two giraffes and one more?

P: Three.

MH: So how many is two and one more?

P: (looks MH straight in the eye) Six.

Children need to connect mathematical concepts to a familiar context but this does not always have to be utterly hands-on. For instance, money is a complicated idea for four-year-olds but Judy Miller showed how two-, three- and four-year-olds were enabled to make sense of purchasing decisions about play equipment. The children had the same number of discs as the pounds limit in the budget. The early years practitioner supported the children as they considered options from the catalogue and counted out the number of discs needed to pay. But soon the children were working with the idea of how much, and not enough, money. The children were also part of the trip to go and buy the equipment, so they experienced a real life context of purchase.

MAKE THE CONNECTION WITH ... OTHER CONCEPTS

- The ideas explored in this section link with other ideas summed up by the whole idea of tuning in to children: an approach that needs to be applied as much to emotional fine-tuning as intellectual.

- I will add my idea of the 'cognitive wobble', drawing a parallel between cognitive and physical development. When young children are in the process of learning physical skills such as balancing or climbing, you can easily identify the gap between learning the skills and being fully confident. You see the wobble.

- Adults have to use more than their eyes to recognise the cognitive wobble. You have to allow that what is obvious to you as an adult, in terms of knowledge or concepts, is far from obvious to a child. You need to back-track to where children are no longer wobbling, where they are cognitively stable and then move on slowly from this point.

The supportive technique of scaffolding

Jerome Bruner studied children's thinking and learning through the way in which they process information. His approach is to look equally at two aspects:

1   How children's experience affects their cognitive development – from external events to internal thinking.

2   How children's ability to think can then shape their experience – inside to outside.

Bruner pointed out that children can enjoy solving problems but that they are not necessarily very skilled or motivated at problem finding. And, of course, in order to identify a problem that needs solving you also need some grasp of the gap between what you currently know and do not know, what you can and cannot do. This kind of identification and guidance is the crucial role of adults who can challenge children without daunting them.

Bruner developed the concept of scaffolding to explain a positive way for adults to intervene in children's learning. The visual image is that of scaffolding on a building. When children are learning an idea or a skill, they benefit from adult suggestions; Bruner does not suggest that adults should take over. Then, as children's understanding or their practical skill grows, adults can steadily remove the scaffolding. This process continues with children's learning at different ages and the adult task is to be alert to the nature and extent of the scaffolding required for individual children.

LOOK, LISTEN, NOTE, LEARN

Jerome Bruner's idea of scaffolding has been described as not so much directing children but more a case of leading by following. You have to observe an individual child before you can judge how best to help.

■   Choose one or two children and focus on something they are currently keen to learn. It might be a physical skill such as learning to button up their coat or the answer to an intellectual search about 'how do we get rainbows?'.

■   Watch individual children carefully to understand how far their learning has progressed. What kind of help might be most useful now: suggestions by words, showing how by demonstration, encouraging a child to talk thoughts out loud?

■   Or might it be helpful to offer an experience to help children make more sense of what puzzles them? For example, several children

> who are perplexed about what exactly happens at the vet's may be
> interested to set up a role play space, so they can explore what it
> means to be a vet. Note that this development arises from the
> children's interest, not because the practitioner has planned a
> topic on 'people who help us'.
>
> ■ Reflect on what you have done and how your contribution seems to
>   have helped children to extend their learning. What have you
>   learned from the experience?

The apprenticeship model

Margaret Donaldson stressed how children want and need sometimes to
learn directly from adults. She pointed out that, 'Young human beings have
a remarkable fitness for the role of novice. They can enjoy accepting new
goals and challenges from other people and can experience great satisfaction
from the achieving of conscious mastery' (1992: 257).

Margaret Donaldson challenged the more extreme interpretations of child-
centred practice. Her view was that learning should be a shared enterprise
to which adults bring their own contribution. Children enjoy solving
problems and making discoveries, but they can only manage this within the
framework of their current understanding and knowledge. A genuinely
child-centred learning environment is not one that leaves children to
struggle when direct adult suggestion could help. She adds that children,
'like to make discoveries and it is good to challenge them to do so, but they
also enjoy and benefit from having things explained to them. They ask
questions and they want clear, honest answers, which, of course, if these are
well-judged, need not close the inquiry but may provoke a further desire to
know' (1992: 257).

Barbara Rogoff developed her ideas of an apprenticeship model of learning
through research that highlighted a contrast in cultural traditions. She
observed children and their families in the USA and in Guatemala. She
noted that the children from Guatemala were expected to learn domestic
skills alongside their parents and other family members and soon had
responsibility for tasks such as care of the animals. In contrast, the children
in the US families were far less likely to be learning in this way. Adults
tended to instruct them but did not expect children to take the same kind
or level of domestic responsibility.

Rogoff developed the concept of learning as guided participation: the
'apprentice' child learns through appropriate conversation, organisation of
the environment and actions and directly from an adult or other child.
Barbara Rogoff also emphasised the concept of a community of learners in

which children learn the socio-cultural meaning of items and actions. She stressed the idea of co-construction of knowledge that children and adults form meaning together, so adults need to tune in to the child's understanding and share control much more than is usual in an instruction model led by adult greater knowledge.

MAKE THE CONNECTION WITH ... YOUR OWN PRACTICE

- **You may well be working within an apprenticeship approach without using that term.**

- **Reflect on how you encourage children to come alongside as you undertake daily tasks. Domestic routines can be a rich source of learning for children in early years settings as much as in family homes.**

- **Can you also see the links with the technique of scaffolding? An active role for the adult that must rest on the child's current skill or understanding – whether it is an idea or a physical skill.**

Are we talking about the same thing?

Penny Munn talked with individual children during their last year in nursery and their first term of primary school. On each of four visits she asked the children the same basic questions including 'Can you count?' and 'Why do you count?'. She found that children generally learn to recite a number sequence at a younger age than they are able to count a given number of objects, or to select a limited number in answer to the question, 'Can you give me three bricks?'.

Four-year-olds tended to believe that counting was the same as saying the number words – rather in the same way that they believed that reading was the same as re-telling the story (page 162). Many of the younger children were perplexed by the question 'Why do you count?'. It was rare for young children to understand the adult purpose of counting until they went to school. Then the children increasingly gave an answer to 'Why do you count?' that focused on 'to know how many'.

Dorothy Caddell describes the implications of research into early mathematical understanding. She draws out the practical strands of number learning for young children and how children need to see adults using numbers for a real purpose. Dorothy Caddell suggests that, much as with literacy (page 161), young children need to see the point of skills. Adult-initiated number activities can appear far too abstract when practitioners require disembedded thinking (page 181).

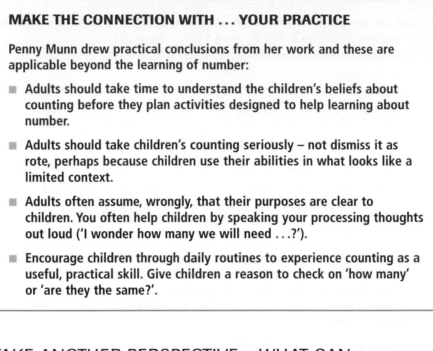

MAKE THE CONNECTION WITH ... YOUR PRACTICE

Penny Munn drew practical conclusions from her work and these are applicable beyond the learning of number:

- Adults should take time to understand the children's beliefs about counting before they plan activities designed to help learning about number.

- Adults should take children's counting seriously – not dismiss it as rote, perhaps because children use their abilities in what looks like a limited context.

- Adults often assume, wrongly, that their purposes are clear to children. You often help children by speaking your processing thoughts out loud ('I wonder how many we will need ...?').

- Encourage children through daily routines to experience counting as a useful, practical skill. Give children a reason to check on 'how many' or 'are they the same?'.

TAKE ANOTHER PERSPECTIVE – WHAT CAN NUMBERS DO FOR US?

Dorothy Caddell shows how young children build firm foundations for numeracy when they have opportunities to learn through daily routines and ordinary events that show how:

- Numbers give information: telephone numbers, prices or your age.

- Numbers help us to make decisions: which bus to catch, the right size of clothes or the temperature to bake this cake.

- Numbers can be fun, part of playful activities: counting before you seek in hide and seek or number rhymes and songs.

- Numbers can be used to impress: when children say they have 'hundreds and hundreds' of something or children may use their age to establish status over a younger child.

Gather observations in your practice and see in what ways children can grasp all these uses of number over the days and weeks and through ordinary activities.

Reflect on your practice – are you trying to promote early mathematical understanding through adult-planned and initiated 'number activities'? Do these activities really work within the children's zone of proximal development?

Look at an action research project in Fife that considered these practical applications: Susan Morton *Promoting number and mathematical development in nursery through staff development* http://www.scre.ac.uk/spotlight/spotlight88

MAKE THE CONNECTION WITH ... DEVELOPMENTALLY APPROPRIATE LITERACY

- In a similar way to supporting writing, helpful adults respond to the three-year-olds' interest in what adults can recognise as early maths, rather than trying to recruit young children into completing mathematical activities such as worksheets, that risk making little sense to them.

- Link these ideas also with Cathy Nutbrown's idea of environmental print (page 160). In what ways can young children experience environmental number – written numbers that exist for a reason?

- Consider some of the toys, kits or posters that claim to promote young children's understanding of number. Which materials are genuinely likely to support learning and how? Young children do not learn by having numbers thrust at them out of context and stuck onto plastic toys.

Shared or non-shared reference

Penny Munn and her colleagues in Strathclyde have explored teacher behaviour with regard to five-year-olds and maths. Catherine Ridler (2002) provides examples from her research of when the teacher and children share the same reference point and what happens when a teacher fails to consider, 'are we talking about the same thing?'. Practitioners need to act differently if the answer is 'no'; there is no point in trudging on with the lesson plan if you have lost the children.

In one example, Catherine Ridler described that children had number lines from 1 to 10 on their desks. Their teacher was asking the children to point to numbers on their line. She asked them to 'find the one with the hat on' and the children all pointed to the number 5. The teacher then asked, 'How do you make a number 5 again?'. And the children used the formula of, 'Down and round and put the hat on'. In this case the adults and children were both talking about the same thing. First of all, they were referring to the written symbol 5. Then they were talking about how you make the symbol 5.

In another example a different teacher wanted to explain how many more cubes child B had than child A. The teacher took four cubes from A (all the cubes that A had). The she said to child A, indicating B, 'What do I have to do to make it fair?'. Child A replied 'Take all of her cubes'. Child A seemed to be thinking of the situation in terms of fairness and social equivalence. Child A had no cubes, so fairness meant taking away child B's cubes as well. But the teacher was thinking about addition and subtraction – that kind of equivalence. She had intended to remove the same number of cubes from B's pile and was then going to ask how many were left in B's pile of cubes. But the teacher's words do not indicate a number operation.

MAKE THE CONNECTION WITH ... YOUR OWN PRACTICE

- It is often easier to spot the gap when you are an external observer. Wise practitioners allow that they may make mistakes and sometimes keep going when odd answers from children and puzzled expressions say very clearly, 'we are not talking about the same thing!'.

- In the first example the children and the teacher shared the same reference point. But can you also spot that the teacher used different approaches to support children's understanding, such as the visual image of 'down and round and put on the hat'?

TAKE ANOTHER PERSPECTIVE

A great deal of research on children's thinking has explored those situations when children do not understand. The practical issues raised in this section put the spotlight on adults' potential failure to understand. Elizabeth Robinson and Peter Robinson focused on what usually happens when adults are puzzled, when children have not got their message across to the more mature partner in the exchange (in Donaldson *et al*, 1983.)

When adults did not understand what children meant, the most frequent response from the adult was to ask for a repetition with 'Pardon?'. The next most common reaction was to ask questions to encourage more information (What? and Who? questions). Some adults would make a guess about what the child meant, or they would repeat and expand the child's message or ignore it. The least frequently used response was for adults to tell children directly, 'I don't understand what you mean' or similar phrases. Several experiments showed that children did not realise adults had failed to understand, unless those adults said so directly.

This research made me think about interactions led by adults. Co-operative young children often repeat themselves or answer adult questions. But a strategy of simple honesty is more likely to promote understanding. Adults can also directly model the difference in words between, 'I didn't hear you (or an honest 'Sorry, I wasn't listening'), please say that again' and the different message of, 'I don't understand, can you say it a different way (or show me)?'.

- Reflect on your own practice, keeping alert to how you handle times when you do not understand what a child says.

- Try letting children know that you are confused about what they are telling you. Use any questions in this context.

From direct experience to concepts

Teaching children road safety is a practical illustration that adults need to understand how young children think. Research projects have highlighted that the traditional approach of a set of rules or safety code fail to transfer into safe behaviour by children at the roadside. The problem can be seen as lack of a shared reference point. But, also young children think from specific examples and then generalise to other similar situations (inductive reasoning). Yet, most road safety training has worked in the opposite way, by stressing general principles and expecting children to apply these rules to specific road crossing situations (deductive reasoning).

Children struggle to apply a rule such as 'Find a safe place to cross', because they do not share adult knowledge of what would be safe or dangerous. Children often thought that the best place to cross was the shortest distance between two points. Children also reason that they if cannot see any cars, then it is safe to cross. They do not allow for their own relative invisibility and may emerge from between parked vehicles. Children also have difficulty in judging the combined effect of the speed of a vehicle and its distance away from the crossing point. A series of studies identified that real practice at the roadside, supported by computer simulations, worked to help children think in a safe way and adjust their behaviour at the kerb.

If you want to find out more:

⭐ **Caddell, Dorothy** 1998a *Numeracy in the early years: what the research tells us.* Dundee: Scottish Consultative Council on the Curriculum.

Summary of research into early learning of numeracy and the implications for good early years practice.

⭐ **Caddell, Dorothy** 1998b *Numeracy counts.* Dundee: Scottish Consultative Council on the Curriculum.

Ideas and examples for developmentally appropriate early years practice.

⭐ **Carter, Rita** 1999 *Mapping the mind.* London: Orion Publishing Group.

More about how brains work in general, rather than childhood in particular – but helpful if you want to extend your knowledge.

⭐ **Cousins, Jacqui** 1999 *Listening to four year olds: how they can help us plan their education and care.* London: National Children's Bureau.

Detailed observational research of young children's language and how their skills relate to, and highlight, the learning process in early years.

⭐ **Donaldson, Margaret** 1978 *Children's minds.* Glasgow: Fontana/Collins.

Discussion of children's thinking, shown through experiments and children's comments.

⭐ **Donaldson, Margaret** 1992 *Human minds: an exploration.* London: Penguin.

Ideas and philosophy as well as practical examples that emerged from Margaret Donaldson's research programme.

⭐ **Donaldson, Margaret; Grieve, Robert** and **Pratt, Chris** (eds) 1983 *Early childhood development and education: readings in psychology.* Oxford: Basil Blackwell.

Wide range of research about how young children learn to think.

★ **Dunn, Judy** 1984 *Sisters and brothers*. London: Fontana.

Descriptions from some of the first research to look in real detail at sibling relationships and ordinary family life

★ **Dunn, Judy,** 1986 'Children in a family world'. In Richards, Martin and Light, Paul (eds) *Children of social worlds: development in a social context*. Cambridge: Polity Press.

Research that highlights the complexity of children's relationships within the family.

★ EPPE: *The Effective Provision of Pre-School Education Project.* http://www.ioe.ac.uk/schools/ecpe/eppe

Report of research into the impact on children of different kinds of early years group experience.

★ **Gopnik, Alison; Meltzoff, Andrew** and **Kuhl, Patricia** 2001 *How babies think: the science of childhood*. London: Phoenix.

What has been discovered by careful research with very young children and the ideas behind making sense of very early development.

★ **Grieve, Robert** and **Hughes, Martin** (eds) 1990 *Understanding children: essays in honour of Margaret Donaldson*. Oxford: Basil Blackwell.

Useful book that placed experiments with children in the broader context of insight into how children think and use their communication skills.

★ **Hughes, Martin** 1986 *Children and number*. Oxford: Blackwell.

Research and practical ideas about what young children understand and how adults can help rather than confuse.

★ **Karmiloff-Smith, Annette** 1994 *Baby it's you: a unique insight into the first three years of the developing baby*. London: Ebury Press.

Research and observations of early childhood. From a Channel 4 series in 1994, also a video (see page 269).

✱ **Maclellan, Effie; Munn, Penny** and **Quinn, Victoria** 2003 *Thinking about maths: a review of issues in teaching number from 5 to 14 years.* Glasgow: Learning and Teaching Scotland.

Practical applications of research about early mathematical thinking to teaching methods appropriate for children at different ages.

✱ **MacNaughton, Glenda** and **Williams, Gillian** 2004 *Teaching young children: choices in theory and practice.* Maidenhead: Open University Press.

Explains communication techniques and how to use them effectively. A good book – although the authors do not understand negative reinforcement!

✱ **Miller, Judy** 1996 *Never too young: how young children can take responsibility and make decisions.* London: Save the Children.

Practical ideas about involving children. Some examples show well that young children can understand and make meaning with familiar reference points.

✱ **Munn, Penny** 1997 'Children's beliefs about counting'. In Thompson, Ian (ed.) *Teaching and learning early number.* Buckingham: Open University Press.

Research explaining how children learn about the skills of counting.

✱ **Rogoff, Barbara** 1990 *Apprenticeship in thinking: cognitive development in social context.* Oxford: Oxford University Press.

Explanation of Rogoff's ideas about the apprenticeship model of learning as guided participation.

✱ **Thomson, J.; Tolmie, A.; Foot, H.** and **McLaren, B.** 1996 *Child development and the aims of road safety education.* London: HMSO.

Description of the road safety research and ways to address how young children think.

✱ **Tizard, Barbara** and **Hughes, Martin** 2002 *Young children learning: talking and thinking at home and at school.* Oxford: Blackwell.

Contrasting the learning experiences of young children in the different settings of home and nursery class – food for thought about practice.

9 How do children learn to behave?

This chapter focuses on children's behaviour, however you can only make sense of what children do within the broader context of their development. Therefore, you will find discussion of how children think as well as what they do. This area of development is also one that throws into sharp relief the impact of children's experience, a large component of which is how adults behave. The main sections of this chapter are:

- Temperament and behaviour.

- Learning from experience.

- Pro-social behaviour.

TEMPERAMENT AND BEHAVIOUR

If you observe several children, within a family or an early years setting, it will not be long before you notice that individual children do not behave in the same way faced with what, to an outsider, look like similar events. If you watch the same children some years later, you will almost certainly notice that the child who looked confident and was central in the play is still very much a social leader. The child who stood on the sidelines or who clung to an adult may not cling so much, but probably still seeks more reassurance, especially in a new or anxiety-provoking situation.

Individual differences

The available research does not suggest that children are fixed from birth; there is plenty of scope for the impact of experience. But there is good reason to say that babies have an inborn inclination towards one kind of temperament, shown through a behavioural style. The word 'temperament' is used to mean inborn tendencies for children's reactions and behaviours that probably build the basis for a more enduring adult personality. The two concepts are both attempts to explain continuities in how the same child, or adult, tends to deal with their experiences.

WHAT DOES IT MEAN?

Temperament: inborn tendencies that shape how a baby and young child reacts to daily experiences.

Personality: usually the term used to describe continuities in how adults react to experiences.

Behavioural style: the individual pattern of behaviour that a child shows from a very young age, reflecting inborn temperament.

Stella Chess and Alexander Thomas led a team that followed children over childhood from the early 1980s. They classified young babies into three broad temperamental types:

1   *Easy babies* – who reacted in a playful way, moved into regular care patterns and adapted readily to new circumstances.

2   *Difficult babies* – whose biological needs did not slip into a regular pattern, behaved in an irritable way and often responded intensely and negatively to unfamiliar situations.

3   *Slow-to-warm-up babies* – who tended to be lower on activity level and responded in a mild way. These babies tended to withdraw from unfamiliar situations, but not in the intense way of the 'difficult' babies. These babies were able to adapt but needed more time than the 'easy' babies.

LOOK, LISTEN, NOTE, LEARN

- Look at the three broad categories described by Stella Chess and Alexander Thomas. How might caring adults – parents or early years practitioners – be affected when they face these inclinations in young babies?

- In what ways could there be an interaction between parental expectations and the baby's inclination? See also the idea of match and mis-match on page 198.

- Draw on your own experience and talk, if possible, with a health visitor or a local Sure Start project team. They could discuss general themes about family support and more or less 'difficult' babies, without breaking confidentiality about individual families.

Other research teams have been interested to explore inborn individual temperament, for example, Arnold Buss and Robert Plomin, also in the USA. The researchers do not all propose the same types, nor use the same terms. However, there are shared themes about individuality, which can be summed up as these dimensions of broad temperament:

- *Activity level*: some children are physically mobile and react in a vigorous way to the possibilities in their environment. Some are considerably less active and may prefer sedentary play activities. Some may react passively, waiting for experiences to come to them.

- *Sociability*: individual differences between children in how they relate to people and to new experiences or objects. Some children are keen to make contact or explore, some are less enthusiastic or out-going in a social way.

Some children may seem more adventurous

▨ *Wariness*: a tendency to react with fear to or to withdraw from new experiences and people. Children who tend to show this kind of anxiety are often called 'shy', but the wariness is not only about people.

▨ *Negative emotions* – children differ in their tendency to react to experiences with anger and irritability. All children feel annoyed at some point, but some children are easily provoked by minor frustrations.

▨ *Effort and persistence* – children vary in how well they are able to focus on what they are doing and to persist despite distractions. Attention control is partly developmental but some older children struggle to concentrate.

MAKE THE CONNECTION WITH ... BALANCE BETWEEN NATURE AND NURTURE

▨ Individual differences in temperament need to be seen as tendencies; they are not proposed as a fixed character for everyone. Temperament operates as a built-in bias: possibilities may be strengthened or weakened through children's experience.

▨ Socio-cultural context determines whether children's temperament is experienced as difficult by themselves, or by the key adults in their lives.

▨ Adults may judge some temperamental inclinations as appropriate, or inappropriate, given this child's sex. Think of some possibilities here.

Interaction between temperament and experience

Longitudinal research about temperament has established that children rated by adults as having a 'difficult temperament' (getting upset very easily, finding it hard to settle and so on) are far more likely to exhibit what adults judge to be behaviour problems. But it is not the case that a 'difficult' temperament inevitably leads to later problems.

For example, newborn babies who cry a lot more than average do not necessarily grow into irritable, easily upset toddlers. Babies whose mothers were rated as highly responsive were crying less by 5–6 months, but those with mothers who were observed as being less sensitive to their baby's crying were still experiencing a great deal of crying at the half-year point. In a similar way, crying babies were more likely to develop into defiant toddlers when their mother had reacted in an angry way to the early crying. Mothers were more able to be responsive to their crying babies if they had the support of family and friends.

TAKE ANOTHER PERSPECTIVE

Consider the idea of match or mis-match. Some adults – parents and practitioners – can feel a wide gap between their own inclinations and the way that a child reacts.

An outgoing adult may be baffled by a reticent toddler, who seems to approach new situations as a worry and not an exciting possibility. On the other hand, a cautious adult may be unnerved by a vigorous young child with an enthusiastic 'leap-then-look' approach.

- Can you think of examples of match and mis-match between children and your own preference and personality?

- What can happen to a child if their important adults insist on a very different style?

- Reflect on your group setting – how do you reduce distractions for children who find it hard to concentrate? Are wary children labelled as 'shy'?

LEARNING FROM EXPERIENCE

You will recall from Chapter 2 that behaviourist theories began with the study of animals and learning through conditioning. Albert Bandura developed a more sophisticated theory of social learning, with key concepts useful to daily life with children.

Using the positives to guide behaviour

Any kind of reinforcement is defined by its effect. You do not know for certain that something will act as reinforcement of behaviour until you observe that its presence increases the probability of that same behaviour. Positive reinforcement comes in many varieties:

- Rewards as tangible treats such as food or sweets.

- Events as a reward, such as extra time with a favourite activity.

- Incentives – rewards for the future, dependent on behaviour (if ... then ...).

- Praise by verbal and non-verbal communication.

- Symbolic rewards such as stars, stickers or certificates, but this kind of reward makes little sense to under threes.

- Intrinsic rewards felt by children as a sense of pride or satisfaction at what they have managed and pleasure at the adults' reaction.

Remember partial reinforcement

When adults are inconsistent, they can unintentionally reward the exact behaviour they are trying to discourage. For example, a young child may wake at night and cry to be taken into the parents' bed. On the first few occasions, the parents stand firm and settle or take the child back to her own bed. Then exhaustion or exasperation takes over and, on the third or fourth crying bout, the child is taken into the parents' bed. Inadvertently, the parents have shown the child that persistence pays off. The child has experienced partial reinforcement: crying does not get you taken into bed straightaway or even every time, but the success rate is good enough. Helpful programmes for parents, whose children wake at night, advise putting a child back again and again, reassuring them and going in only briefly. Supportive advice must also acknowledge that it is tough for exhausted parents to be consistent.

Being cautious about rewards

Early years practitioners may be aware of the risks of using sweets as a reward. However, some teams have found that their use of symbolic rewards, such as stars or certificates, appears to have reduced, not increased, a wanted behaviour in a group of children. When children are given stickers for specific tasks, they do not necessarily increase this behaviour when given a free choice. The claim then is sometimes that 'reward does not work' or that 'it does not have a long-term effect'.

Social learning theory explains that the use of tangible rewards has shaped children's perspectives on this particular activity. Instead of developing a sense of internal satisfaction – 'I lay the table because it's interesting and I enjoy helping' – children now think of the task as something they do for the reward – 'I only do this if I want a sticker today'. Some children experience a sense of pressure that operates as a disincentive, for instance that they are only liked and valued if they earn enough stickers.

MAKE THE CONNECTION WITH ... CHILDREN'S THINKING

Social learning theory reminds adults that children are the experts on whether something is a reward or a punishment.

- A child who seeks immediate attention by throwing toys or shouting may experience adults who tell her off at some length. The adults judge that they are dissuading her from being so 'demanding'. Yet, from the child's point of view, her behaviour was successful (reinforced); she gained the full attention of one or more adults. Children with little experience of pleasant adult attention can be motivated to attract reprimands, even anger.

- Primary school teams need to reflect on the symbolic reward systems as part of their behaviour policy. Some children enjoy public praise. Others find it embarrassing to receive 'best behaved child of the week' certificates and, especially for some boys, the event threatens their playground credibility. What is supposed to reinforce good behaviour through reward can operate as a disincentive, more of a punishment.

The conclusion of this example is not that adults should avoid celebrating behaviour they want to encourage, but that they should consult children in order to understand what they find genuinely rewarding!

- Can you think of examples from your work or personal experience that highlight unexpected patterns of reward and punishment?

Using encouragement

The Adlerian approach to using encouragement rather than tangible rewards or spoken praise was a practical response to this type of dilemma. Rudolf Dreikurs and other writers in this tradition, have stressed the difference between spoken praise or tangible rewards and a pattern of encouragement. These are the main differences:

- Conventional praise focuses on the end result whereas encouragement is freely given for effort and improvement.

- Praise or rewards stress a fixed quality about a child, but encouragement focuses on what a child has done. Can you experience the difference between 'Well done for waiting your turn' rather than 'Good boy', and 'Thank you for helping' instead of 'You're such a helpful little girl'.

- Encouragement focuses on feelings: of the adults when they express appreciation for help and on the children by acknowledging their pleasure in a job well done or finished, despite the difficulties.

- Encouragement taps into children's feelings of satisfaction and their strengths. Patterns of praise and reward can be unforgiving of mistakes or times when children do not feel like being 'patient' or 'helpful'.

Negative reinforcement in action

Negative reinforcement is an unpleasant event such that, when it stops, the cessation acts to increase a particular behaviour. It is a useful concept to grasp, because adults can behave, unintentionally, in a way that is negatively reinforcing for children.

Imagine a harassed early years practitioner who tries to get some children to tidy up before lunch. She tells them to put the blocks away and then she tells them more firmly. She calls them 'inconsiderate' and says they will not get any 'helpful' stickers this week. She threatens that they will not be able to have the blocks out this afternoon ... she runs out of steam, lunch is ready. The children have not tidied up, they need to eat lunch and the practitioner tidies up the blocks, muttering and giving unfriendly stares all the time. What has happened here and what are the alternative options?

- From the children's perspective their behaviour, of not tidying up, has been negatively reinforced. They have learned that if they ignore the practitioner, they can carry on playing and avoid tidying up, which seems like a boring chore to them. They may also know from experience that the practitioner will forget about her threat of 'no blocks this afternoon'.

- The practitioner believes she has been using punishment by telling off and withdrawing positives such as playing with the favourite blocks or having a sticker. In fact, she has been using the ineffective 'hot-air' punishment strategy where children learn that, if you ignore adults' nagging, they give up in the end.

- If the practitioner asks for help, sound advice will include awareness of the situation from the perspective of the children. They need a friendly time warning and positive incentives to be involved in tidying up time.

This example highlights how the concept of negative reinforcement is confused with punishment by some childcare writers. The term seems to be applied to the practitioner's nagging behaviour and not to the importance from the children's perspective of when that nagging stops.

LOOK, LISTEN, NOTE, LEARN

- Visualise the scene at the supermarket checkout. A young child asks for some sweets, asks in a louder voice, grabs a packet, whines when the adult takes it away and then goes into a full-scale tantrum. Her carer has said 'No' several times increasingly loudly, taken the packet from the child's hands twice but is now deeply embarrassed at the scene and hands the sweets back.

- What has happened here and what are the patterns of reinforcement for the child and for the adult? What could be the alternative options?

- Are you facing similar situations with children?

MAKE THE CONNECTION WITH ... AN AUTHORITATIVE STYLE

- Open discussion about handling children's behaviour often poses two stark options: strong adults laying down the law or weak adults letting children run wild. But there is a more effective third option. Authoritative adults show kindness and set boundaries for children's behaviour, explaining their reasons. As you will guess, the research is complex but the authoritative style works best to support children and teenagers.

- Strict, punitive adults often provoke rebellion or children who copy their harsh role model. Children soon do not like permissive, uncertain adults, because they want grown-ups to take appropriate responsibility. The authoritative adult offers emotional warmth and safety through being firm but fair.

Imitation and modelling

Albert Bandura emphasised the importance of imitation and adult role models in how children learn to behave. However, his theory also acknowledges that children use their skills of observation and thinking.

Bandura found that, when adults' behaviour did not fit their words, then children were most likely to copy what the adults did. So, research does not lead to any optimism about adult approaches of 'Do what I say, not what I do!'. Children consider what they are told and do not simply accept a behaviour rule, especially if the adult's behaviour is inconsistent. Children do not only imitate real people, they also copy role models on the television.

Research across cultures has shown how adults behave in ways that shape children's behaviour to fit the values and priorities of that society. Adults are often not alert to the differences; the pattern of behaviour within their own group is 'normal'. Janet Maybin and Martin Woodhead describe the contrast between an Inuit community (the Utkuhiksalingmiut) in northern Canada and American children in south Baltimore. The Inuit parents modelled their preferred behaviour pattern of being nurturing, protective and even-tempered (summed up as naklik). Parents did their best to avoid scolding children or showing anger. They re-interpreted unacceptable actions, for instance, treating an expression of annoyance from a child as if it were amusing. They also commented with disapproval on un-naklik behaviour from other people.

In contrast, the American parents guided their children to stand up for themselves through verbal and physical aggression. Mothers provoked their daughters by teasing and pretend fighting. Adults recounted how they had handled an incident with aggression, or imagined how they would retaliate. However, if the girls directed anger at their own mothers, they were reprimanded and labelled as spoiled.

MAKE THE CONNECTION WITH ... PRETEND PLAY

Children who manage to behave well often let off emotional steam through play. Carmel Brennan provides the story of 'The bold girls' – a pretend play sequence in an Irish playgroup. Several four-year-olds developed a rich imaginative sequence in which they enjoyed taking the role of badly behaved little girls. They made a mess in the home corner (that they were ready to tidy up later) and were chided by 'Mammy' and then by the 'babysitter', two roles taken by children. (Non-Irish readers need to know that 'bold' is the word used to mean 'naughty' or 'being rude' in parts of Ireland and also often by gypsy/traveller communities.)

Gather examples of how you have observed children show their understanding of adult expectations for behaviour and reactions through pretend play.

Using consequences

Punishment is the addition of something negative to the situation, or the removal of something positive. Some adults are confident, even enthusiastic, about the likely success of punishment to change behaviour. However, punishment by words, removal of privileges or harsh actions can, just as successfully, make children secretive. Children learn not to let the adults see them doing what is forbidden. The learning dilemma for young children is also that conventional punishment does not direct them towards what they could do, it only communicates 'don't' and 'stop it'.

The Adlerian approach to guiding children's behaviour offers a constructive way to avoid difficulties raised by the word 'punishment'. Rudolf Dreikurs and Vicki Soltz explain the value of using the consequences of children's behaviour. Behaviour that you want to stop or re-direct can be guided by ensuring that children experience the consequences of their actions. Dreikurs distinguished between using natural and logical consequences as a way to encourage children to experience responsibility for their own actions. Some writers use the word 'sanctions' with a similar meaning.

- Natural consequences follow as part of the child's behaviour. For instance, a child who insists on tearing the pages of her favourite book may be sad that it cannot be mended as good as new. (Of course, responsible adults do not allow children to experience dangerous consequences of an action.)

- Logical consequences are adult-determined but relevant. A child who persists in throwing blocks after fair warning is moved away from the construction area. Caring adults do not allow the natural consequence that somebody may be hurt.

Any consequence needs to make some sense, given the children's behaviour. Children feel resentful if they lose a trip to the local park because they did not finish their lunch. This artificial consequence operates as punishment. A great deal depends on how adults behave, because an apparently similar action can be punitive, or a calm use of consequences. For example the strategy of a short time-out can be operated calmly as a logical consequence or made into a punishment by rough, adult words or actions. Studies suggest that children are best guided towards the behaviour adults want when:

- You react early within a sequence of misbehaviour. For instance, a toddler is removed swiftly from his explorations of the waste bin, and not after a great deal of ineffectual 'Don't do that' from the adult.

- As appropriate, you offer an alternative: something equally as interesting as emptying the bin. You also go beyond, 'don't do that'. You do not want a toddler to shriek every time another child tries to take the toy he is holding. But maybe he knows no other way to communicate 'I'm using it!'.

- You deal with the incident with as much calmness as possible. When adults shout, they model a behaviour that children are likely to imitate.

- You use the mildest sanction possible and do not increase the level because you feel angry or embarrassed by being watched by other adults.

- You resolve issues at the time and do not drag on for ages, whether with loss of privileges or adult harking back to the incident.

- You are generally warm in your interaction with children, consistent and clear about the rules involved.

WHAT DOES IT MEAN?

Natural consequences: results that inevitably follow from a course of action.

Logical consequences: adult-determined and pre-warned consequences that make sense given a child's persistent pattern of behaviour.

TAKE ANOTHER PERSPECTIVE

There has been a strong cultural tradition in the UK that it is acceptable to hit children as a form of discipline. Use of physical punishment has been withdrawn as an option in care and educational settings. However, at the time of writing (2004), children in the UK do not have the same legal protection as adults against assault.

- Supporters of parents' right to hit their children prefer to say 'smacking' ('spanking' in the USA). Look at a range of childcare books for parents, published in the last 15 years. Search for these words in the index. What does it say in the main text? Some books are clearly against smacking and offer alternatives. Some remain open to the possibility of hitting children, even books that otherwise have sound advice to offer.

- For example, Christopher Green (*New toddler taming*, 1990) suggests on pages 83–88 to avoid smacking if possible. But then he has a section headed 'Smacking used correctly'. In *Beyond toddlerdom* (2000), Green says that 'school age children should not be smacked' (section pages 44–45). Why do you think this paediatrician and author makes the age distinction?

▨ Look at what H. Rudolf Schaffer has to say about 'Is physical punishment psychologically harmful?' (1998: 210–19). I think this is a useful book and refer to it in Chapter 4. However, this section rests upon an assumption that parents should not be banned from using 'normal' physical punishment unless their actions can be proven through research to be harmful to children.

▨ Reflect on whether such an approach would be taken over adults who hit their 'badly behaved' partner or work colleague. See if you find smacking or hitting in the index of advice books about adult relationships.

PRO-SOCIAL BEHAVIOUR

The four national early years curriculum guidance documents within the UK all promote patterns of pro-social, rather than anti-social, behaviour. The English Foundation Stage is the most ambitious in having an early learning goal that five-year-olds will be able to 'Understand what is right, what is wrong and why'. This goal only makes sense when firmly grounded in an understanding of child development.

Children's ideas of right and wrong and their understanding of what is expected of them are a blend of several different aspects to development.

▨ *Social relationships*. Babies are born morally neutral but inherently social. A growing sense of morality is partly a social development. Rights, wrongs and expectations make sense to children because ideas are grounded in relationships with other people. With positive early experiences, young children are motivated to please their carers and get along with other children.

▨ *Moral behaviour*. Young children do not understand adult moral judgements of 'messy' or 'destructive', but they notice adult disapproval. Adults can over-focus on ideas such as, 'It's nice to share'. Young children start with actions; an abstract concept such as 'sharing' only makes sense from 'what does sharing look like?'.

▨ *Moral reasoning and judgement*. So moral development for children is first about behaviour; ideas are harder to grasp and come later. Understanding 'why' and making the 'right' decision are related to children's growing ability to think and reason. They begin to follow a pattern of what is expected, of rules about acceptable and unacceptable behaviour. Older children increasingly understand the reasons and values behind moral judgements. They make judgements in their turn.

TAKE ANOTHER PERSPECTIVE

As an adult it is unwise to set moral standards that you are unlikely to meet yourself. Many grown-ups know very well what is right, what is wrong and why, and still do not always take the moral option. In your interaction with children it is crucial to recall that:

It can be very hard sometimes to do the right thing.

Supportive adults use their observation and reflection skills to work out the source of the difficulty for children. (Thank you to Balham Nursery School, London, who use that phrase within their approach to behaviour.)

LOOK, LISTEN, NOTE, LEARN

You may have encountered the poem *Children learn what they live* that starts with these lines:

■ If children live with criticism, they learn to condemn.

■ If children live with hostility, they learn to fight.

And continues with other wise connections such as:

■ If children live with encouragement, they learn confidence.

■ If children live with tolerance, they learn patience.

The entire poem is 19 lines long. But it is often quoted in part, and without acknowledgement of Dorothy Law Nolte, who first wrote the ideas in 1972 and has developed the content since then.

■ Consider the ideas in the entire poem. Can you see connections for children you know between how they are treated and how they have learned to behave and view their world?

The full version of the poem is given in Dorothy Law Nolte and Rachel Harris (1998) or download from www.EmpowermentResources.com

Potential development of pro-social behaviour

Practical researchers such as Nancy Eisenberg, Judy Dunn, and Ronald Slaby and his team highlight whether children's early experience supports them to be able and willing to:

■ Tune in to the feelings of other children or to adults – empathy.

■ Behave with a selfless concern for the well-being of others – altruism.

The combination of empathy and altruism is called pro-social behaviour. The key features are that children show intentional, voluntary behaviour that is intended to benefit someone else. It is not inevitable that children learn empathy, nor that they choose sometimes to act with altruism. These skills and choices arise from experience. The events of their early years can just as easily teach children that life is competitive and 'he who shoves gets'.

WHAT DOES IT MEAN?

Empathy: the ability and willingness to tune into the feelings of others – children or adults.

Altruism: acting with a selfless concern for the well-being of others.

Pro-social behaviour: children show intentional, voluntary behaviour that is intended to benefit someone else.

Judy Dunn and her team showed how actions, allowed and not allowed, are learned within a context that is given sense by the emotional link integral to family relationships. Children as young as 18–24 months of age had a good grasp of the family ground rules, to the extent that they could talk about them with parents or siblings and deliberately break rules as a source of joking.

If toddlers feel emotionally secure, from about 18 months of age they are able to notice the distress of others. They get your attention as an adult, and point out that another child is crying or hurt. Toddlers also sometimes take the initiative to help. Young children may offer another distressed child their own comfort object – an act of great generosity in itself. But soon, young children who know each other well (in the same family or early years setting) offer the other child's favourite blanket or teddy. Young children may also pat the hand of a sad-looking adult. By three years old, children may imitate and suggest you have a 'nice cup of tea'.

Children like to have opportunities to be a helper

MAKE THE CONNECTION WITH ... YOUR OWN PRACTICE

Early years settings, like family homes, are undoubtedly happier places for everyone if children behave in a pro-social way, so how can you help?

- Create an affectionate and warm environment. Young children who feel they have to compete with peers for the attention and affection of adults, have little emotional energy left to give to each other.

- Be clear about your rules for considerate or helpful behaviour. Be ready to give children simple explanations of why 'we ask – we don't just grab'.

- Just telling a child, 'you mustn't hit people' is less effective than alerting him to the consequences, for example, 'when you bit Sam, you really hurt him and made him cry'.

- Create opportunities for even very young children to do something helpful and acknowledge what they have done. Recognise considerate behaviour but avoid trying to make children feel guilty if today they feel less than helpful.

- The most important step for adults is to behave in line with what you would like children to do: model thoughtful and generous behaviour.

In summary, aim for tell–show–do. It is the combination that works.

TAKE ANOTHER PERSPECTIVE

Young children use their perceptiveness and knowledge of others both to comfort and to annoy siblings or friends.

■ In my own family, I noted that at 16 months Tanith brought Drew his quilt and monkey (his personal comfort objects) when she saw he was sad. Nobody ever told Tanith to do this; her actions resulted from her own observations and a wish to comfort. But she used the same objects to provoke him into playing with her, when he wanted to sit and look at his books. Tanith would take Quilt or Monkey, stand at the door to the room and wave them at Drew until he was provoked enough to chase her.

■ Can you recall times when a young child you know well showed a similar level of subtle understanding of the feelings of another child? What happened?

■ It is important that your adult concern about the provocation does not make you overlook examples of a child's pro-social behaviour based on the same knowledge.

Support for social skills

Ronald Slaby and his team looked at applications of the research on pro-social behaviour. Their concern also arose from a goal of re-directing children away from aggressive patterns. The team re-defined the area as an adult task to coach children in specific social skills.

■ The project worked to identify the kinds of behaviour that children needed to learn if they were to develop, for instance, an assertive way of dealing with conflict rather than turn to aggressive methods.

■ They focused on adult behaviour and how practitioners could shift from telling and directing behaviours ('You must share') or stepping in on behalf of children ('Let him have a go').

■ Attention was paid to how settings operated on a daily basis and the unspoken messages from layout and organisation. Was it relatively easy or hard for a child to take the pro-social option?

■ Strategies were also developed for adults to model the pro-social options and find ways for adults to coach children in how to handle situations themselves.

The approach of Ronald Slaby and his team supports reflective practitioners to consider the real meaning of moral rules such as 'sharing': what do adults mean in terms of recognisable behaviour and what children think is expected of them? For example, the team recognised that 'nice sharing' should not have to mean that children simply feel obligated to hand over an important play item. Practitioners can model phrases such as, 'You can have it when I've finished' or 'I'll swap you the car for your truck', just as much as how to ask courteously rather than seize what you want.

MAKE THE CONNECTION WITH ... PRESSURE AND TIME

Vivian Gussin Paley (2004) comments about making the time to be kind and the sense of pressure felt by practitioners in US kindergartens. She describes a conference at which practitioners talked about ' the gradual lessening of "ordinary niceness" in the classroom' (page 53).

A kindergarten teacher explained how she and the special education teacher had re-introduced long play periods. The change was led by the needs of children who could not possibly go 'from task to task' as was expected of their peers. It dawned on the two staff that all the children needed the ordinary, therapeutic support of uninterrupted play. The staff had then observed that these young children were generally 'nicer' to each other. But the adults had not talked more about kind behaviour: 'There is more time to be kind, to solve problems by playing in different ways, to include more kids and let them have a say' (page 54).

■ Does this dilemma sound familiar? What happens when early years practitioners feel harassed to achieve a long list of targets?

■ Look also on page 227 for discussion about time and children's awareness of adult priorities.

Skills of conflict resolution

In early childhood children have to negotiate many situations of minor or more major conflict on issues that are significant for them. For instance, more than one child wants the favourite bike, to go first up the ladder of the climbing frame or to stay longer at the painting easel. The observations of Vivian Gussin Paley show that the emotional temperature can rise when children argue over how a play theme should be worked out or who should be involved. Additional social skills are needed when words at normal volume have not resolved the problem. Children need adult help to learn and use skills of conflict resolution.

Betsy Evans described the research and theoretical concepts underlying the High/Scope approach. These practical ideas combine insights from emotional literacy and applications to early childhood from research about conflict resolution between adults. The six-step approach requires that adults understand and are committed to using these skills. In using the steps, your aim is to help children with the immediate problem. But equally important, you can support them to learn general skills of resolving problems when emotions run high.

MAKE THE CONNECTION WITH ... YOUR OWN PRACTICE

These are the six steps in the High/Scope approach. To what extent can you recognise some actions you follow in your practice? Which steps do you feel you tend not to reach or try to rush? To what extent do you, or your colleagues, think 'I must resolve this quickly' or feel self-conscious because you are watched?

The steps draw on good quality communication skills. Remain close to the children, on the child's eye level and use touch as appropriate. It is impossible to support conflict resolution with children from across the room.

Step 1: Approach swiftly and calmly. Stop any hurtful behaviour between the children, use gentle touch if they have started to fight. Be calm as an adult and do not raise your voice.

Step 2: Acknowledge children's feelings. Make simple statements such as, 'You look cross' or 'Yes I hear that you want the bike'. Even if the reason for arguing seems minor to you, recall what it was like to be a child and what could really, really matter. With younger children, you use your words to name the feelings and say what is happening.

Step 3: Gather information from the children. By asking, 'what has happened?' or 'what's the problem here?'. Listen, show that you are fair and impartial and let children feel confident they are heard. With very young children you describe what is happening ('You want the book and he wants the book too') and you explain, ' We have a problem here'.

Step 4: Restate the problem Use the children's words but help them with the communication exchange. Ease the interaction and restate potentially hurtful language.

Step 5: Ask for solutions. 'What can we do here to solve this problem?' Listen to what children suggest and avoid filling a silence with your ideas. Give some time and help the children to find a way out of this situation without a loser.

Step 6: Be prepared to give follow-up support. Be alert and pleased when children have resolved the situation.

Moral reasoning and judgements

Children apply their growing powers of thinking and reasoning to try to understand ideas of right and wrong and why. The same head that is coming to grips with the meaning of number or that some squiggles are 'writing', is also trying to make sense of social situations and the behaviour of others.

TAKE ANOTHER PERSPECTIVE

- Three- and four-year-olds have the thinking skills to build a working theory about moral standards. They tend to focus on what happened, rather than allowing for intentions. The actual consequences of an act are seen as the same as intentions. Also behaviour is judged by the seriousness of the consequences: a major mess means a 'naughtier' act.

- But informal observation of children and adults will show you that adults often get more angry about bigger messes. Parents and practitioners under pressure do not always pause to explore children's intentions before criticising the consequences.

- So the conclusions of young children may arise at least as much from their observation of how adults behave as from immature thinking processes.

Lawrence Kohlberg studied the moral reasoning of children and young people. He built on Piaget's views to develop a stage theory of moral development, supported by research into how children of different ages resolved a series of hypothetical dilemmas ('What if . . .' problems). Kohlberg's stages depended not so much on the choice that children made for the characters in the story, but how they explained their chosen option. He argued that children operate at a level of 'pre-conventional morality'. Young children decide something is only wrong if it is punished. They judge the rightness of an act by whether it feels good or could benefit them in turn.

Kohlberg suggested, and studies support him, that a second level, 'conventional morality', develops in adolescence as older children view 'being good' as worthwhile for its own sake and to live up to the expectations of important people in their life. Their moral reasoning moves into a broader social context, including the laws of society. Kohlberg argued that adults move into a third level of 'principled or post-conventional morality' when there is an awareness of a social contract: that moral behaviour takes account of the good of the many and not only individual wants.

TAKE ANOTHER PERSPECTIVE

- Recall that Lawrence Kohlberg's stage theory is based on the reasons children give to explain why somebody ought to behave in a particular way in the story. You will observe children behaving in a pro-social way at an age much younger than that at which they typically use this kind of reasoning.

- Psychological research into adult attitudes and behaviour has established only a tenuous link between what adults say is the right thing to do and how they actually behave faced with this situation.

- So we should not be surprised if children say firmly you should be honest, and then do not behave in line with expressed moral values. Children, like adults, have their reasons for actions – why this situation was different.

Nancy Eisenberg looked at how children explained considerate behaviour by giving them hypothetical dilemmas in which there was a clash between self-interest and helping someone else (the pro-social option). Children younger than five years might choose the pro-social option, but their reasoning was different to that of older children who chose to help over self-interest. The younger ones were more likely to help for personal reasons, such as, 'If I'm nice to her now, she might be on my side another time'. Eisenberg called this pattern 'hedonistic reasoning'. This orientation gradually shifted through childhood to a focus on the needs of the other person, that 'she would feel better if I helped'. Eisenberg called this pattern 'need-oriented reasoning'. It was not until adolescence that options were chosen on the basis of general principles, such as 'society is better if people help each other'.

TAKE ANOTHER PERSPECTIVE

Children may know very well what is expected of them but, for various reasons, be unable to control their impulses. Carol Hayden and Derek Ward interviewed children who had been excluded from primary school.

The children (all but one were boys) knew they had broken the rules, although they sometimes felt that the incident that led to exclusion was not bad enough to justify the punishment. Children knew what they should not do, but they had been unable to control their own behaviour. Motivation and impulse control were the problems and not a lack of knowledge or mis-understanding of the rules. This research was reported in the journal *Children and Society* December 1996, Volume 10.

- Reflect on whether you assume children do not know the rules, so your efforts are best aimed at reminders.

- Sometimes your efforts may be better aimed at helping a child to resist an impulse or coaching them in skills for resolving conflict situations.

Aggressive or just playing?

Parents and practitioners are concerned that children do not get hurt as a consequence of their play and worried that they, the adults, should not be blamed for incidents. Early years and school settings have long been concerned about play that looks aggressive. Teams have frequently discouraged or actually banned play fighting, lively games or pretend play themes that are judged to be rough or violent. Researchers in school and early years settings have gathered observations to challenge the swift judgements.

Games in the school playground

Mechthild Schafer and Peter Smith showed children and primary school teachers video footage of play fighting incidents. They found that:

- Children and teachers broadly agreed on how to tell the difference between play fighting and real fights (from facial expressions and the actions) and they also agreed that play fights could turn into real ones. But there the agreement ended.

■ Teachers' estimates were that about 60 per cent of fights were play and over one-third real and that up one-third of play fights would turn into real ones.

■ The children's estimates were that the overwhelming majority of fights were play and that very few turned into real ones. Observations made by the researchers supported the children's claims.

The explanation seemed to be that teachers generalised from the small number of children whose behaviour was habitually aggressive and whose play fighting often turned into real fights – and of course worried the adults. The behaviour of these children was not typical of the pupils as a whole, a fact that the other children knew from observation and experience.

David Brown showed children exchanges recorded on video and they were in agreement about what was genuinely aggressive. Children explained how observers should use changing gestures and expressions to identify the point at which a play fight turned into a bullying incident. Brown reported that the adults who viewed the videos were far less able to read the body language. Michael Boulton also noted that it was harder for adults to read the subtle clues for play fighting than the children involved in the game. Boulton's observations suggest a cautious approach by all adults, since men were no more attuned to the reality of incidents than women. In comparison with children, the adult males were more likely to classify an aggressive incident as playful and the females to judge a playful fight as aggressive

Mechthild Schafer and Peter Smith view play fighting as potentially positive. They stress that play fighting is one way that relationships are formed and friendships gel, especially with boys. It is an enjoyable activity and, in the main, low risk. Their conclusions are notable because Peter Smith has also undertaken studies of bullying. As a researcher, he is well aware of the significance of genuine playground troubles to children.

WHAT DOES IT MEAN?

Play fighting: physical games between children, usually boys rather than girls, in which the play develops into wrestling and close body contact.

Superhero and weapons play in early years

Vivian Gussin Paley documented her change in approach about superhero play. She described why she did not initially value the boys' superhero play in her kindergarten and was more concerned about potential disruption, because the play was lively. Paley describes her awareness that, once she stopped trying to control the play, she was able to see much more that the pretend play was not aggressive at all. Practical issues revolved around negotiation of space, but there was no justification for treating the games as problem behaviour.

Penny Holland undertook an action research study while she was working in a London early years centre. In common with many early years settings, this centre had a long-term commitment to stopping 'aggressive play'. As Penny Holland documents, a approach of zero tolerance had developed in UK early years settings over about three decades. An initial concern about 'no guns in nursery' had spread to stopping any kind of pretend play that involved weapons or what was seen as war play. The ban usually spread to imaginative play around monsters, superhero play and pretend play themes built on favourite cartoon characters. Such an approach became an 'everyone knows' plank of good practice and was rarely challenged.

Penny Holland and her colleagues faced up to the dilemma:

- The ban was not working. Despite continued efforts by practitioners, children, usually boys, were busy making pretend weapons and playing their superhero games.

- Continuous discouragement gave the boys no choice but to be devious. Children developed verbal strategies to deflect practitioners with remarks such as, 'It's not really a batmobile, it's a fire engine' and the fair, 'we're not fighting, we're just pretending'.

- It was hard for young boys to interpret the nursery ban as anything other than personal rejection of their interests and play preferences. There was real concern from the team that such an experience promoted disaffection that could continue with the boys into school.

The team agreed to try a removal of the ban, explained by letter to parents and then observed what happened. The children initially increased their time on previously forbidden games, especially with pretend weapons. However, Penny Holland and her colleagues tracked that, now they did not have to be secretive, the boys' play flowed into complex imaginative games. Children used the play resources of the centre to build, draw and otherwise extend their play. The pretend games did not dominate the centre and the boys were happy for adults to become involved and make suggestions for the game. The team had been concerned that girls' play might be marginalised by lifting the ban. On the contrary, girls become more involved in the active group play, having judged accurately that such play was no longer unacceptable behaviour.

LOOK, LISTEN, NOTE, LEARN

Vivian Gussin Paley and Penny Holland raise legitimate concerns about what can happen to children, boys in particular, when their pretend play is treated as a behaviour problem.

- Do you operate a war and weapons ban in your setting? Do you effectively extend it to a wide range of superhero and good guy–bad guy play?

- What are the genuine consequences of the ban?

Penny Holland describes developments in other centres, where an equivalent ban had been lifted. Use her ideas to pull out the main themes and, if possible, talk with a team who have re-thought their strategy. Bear in mind that practitioners do more than lift the 'weapons play' ban.

- They observe the themes and actions in pretend play with an open mind.

- Practitioners continue to deal constructively with genuine aggression.

Look also at the parallel drawn with home corner play in my book *Understanding children's play* (2001: 115). Real babies arise from sexual relationships. Do practitioners ban pretend baby care and being Mummies and Daddies as 'sex play'?

Does television make children aggressive?

A considerable number of studies, many undertaken in the USA, have shown a link between watching of violence on television and the children's own patterns of behaviour. There is not a simple causal link but the evidence is sufficiently strong for adults to take children's viewing habits seriously.

Experiments with children show at least a short-term effect on children's behaviour of watching programmes with aggressive content. The themes of the programme can be observed in their later free play. In the USA, children who watch more television are almost always found to be more aggressive in their behaviour than their peers who watch fewer hours. Careful analysis explains this finding partly by the fact that children who are already more aggressive than the average child, choose to watch more television and select the more violent programmes. However, the children who watched the most television within this more aggressive group, emerged as the more violent and delinquent adolescents and adults.

Another group of studies has looked at changes over time within societies following the introduction of television or increased ownership of televisions. In small communities who previously had no television, there have been patterns of an increase in children's aggressive behaviour in play. Levels of violent crime in several countries have been seen to rise dramatically some 15 years after television became widely available to children.

In contrast, Tony Charlton and his team tracked the introduction of television in 1995 to St Helena, a small island community in the southeast Atlantic. Children's behaviour was tracked before and after their exposure to television, by observation in the playground and survey of the views of parents, teachers and the children themselves. The children did not become more aggressive in their behaviour. If anything, the team observed less playground squabbling and teasing, which they suggest might be linked with the shared experience of the television programmes that fuelled conversations. This project highlights that television works within a socio-cultural context. In St Helena, parents watched television with their children and the strong sense of community created an atmosphere in which children's behaviour was strongly influenced by the role models provided by parents and teachers.

LOOK, LISTEN, NOTE, LEARN

- Over a period of several weeks, make notes in your setting of any children's games that include themes from television programmes.

- What themes are children using – phrases, characters, physical moves?

- Children's imitation will not always be negative. Identify some of the patterns that could be positive for children's development or behaviour.

- Are the children enjoying themselves?

If you want to find out more:
Some concepts in this chapter are summarised from a range of research studies and theoretical perspectives. You will find more detail in:

☆ **Bee, Helen** and **Boyd, Denise** 2004 *The developing child*. Boston MA: Pearson Education.

☆ **Cole, Michael** and **Cole, Sheila** 2000 *The development of children*. New York: Worth Publishers.

☆ **Boulton, Michael** 1994 'Playful and aggressive fighting in the middle school playground'. In Blatchford, Peter and Sharp, Sonia (eds)

Breaktime and the school: understanding and changing playground behaviour. London: Routledge.

Research into play that adults believe is aggressive. Other chapters in this book are also useful for an insight into children's perspective on break time.

⋆ **Brennan, Carmel** (ed.) 2004 *The power of play: a play curriculum in action* Dublin: IPPA.

Learning stories, in words and photos, of young learning in Irish playgroups.

⋆ **Brown, David** 1994 'Play, the playground and the culture of childhood'. In Moyles, Janet (ed.) *The excellence of play*. Buckingham: Open University Press.

Valuable observations of children's play in primary school and the sense that they make of what is happening. Other chapters in this book are also useful.

⋆ **Buckingham, David** 1996 *Moving images: understanding children's emotional responses to television*. Manchester: Manchester University Press.

A discussion of how children react to children, supported by interviews with children of different ages.

⋆ **Charlton, Tony; Gunter, Barrie** and **Hannan, Andrew** (eds) 2002 *Broadcast television effects in a remote community*. New Jersey: Lawrence Erlbaum Associates

Report of a longitudinal study of the arrival of television to the island of St Helena.

⋆ **Dreikurs, Rudolf** and **Soltz, Vicki** 1995 *Happy children: a challenge to parents*. Melbourne: Australian Council for Educational Research (ACER).

A practical book on taking a positive approach to children's behaviour. This book and other materials that link feelings and children's behaviour can be bought from Adlerian Workshops and Publications, tel. 01296 482148; http://www.adlerian.com

☆ **Dunn, Judy** 1993 *Young children's close relationships beyond attachment.* London: Sage.

Shows how much children's social development is intertwined with their cognitive and language development, and so with their behaviour.

☆ **Eisenberg, Nancy** 1992 *The caring child.* Cambridge MA: Harvard University Press.

An exploration of pro-social behaviour and the role of adults in promoting this development.

☆ **Evans, Betsy** 2002 *You can't come to my birthday party: conflict resolution with young children.* Ypsilanti: High/Scope Press.

Practical discussion and explanation of how to coach even young children in the skills of conflict resolution. High/Scope also has videos – see page 268.

☆ **Holland, Penny** 2003 *We don't play with guns here: war, weapon and superhero play in the early years.* Maidenhead: Open University Press.

Action research in nursery to explore the effects of lifting a ban on weapons play. Discussion of how such a ban became common in early years settings.

☆ **Lindon, Jennie** 2001 *Understanding children's play.* Cheltenham: Nelson Thornes.

Review of perspectives and research about how and why children play.

☆ **Maybin, Janet** and **Woodhead, Martin** 2003 'Socializing children'. In Maybin, Janet and Woodhead, Martin (eds) *Childhoods in context.* Milton Keynes: Open University Press.

Discussion of the ways in which adults behave in order to raise children within their values.

☆ **Paley, Vivian Gussin** 1984 *Boys and girls: superheroes in the doll corner.* Chicago: University of Chicago Press.

One of Vivian Gussin Paley's thoughtful descriptions of a kindergarten year. This book focuses on the value of boys' lively pretend play.

✩ **Paley, Vivian Gussin** 2004 *A child's work: the importance of fantasy play*. Chicago and London: University of Chicago Press.

Broad discussion of Vivian Paley's observations and ideas.

✩ **Schafer, Mechthild** and **Smith, Peter** 1996 'Teachers' perceptions of play fighting and real fighting in primary school'. *Educational Research* 38 (2), 173–181.

Details of the research described on page 215.

✩ **Severe, Sal** 2004 *How to behave so your children will too*. London: Vermilion.

Practical application of ideas of reward, modelling and other aspects of a positive approach to behaviour – equally useful in out-of-home settings.

✩ **Slaby, Ronald; Roedell, Wendy; Arezzo, Diana** and **Hendrix, Kate** 1995 *Early violence prevention: tools for teachers of young children*. Washington DC: National Association for the Education of Young Children.

Practical ideas showing how adults help children learn social skills, including sharing. Consideration of adult behaviour and how a setting is organised.

10 Children as part of a social and cultural community

Children's early life unfolds within a particular time, place and social context. The socio-cultural framework has increasingly influenced the theoretical approach within early childhood studies. It can, however, still be challenging for researchers, as well as practitioners within early years, to turn that awareness on to their own studies and practice.

This chapter draws on a very wide range of sources. So, only the more general resources are given in 'If you want to find out more'. Many references are given in brief here and then fully in the bibliography from page 257. The main sections to this chapter are:

- Childhood experienced in a time and place.

- Early education and childcare in context.

- Children within families and a community.

CHILDHOOD EXPERIENCED IN A TIME AND PLACE

The details of childhood are shaped by the cultural traditions that children experience through family life and other settings influenced by the predominant culture, such as early years centres and school. Socio-cultural traditions are not fixed forever; they can and do change over time. Some knowledge of recent social history can help an understanding that there can be changes within a culture as well as differences between cultures that co-exist within a diverse society. This section offers a range of ways to step back and reflect on childhood in a time and place.

Raising children to fit society

Beatrice Whiting and Carolyn Edwards explored how young children start out with potentials that are shaped by adults. The older generation is not necessarily reflective about how they behave; it seems the right way. Whiting and Edwards suggested that cultural forces operate through:

- Adults' expectations of children.

- What they give children most opportunity to practise.

- Which behaviours adults make meaningful for children in terms of the central cultural goals and values.

Whiting and Edwards concluded from observations in many societies that children were disposed to respond in a nurturant way to what they called 'lap children' (under one-year-olds), in a dependent way towards adults and in a playful and challenging way to child companions. Adults then set boys and girls on different paths, sometimes very different, by allowing them varied amounts of autonomy in daily life, giving them a different pattern of responsibilities and limiting the company they kept (Whiting and Edwards, 1988).

WHAT DOES IT MEAN?

Socialisation: the process by which children learn what is expected of them in terms of behaviour and attitudes within their society, or social and cultural group.

Socialisation does not only operate within the family. Joseph Tobin and his colleagues studied the pattern of interaction between teachers and children in pre-school settings in different countries. How teachers behaved and what they believed they should be doing varied between cultures. Teachers from Japan and the USA were shown a video of a pre-school day in the culture unfamiliar to them. Japanese teachers felt that the Americans intervened too much in children's behaviour and conflicts. On the other hand, American teachers thought the Japanese ignored behaviour that should have been tackled directly.

American teachers were behaving so as to promote what they viewed as independence and self-reliance in the children. Japanese teachers stressed co-operation and a sense of inter-dependence in the group. Both sets of teachers judged they were active, in the best way, to promote the social learning they valued.

MAKE THE CONNECTION WITH ... CULTURAL TRADITIONS

Any services for children will reflect in obvious, and more subtle, ways what is valued by society. When several cultures co-exist within a community then such differences become more obvious. For example:

- The behaviour valued in one culture as 'courtesy' (not pressing one's opinion, nor disagreeing with a teacher) may be judged as 'passivity' and 'low self-confidence' within another culture.

- Ground rules about gesture and other forms of non-verbal communication can vary considerably. In some cultures children are taught not to look an adult in the eye when being reprimanded. In a diverse community, children can meet an adult who interprets lack of eye contact as 'shifty' and requires, 'look at me properly when I'm talking with you!'.

TAKE ANOTHER PERSPECTIVE

- Socialisation, like cultural tradition, is not something that only happens to other people. Until you reflect, it may be harder to spot the main themes within your own culture; it just seems like 'normal life'.

- Fierce, state-led socialisation programmes may stand out as propaganda. See for instance, Guido Knopp's *Hitler's children* about Germany in the 1930s and 1940s (2002) or Jung Chang's *Wild swans* about three generations of growing up in China (1991). However, all children experience the process of socialisation.

- Study of street children, forced to fend for themselves, shows that the older children sometimes 'parent' the younger ones and socialise them into the behaviour, including stealing, that will ensure survival (Konner, 1991).

In the best interests of the child?

Margaret Humphreys documented the emigrations from UK residential children's homes to America and Australia, which only finally stopped in 1967. This mass movement of children was purportedly to provide them with a better life. Yet the children's welfare and emotional well-being were strikingly ignored. There was no follow-up of the children, many of whom experienced harsh, sometimes abusive, conditions. Most of the children were given no information about themselves, such as their birth certificates. Some were told lies: that their parent(s) had died. Attitudes towards children and their well-being have changed, but it would be an unwise practitioner who pronounced that children's well-being would never be so ignored again. The phrase 'in the best interests of the child' developed strongly from the different UK Children Acts or Orders from the 1990s. However, it can be challenging to weigh up priorities.

Mary Pipher, a child and family therapist from the USA, has been constructively critical about the tendency for therapy to ignore the broader influences on the struggles of children or teenagers. Pipher argues persuasively that even family therapy does not properly acknowledge the immense social and commercial pressures on families. She documents how she shifted the balance towards more advice to parents that they go out as a family and to the outdoors, not the shopping mall.

Dan Kindlon and Michael Thompson describe their concern for those boys and male teenagers referred to them by parents or schools. They argue that young males are not helped for emotional literacy in the USA, nor western culture in general. Kindlon and Thompson also express serious concern about families or schools who want to medicate ordinary boyish exuberance, because it is inconvenient for adults. Their concerns are echoed in the UK about over-diagnosis of Attention Deficit (Hyperactivity) Disorder and serious unease that pressure on educational targets runs the risk of labelling normal, lively behaviour as 'unacceptable', even in the early years.

LOOK, LISTEN, NOTE, LEARN

For a period of two weeks, cut out any news article about children in your regular newspaper. If you can do this activity with colleagues, you could cover several newspapers. What range of images do you find?

■ Are children portrayed as innocents in need of protection – 'no child is safe anymore'? Are they described as instruments of 'pester power' to get their parents to buy a brand of biscuits or designer clothing?

■ What has made these children newsworthy? Do they have to be extraordinary: tragic little angels battling illness or terror tots whose outrageous behaviour has led to exclusion from nursery?

■ What does choice of material and language tell you about the images of children and childhood promoted within our society?

■ Imagine these reports were your only source of information about childhood. What beliefs might you develop about children in UK society?

A view on time

You could make the case that time pressure is a feature of current childhood experience in the UK. The concept of quality time underpins much of the advice of 'make the most of your time' in advice to parents. The original meaning was that mothers did not have to be constantly available to ensure their children's well-being – a challenge to John Bowlby's influential views (page 86). The original idea envisaged generous amounts of attention. Re-working of quality time, especially in family magazines, has moved much more towards fitting children in for very short amounts of time.

WHAT DOES IT MEAN?

Quality time: the concept that children thrive with periods of full attention and do not require the continuous presence of their main carer.

LOOK, LISTEN, NOTE, LEARN

- Take a look at a range of childcare advice books for parents. How many titles imply time given to children has to be squeezed in between other competing priorities?

- Make a brief survey of family or women's magazines. What are the messages – perhaps also amid sound advice – as in the books?

- How might such an approach affect children?

- Sylvia Ann Hewlett describes how Hallmark cards in the USA now have a range for absent parents, with messages such as, 'I wish I were there to tuck you in'.

Early years practitioners can feel anxiety about how much has to be completed in a day or the sense of pressure about 'getting the children ready' for the next stage. Jacqui Cousins showed that many four-year-olds recognised adult priorities. She quotes Sonnyboy's challenge that, when you are enthused, 'time's as long as it takes'. Another boy was keen on a model-making kit but had stopped playing with it because, 'when I build a house it takes me a long time ... and then I got to break it ... tidy up time'. And a girl expressed her heartfelt frustration with, 'All the time it's 'Hurry up! Hurry up! ... It's time'. What it time for? Packing up ... I hate hurrying up' (1999: 36).

Many UK practitioners have been interested and enthused by the approach taken by the early years centres of Reggio Emilia, in northern Italy. *The Hundred Languages of Children* exhibition has brought a visual explanation to parts of the UK. Ideas from the Reggio approach have challenged existing practice and priorities, especially about using space, relaxed time and tuning in to children's interests. Marianne Valentine explains that how children and adults use time is central to the reflective philosophy of the Reggio approach: 'Children who become involved in a learning activity should be given the opportunity to continue with it for as long as they need. Teachers need to find ways of making space for work in progress rather than simply telling children to clear up at the end of the day' (Valentine, 1999: 27).

There are over twenty years between these two photos. The young toddler with his saucepans is now the adult who helped me with page 52. Society is different around the baby with the treasure basket, but the needs of children have not changed

EARLY EDUCATION AND CHILDCARE IN CONTEXT

Services exist within a social and cultural framework. Early years practitioners are familiar with the pattern within their own society and, without any point of comparison, can assume that these services are the norm.

A split service for early years in the UK

The four nations that make up the UK have increasingly determined the details of their own early years services. However, all share a common history of division between services known as 'childcare' and 'early education'.

The many initiatives from the last years of the twentieth century have laid over the top of this basic division. Despite the hard work of teams and different combined centres since the 1970s, there are still two systems:

1   Childcare services provided by group settings or by childminders in their own home, to fit the hours of cover needed by parents who have jobs or are students. The cost of this service is mainly met by parents.

2   Early educational provision is available for children from two or three years old through to their entry into primary school. This kind of provision is usually free, offered on a sessional basis and follows a school year.

Public statements from politicians have happily merged the terms, often talking of part-time early education as a form of childcare. But, of course, this part of the fragmented service cannot meet parents' childcare needs without additional provision. Developments in England at the time of writing (Autumn 2004) include claims that parents' rights to new, highly flexible use of part-time places constitutes 'educare'. This term originated within integrated early years services, for instance in Scandinavia, and bears no relation to the disruptive patchwork that is likely to result.

WHAT DOES IT MEAN?

Educare: an approach that integrates care and support for young learning. This philosophy and practice avoids a school model that parts of the day are more valued and 'educational' than others. See for example in Miller and Devereux (2004).

Peter Moss and Pat Petrie track how the prevailing view of childhood works to shape services for children and their families. One chapter sums up the link from adult attitudes to children's direct experience with the title of, 'Children – who do we think they are?'. Peter Moss and Pat Petrie are based at the Thomas Coram Research Unit in London, where the team undertook a major rethink of approach in the late 1970s and early 1980s. They challenged the predominant way of thinking about early years and childcare, which the unit had shared up to that point. The team re-focused on family, more than childcare or maternal employment as separate topics for study.

The Unit has also been to the forefront of bringing perspectives to the UK from other countries, often just across the channel in mainland Europe. The UK patchwork of early years services is not the only pattern and Peter Moss has been a strong advocate of a publicly funded early years service, more like the system in parts of Scandinavia. The development of early years curriculum frameworks since the 1990s has been strongly influenced by perspectives outside the UK, especially early childhood education in Australia, the bicultural Te Whāriki approach in New Zealand and the philosophy and practice of the Emilia Reggio region in northern Italy.

TAKE ANOTHER PERSPECTIVE

- Some other European countries, notably in Scandinavia, chose to create a coherent, publicly funded early years service, with a single early years profession. This approach takes the view that provision is a public service: a contribution to raising the next generation needed by everyone in society.

- In contrast, the dominant philosophy in the UK has been that the task of early years settings is to prepare children for school. This priority is reflected in the language of 'pre-school': a phrase often used for the three- to four-year-olds' room within a day nursery and for the whole setting by groups that are members of the Pre-school Learning Alliance.

- Track the development of the UK early years patchwork: nursery schools, nursery classes, pre-schools, playgroups, day nurseries and different kinds of combined centres. You will find lines of enquiry in Jennie Lindon *Early years care and education in Europe* (2000) and Peter Moss and Pat Petrie (2002).

LOOK, LISTEN, NOTE, LEARN

Sue Miller and Kay Sambell share the experience of their Early Childhood Studies team working to put childhood and services in context. The team use a range of methods: visits, outside speakers, visual material (photos and videos) and students' own experience on which to reflect. Mel Gibson's chapter, entitled 'I'd no idea there was so much going on under the surface' sums up the need to step back from 'that's just normal life'.

Try this activity, modified from one used at the University of Northumbria.

- Collect a series of photographs of the entrance areas of settings available for children: nurseries or pre-schools but also the local library and health clinic. Of course, ask permission before using your camera, even if there are no children in focus at the time.

- Consider the images – on your own and with colleagues. What messages does each layout give to children as they come in to this setting or part of the building? Is it 'we're pleased to welcome children' or 'we're a place for grown-ups'? Is it 'be lively and please touch' or 'quiet, ask before you take'?

- What messages might the environment give to parents and other carers who accompany the children?

> ■ I would add that the entrance area of a nursery should feel very personal. It is not only the 'welcome' area; it is the 'goodbye' area as well. The entrance area can tell children, 'we're pleased to see you again, this is your nursery'. But it also gives the message of, 'See you again soon. We will keep you in mind while you are gone. You still have a place here'.
>
> For other ideas look at Miller and Sambell (2003).

Partnership with parents

Good practice in early years, school and out-of-school services now incorporates partnership with parents. However, this phrase does not carry the same meaning whenever it is used. The different working definitions make it difficult, probably impossible, to compare research studies because 'partnership' can mean very different activities, as well as underlying assumptions. Gillian Pugh *et al.* provide an overview of the tremendous variety of support programmes and underlying attitudes. Helen Barrett's review shows how working definitions are so diverse that it is a serious challenge to compare studies of parenting programmes and evaluate their effectiveness.

MAKE THE CONNECTION WITH ... YOUR PRACTICE

- ▓ The concept of partnership has grown from several distinct strands. The divergence explains how discussion of practice can become confused.

- ▓ Please reflect on each strand in turn and make the connections with your own practice. What does 'partnership' mean to you and your team?

- ▓ Can you recognise the strand of social history in partnership that has most affected the part of early years services familiar to you?

Parents need to be involved to help children

Successful early years intervention programmes, especially in the USA from the 1960s involved parents in the programme, directly through group work or regular communication about children's learning. These programmes were designed to counteract the effects of social disadvantage and parent involvement was crucial. Over a similar period, professionals in social work and social psychiatry concluded that problems experienced by children could not be understood or improved in isolation from their family.

This approach led to developments of family therapy and settings such as family centres, where parents and children attended. The community focus developed significantly through centres such as Pen Green in Corby, but also through national initiatives such as Sure Start that have aimed to bring services together in a more integrated way.

LOOK, LISTEN, NOTE, LEARN

- The EPPE project (http://www.ioe.ac.uk/cdl/eppe) found that the most effective early years settings shared their educational aims with parents. But in order to share the 'what and how' of good early years practice, you need to be clear and consistent within the team about your methods and the reasons why they are developmentally appropriate.

- Look back over page 155 about early literacy or the importance of the positive disposition to learn on page 103. How do you, could you, share those important aims and approaches with parents?

Sharing skills with parents to help children

Through the 1970s some professional teams re-thought the medical model in which children attended for specialist sessions, possibly without their parent even being in the room. The Hester Adrian Centre in Manchester and the Wolfson Clinic in London are two examples of teams who re-designed their programme and shared direct suggestions of activities for parents to do with their children between sessions. Schemes such as the Portage programme and Home-Start went one step further, by visiting families in their own home. The key assumption underlying this development was that parents were motivated and competent to help their own children. Local Speech and Language teams have also often moved towards direct advice for parents, and also early years practitioners.

MAKE THE CONNECTION WITH ... THE MEDICAL MODEL OF DISABILITY

- Into the 1980s, the dominant approach to disabled children and their families was to focus on disability in medical terms: diagnosis, treatment and management of the condition when, as often, no cure was possible.

- Challenge to the medical model came from disabled adults, who shared their childhood memories and parents who objected to an approach that treated their disabled sons and daughters as 'cases' rather than children.

- An alternative *social model* of disability has been promoted which focuses on children, then disability. This model also highlights social conditions that can cause children to be disabled unnecessarily by circumstances, such as difficult access to a play area or a rule that no medicine can be given, when normal life for some children requires regular medication.

- The social model approach does not deny the value of appropriate medical interventions, but stresses that children's life should not be driven by the disability label they are given, nor by a regime of treatment.

- Look also at Mary Dickins with Judy Denziloe *All together: how to create inclusive services for disabled children and their families* (2003).

Direct advice and leaflets for parents is so usual now, that it is easy to forget that many professionals, not only in the medical sphere, resisted sharing skills or ideas. A key argument was that 'mere' parents would fail to understand or would disrupt the professional input. It is now normal life to see nursery, reception and primary school children with their book folders. Yet, innovations such as the Haringey Project in London during the late 1970s, faced strong resistance from many teachers. They were convinced that parents would disturb the reading process as taught within school.

Many parents are already involved with their children

Barbara Tizard led a research project into parent involvement in the second half of the 1970s. The report offered constructive criticism that, 'It was generally the case that staff implicitly held a "one-way" model of parent involvement – they wished to change some aspects of the parents' behaviour in order, as they believed, to benefit the children educationally. They did not see a need for school practice to change in response to input from the parents' (Tizard *et al.*, 1981: 51).

The insights from this research are equally relevant now. Barbara Tizard and her team reported that many parents of children in the 1970s nursery and infant classes were doing much more with their children at home than the teachers believed. The EPPE team, working nearly a quarter of a century later, concluded that, in some early years settings, parents engaged in as much, if not more, sustained shared thinking (page 174) with their children at home than practitioners undertook within the setting. The team's findings confirmed that parents, who enjoyed activities such as reading books with their children at home, made a difference to their children's progress. Parents were already involved in these ways with their children; they did not need early years practitioners to tell them to do so.

There is good reason to assume that some early years and school practitioners still underestimate how much is happening at home. Liz Brooker turned researcher after her time as a Reception class teacher to track children through their Reception year in a London school. Brooker documents that, despite an avowed open communication system between staff and parents, some of the families experienced greater difficulty in approaching the Reception team – and not only because of different home languages. Brooker describes how families, some of them Bangladeshi, were keen to support their children's learning at home – both in general life skills but also from anxiety that school methods were not effective.

MAKE THE CONNECTION WITH ... YOUR BELIEFS ABOUT PARTNERSHIP

- Barbara Tizard reported that most parents were very interested in their own children and wanted to discuss their progress. However, practitioners sometimes decided parents were uninterested, because they chose not to participate in the form of involvement offered by the staff.

- Partnership in action is still sometimes defined from a practitioner's perspective. I encounter teams who judge parents as 'uninterested' or that 'involvement does not work' because some parents resist being on the rota (defined as parent involvement in some pre-schools) or do not attend open sessions (planned and scheduled by some nurseries without consultation).

- Reflect on your own practice, even if you feel you avoid the extremes of one-way partnership.

Parents as people with rights and responsibilities

An alternative perspective emerged from growing pressure that parents had a right to be involved and consulted since they were users of a public service, such as childcare or education. Organisations such as the Advisory Centre for Education supported parents' rights to information about their children's schooling and access to their child's records. This theme of consumer, or service-user, rights has continued against a social background of greater accountability in any service.

TAKE ANOTHER PERSPECTIVE

- This approach to partnership can raise another issue of balance between professional judgement and parents' preferences.

- What happens if teams feel partnership means agreeing to anything that a parent asks? What if a parent wants a harsh approach to discipline or requires that their two-year-old is taught letters and numbers?

■ Quality in early years practice is based in values and knowledge of child development. Genuine partnership sometimes means explaining why it will not be possible to agree to a parent's request.

■ Partnership raises issues around power, as well as a two-way relationship. These themes are discussed in more detail in Lindon (1997: part four).

Parents with skills and experience to offer

A challenge has grown to the view that professionals, in early years or other children's services, were the people with expertise and parents had nothing special to offer; they were 'just parents'. The playgroup movement developed in the 1960s in response to insufficient sessional nursery provision. Leaders took what was then a radical approach in involving parents, mainly mothers, in the daily running and sometimes the management of the playgroup.

LOOK, LISTEN, NOTE, LEARN

There can still be an uneasy balance for partnership in early years or school. Is an approach of skills-sharing a genuine two-way relationship, or a one-way process from knowledgeable professionals to allegedly less competent parents?

■ Some materials acknowledge that learning at home can and should be different from nursery. However, some leaflets imply parents should use activities to deliver the early years curriculum at home.

■ Gather some different resources aimed at parents. Does the approach show respect for family life? Was it really a compliment for parents to be told 'you are your child's first teacher'? Now the more usual phrase is 'your child's first and continuing educator'. Is that an improvement?

■ Be observant about the approach shown through features in early years magazines. Is partnership presented as a relationship of equals? When partnership is tough, who is seen to be the main problem? Are parents, but not practitioners, stereotyped with labels such as Mrs Pushy or Mr Anxious?

■ For a well-rounded approach, look at Dorothy Caddell (2001).

Schools had long acknowledged parents' skills through Parent Teacher Associations. But the traditional PTA role was restricted to fund raising and did not offer direct involvement in educational decisions. By the 1980s some nurseries and primary schools had developed more of the playgroup approach to involvement, encouraging parents to help out, often with specific activities or hearing children read.

Learning through play

Early years practice in the UK is very influenced by the perspective that children learn through play. Historical and cross-cultural data show that all children play unless they experience persistently restrictive, depriving or abusive circumstances. However, the phrase 'learning through play' has come to have a particular meaning for early years settings.

The focus on the value of spontaneous play grew in western Europe from the 1930s to become established by about the 1970s. The origins are often traced to the forms of early education pioneered by Frederich Froebel and Maria Montessori. But their approaches took a very broad view of playful activities and both placed a high value on children learning life skills through involvement in daily routines, not only by more recognisable play materials.

Peter Smith describes how spontaneous play came to be promoted as an essential support to children's early learning. The Plowden report in 1967 was probably the first official statement, but Peter Smith suggests three main strands had supported the development of what he calls the play ethos:

1   Theoretical perspectives from the psychoanalytic tradition (page 22) focused on play as vital for children to express their emotions and resolve what were seen to be inevitable conflicts of childhood.

2   Studies from evolutionary biology (page 21) proposed that playing was an important part of how all young mammals learn skills during their years of immaturity.

3   Socio-economic changes within western Europe, along with smaller families, led to a separation of work from home life. Children largely ceased to contribute to the family income and a commercial toy industry promoted a focus on play with bought playthings.

DEFINITION

Play ethos: an approach that stresses the crucial importance of children's play within their development.

TAKE ANOTHER PERSPECTIVE

- There is every reason to argue that young children can learn a great deal through relaxed play opportunities within an accessible learning environment.

- But the play ethos has led to some adult-determined interpretations of learning through play. Professional discussion about play and learning from the 1970s and 1980s included ever-increasing use of phrases such as 'play with a purpose', 'well-planned play' and 'structured play'.

- You need to ask whose purpose and whose structure? In many cases the answer is not that of the children, especially if practitioners follow a working definition of planning that incorporates many adult-planned and -initiated activities, designed to deliver specific educational outcomes and products.

Elizabeth Wood and Jane Attfield home in on the situation that can be created when adults become invested in the value of play for their own professional purposes. The authors explain their goal of linking play closely to the task of teaching and the early childhood curriculum as '... a direct response to the fact that play has too often been found as limiting, stereotypical, unchallenging and occupying rather than extending. The claims made for play do not seem to be realised in practice' (1996: x).

It is important not to take this quotation out of context. Elizabeth Wood and Jane Attfield acknowledge, like Peter Smith, that researchers and educators have sometimes made inflated claims that play can directly boost aspects of development, especially intellectual. They go on to challenge the validity of some attempts to define 'quality' in play and the risks of taking control to make play 'educationally worthwhile. A further problem is that we often make value judgements about "good" and "bad" play and potential learning outcomes' (1996: 6). When practitioners feel justified in evaluating the quality of play, without much reference to children's views, those adults

Children happily learn a very great deal through child-initiated play from a rich choice of resources

may decide that child-chosen play activities can be interrupted at adult whim or stopped, without much reflection or consultation.

Play, as adults sometimes define it, is not the sum total of children's activity and they can be very interested and motivated to have an active role in how an early years setting is run day by day. They learn a great deal from helping out – a point made by Margaret Henry (see also page 89) and supported by informal observations in home settings. Henry argued that the appropriate model for young children should be what works well in a family home and not a model from school, slightly adjusted. Children want and need relaxed time to spend with adults. An exclusive learning through play approach can reduce the opportunities for children to learn from direct coaching from adults: the pleasure in the role of novice described by Margaret Donaldson (page 186) and apprenticeship in thinking from Barbara Rogoff (page 186).

The role of the early years practitioner

The innovatory work of pioneers such as Margaret McMillan was a deliberate reaction against rigid school methods in the early twentieth century. Difficulties have arisen over the last years of the twentieth century and early twenty-first precisely because the job of early years provision has been seen increasingly to be that of preparing children for school. An exploration of the meaning in practice of 'learning through play' raises the importance of how early years practitioners behave towards young children.

TAKE ANOTHER PERSPECTIVE

- I would argue that much of the confusion about how best to support young learning arises from the whole framework created by 'pre-school' (see also page 230).

- Is primary school or a Reception year ever described as 'post-nursery'? What does that tell you?

The nature of the problem can be seen in the English Foundation Stage. The guidance uses the term 'practitioner' to refer to all adults involved in supporting children's learning, but the words 'teach' and 'teaching' are used to describe adults' behaviour. Some early years practitioners have what Colwyn Trevarthen has called an image of 'teacherly' behaviour. In the absence of specific guidance, some have concluded that they should behave close to their primary school memories of what a 'teacher' does. This classroom model includes greater adult direction of children's activities, including a balance towards sit-down, indoor activities, often those which all children complete, regardless of interest.

WHAT DOES IT MEAN?

Pedagogy: holistic approach to supporting children in learning, including the behaviour of practitioners and the learning environment they create.

However, good nursery-trained teachers do not behave like primary school teachers. As the EPPE project has described, the more effective early years settings were led by a nursery teacher who created a genuinely play-based curriculum, following the threads of children's current interests (*Effective Provision of Pre-School Education* available at: http://www.ioe.ac.uk/cdl/eppe). The research findings challenge the kind of top-down model that makes early years practitioners think they should copy school methods.

The EPPE team found that:

- Good learning outcomes for children are linked to adult–child interactions that involve 'sustained shared thinking' (see page 174 in this book).

- Practitioners need thorough knowledge of their early years curriculum, but these details have to be grounded in sound child development knowledge.

■ Children benefit from brief, constructive feedback from adults, given at the time, about what and how the children were doing (see page 110).

■ Teams need to establish a positive approach to behaviour. Such an outlook supported good learning outcomes for children, since they learn to be assertive and to use language to talk through conflicts (page 212).

The good practice observed depended on choice for children, that the nursery environment was not a primary classroom. The most effective settings provided a balance between adult-initiated activities and play activities freely chosen by the children.

The REPEY team made detailed observations of 12 effective settings. Early years practitioners who were trained nursery teachers were observed to undertake the most effective interactions with children, with greater amounts of sustained shared thinking. Non-teacher trained practitioners were most effective when working under the guidance of trained teachers. The possible dynamic here, although not one described specifically in the REPEY report, is that the teacher-trained practitioners were able to show colleagues not only a supportive style of interaction, but also showed by example how good 'teachers' behave with younger children. More information about the REPEY project is available at http://www.dfes.gov.uk/research/data/uploadfiles/RB356.doc.

The SPEEL project (Study of Pedagogical Effectiveness in Early Learning) also evolved from the EPPE research. This team explored that teaching in the early years is qualitatively different from the rest of the educational system. Genuinely helpful adults need to share control with young children and avoid following an adult-determined plan. This approach can feel difficult if practitioners do not trust learning through open-ended play and at the child's pace. Practitioners can also feel they are 'not doing much' unless they are directive by words or action.

In the SPEEL project, early years practitioners were asked to produce a video showing what they believed to be effective adult behaviour to support the children's learning within their own practice. Despite the rhetoric about the importance of learning through play, few practitioners chose to video play situations. Far more often, they selected literacy and numeracy sessions. The explanation seems to be that in these sessions they judged they were more active in advancing children's learning. A fair interpretation seems to be that they felt they were behaving like a teacher, and in England teams have felt under particular pressure to deliver literacy goals (page 158).

More information about the SPEEL project is available at http://www.dfes.gov.uk/research/data/uploadfiles/RB363.doc.

The learning environment

The focus on the learning environment has been part of the shift away from a primary school model. In some ways there is a return to the first traditions of UK nursery school practice, including a high value for the outdoors (page 130). Several strands support this aspect of good practice:

- The High/Scope approach has included a strong focus on layout of the room for children, with storage that enables even young children to operate the plan–do–review cycle, supported by find–use–return.

- The approach to early education that developed from the work of Maria Montessori has also had a strong focus on the layout and resources of the learning environment.

- The team at Community Playthings has drawn on US, UK and other European sources to take a strong practical approach to use of space, colour and furniture to create a supportive environment for young children and their carers.

Extensive interest in the Reggio Emilia early years centres also brought a focus on the learning environment. Marianne Valentine explains that the Reggio approach rests on the belief that 'teachers' are also learners, with a high awareness of what can be learned by watching and listening to children. The environment matters because, 'Once the adults involved move their focus from how to teach the child to being concerned with how the child learns, then the way in which space needs to be organised must also change. The teacher no longer considers how to use the space to enable her to teach but how the space can be used by all concerned to create valuable learning experiences. The focus therefore moves from the adult to the group' (1999: 19).

MAKE THE CONNECTION WITH ... YOUR OWN PRACTICE

- In what ways do you focus on an accessible, interesting learning environment?

- This approach enables adults to share control with children, who are able to find their own materials, make choices and reach decisions. Supportive practitioners can move away from completing a list of adult-planned activities. Instead you create resources that offer opportunities and experiences to support learning. A focus on the opportunities of the learning environment challenges the more adult-led school model and how it is developmentally inappropriate for young children.

- Look at Glenda MacNaughton and Gillian Williams (2004) who start their practical book about teaching techniques with a section about the environment.

- Also look at the visual explanation offered by *A place to learn: developing a stimulating learning environment* (2002; LEARN, tel. 020 8695 9806).

CHILDREN WITHIN FAMILIES AND A COMMUNITY

This section covers key concepts around the recognition that children are active learners within their own family or out-of-home care and are young citizens of their local community.

Children have a viewpoint and expertise

Berry Mayall has challenged the regular statement that early years settings in the UK are 'child-centred'. She takes the thought-provoking view that the philosophical statement does not necessarily produce settings genuinely attuned to children's needs. She argued from observation that in so-called child-centred settings, adult priorities are often most dominant. Yet the claim to be 'child-centred' means that children, whose behaviour is less than easy to handle, can be labelled as problems. Practitioners deny that it is their actions that could be responsible, because the setting is child-centred – a circular argument.

It is a respectful approach to recognise that the children have their own perspective on events. The narrative approach to the study of children has been one means with which to document children's views and understanding. The work of Vivian Gussin Paley (page 169) and of Jacqui Cousins (page 157) has highlighted that children have considered opinions and are happy to express them to adults who show genuine interest.

The awareness shown by Jacqui Cousins' four-year-olds sharpens through their experience in primary school. Wendy Titman showed that children had valuable expertise about the quality of their school grounds and good ideas about resolving problems. She also demonstrated that children made sense of adult priorities through rules such as keeping off the grass. Children concluded that protecting this part of the grounds was more important to the school than their play and well-being. When the school grounds were poorly maintained, children assumed that the adults did not care much about them.

LOOK, LISTEN, NOTE, LEARN

- Wendy Titman's ideas and some of the methods are applicable for early years as well as school settings.

- You can read about the action research in *Play, playtime and playgrounds* (1992) and *Special places, special people: the hidden curriculum of school grounds* (1994) published by Learning Through Landscapes. This organisation still works with schools, but is now also active with early years settings. Tel. 01892 845811; http://www.ltl.org.uk

Consultation methods with children have been developed in recognition that even very young children have views, insights and preferences – and that adults should listen. Alison Clark and Peter Moss describe the Mosaic method: five broad techniques to gain the ideas of children about their daily experiences in their early childhood centre.

1   Observation by adults that enabled the gathering of 'nursery stories' that were then considered in an open-ended way.

2   Child conferencing: a short interview with children, which could be on the move.

3   Cameras given to the children so they could take photos of anything that was 'important' to them in the centre.

4   Individual children led the adult on a tour of the nursery – indoors and outside. Children were the experts over what was to be shown.

5   The Mosaic approach then enables a visual and very personal mapping of the nursery through all the material gathered with the involvement of the children.

This consultation work is one of the strands in *Listening as a way of life* – a set of leaflets produced by the Early Childhood Unit (2004). See http://www.earlychildhood.org.uk

---

MAKE THE CONNECTION WITH ... YOUR OWN PRACTICE

Look at some of these consultation projects. All of them offer practical examples of how to engage children as genuine partners. What could you use in your work?

- Clark, Alison and Moss, Peter 2001 *Listening to young children: the Mosaic approach*. London: National Children's Bureau.

- Fajerman, Lina; Jarrett, Michael and Sutton, Faye 2000 *Children as partners in planning: a training resource to support consultation with children*. London: Save the Children.

- Kinney, Linda and McCabe, Jerry 2000 *Children as partners: a guide to consulting with very young children*. Stirling: Stirling Council (tel. 01786 471177).

- Miller, Judy 1996 *Never too young: how young children can take responsibility and make decisions*. London: Save the Children.

Several projects have shown the power of visual methods such as using happy and sad faces or enabling children to take photos and then talk about why this image is important or special to them. Linda Kinney and Jerry McCabe show, in their project at Stirling, that young children make perceptive and possibly uncomfortable comments.

Staff wanted to hear the children's views about where the adults were best placed for the indoor and outdoor spaces. Children were given play figures and a paper diagram of the nursery. However, the children did not stop at placing the figures, 'they began also to give the figures names of nursery staff and to make comments about why they were putting certain staff in particular areas. This was done spontaneously and without prompting. Their comments were full of insight, flagging up the strengths, skills, but also weaknesses, of particular people' (2000: 21). The report describes that the nursery team, although rather taken aback by constructive feedback from such young children, were prepared to learn from the comments in staff development sessions.

MAKE THE CONNECTION WITH . . . HOW DO YOU FEEL ABOUT CONSULTATION?

- It is important that consultation is genuine. How do you feel as an adult if you spend your time expressing your views (spoken or written) and then discover that the decision was already made or nobody appears to have taken account of your preferences?

- Young children may say, 'you could have asked us', if you go ahead without having a conversation with them. But they are really cross if, 'we told you the bush was really important – it's a special place, where we play the Monster Game. So why did you cut it down?'.

TAKING ANOTHER PERSPECTIVE

Consultation with children is sometimes described as 'giving children a voice'. As Priscilla Alderson (2000) points out, children already have a voice; the problem is whether adults listen. She gives many examples of how children want to be involved and consulted and can, with information, partake in even complicated medical decisions that affect them.

Anti-discriminatory practice

Early years services operate within society. The view of good practice has incorporated an awareness of discriminatory attitudes and behaviour, and that early years practitioners have a responsibility to make a difference. Some discussion about anti-discriminatory practice implies that the term is exclusively about discrimination based on ethnic group differences. The term more appropriately covers any social or cultural grouping: ethnic and linguistic background, faith, gender and disability. In some neighbourhoods it may be especially important to address attitudes towards gypsy/traveller communities, to refugee families or to children distressed because a parent or other family member is currently in prison.

Young children are in the process of developing their attitudes, so early years practitioners are expected to be active in:

- Promoting equal opportunities for all children and families who are in contact with the service.

- Working to equalise opportunities for those children and families whose situation or group identity may place them at a disadvantage.

- Fostering respect and mutual understanding between children and families who see themselves as different from each other. Such respect is a two-way process; it is not good practice to assume that offensive attitudes or action only emerge from one group.

Words matter, but it does not help good practice if early years practitioners become anxious about using the 'wrong' words. What matters most is what you do with and for children and their families. All strands to anti-discriminatory practice need to find a balance between understandable anger over inequalities in society and the strategies that are most likely to bring about change in attitudes and behaviour of individual adults.

WHAT DOES IT MEAN?

Equal opportunities: daily practice to ensure that all children are enabled to have positive experiences to support personal identity and that action is taken if children's opportunities are blocked.

Anti-discriminatory practice: an active attempt to promote positive attitudes and behaviour, to challenge and change negative outlooks and actions, on the basis of any group identity. An approach that stresses practitioners should take the initiative, not wait for issues to arise.

Anti-bias curriculum: a framework of activities, play materials and experiences that avoid stereotypes and actively promote understanding and knowledge of all the groups within society.

Children are not born prejudiced or bigoted, but they are enthusiastic learners and they imitate the words and actions of familiar adults and other children. Adult divisions can then be reflected in what children say, their beliefs about groups in society and their choice of play companions. Parents and early years practitioners may prefer to underestimate the extent that even three- and four-year-olds hear and imitate negative attitudes rife in their local neighbourhood.

Research in the USA from the 1940s and the UK from the 1960s, established that young children did notice ethnic group differences David Milner's review draws on research into how children develop race awareness and related attitudes (1983). However, it was a separate step, sometimes a swift one, to place social meaning on those differences. Most of that research focused on the ethnic group indicator of skin colour. So it is important to realise that children do not need such apparently obvious group markers to learn social distinctions that adults judge to be significant.

A significant part of anti-discriminatory practice in Northern Ireland involves anti-sectarianism. Similar issues also arise in some cities in Scotland, where the depth of sectarianism can shock outsiders. Paul Connolly *et al.* have shown that young children are aware and begin to understand the importance of the different symbols that relate to Catholic and Protestant groups in the Province, such as flags, football teams and symbolic annual events such as marches. They observed a few three-year-olds who were already aware of distinctions between the religious and social groups. But, by five years of age there was a high awareness of the impact of sectarianism. Apart from children's likely increased understanding as a result of age, most children in Northern Ireland attend primary schools with a clear religious affiliation. There are few integrated schools in the Province.

The traditions of anti-discriminatory practice for gender and disability have emerged along different paths from awareness of ethnic group or faith differences (see Jennie Lindon, 1998). Concern about equal opportunities on gender was strongly shaped by feminist concerns about discrimination against women and girls. The cycle has turned towards more even-handedness with a concern about what can happen to boys, especially in a female-dominated environment such as early years. Disability awareness emerged through a challenge to the medical model (page 232) and an inclusive approach requires thinking of children first, then their disability or chronic illness.

Young children start by finding differences of interest, or not, but they do not automatically believe that different is wrong or less acceptable. Young children extend their general knowledge about people who seem to be different from themselves. But over the same period of time, they are also building their own sense of identity. Children younger than four or five years of age view the world from their personal perspective outwards into what they recognise as the broader social network for themselves and their family. They need a sense of themselves, of personal identity and a secure sense of self-worth, before they can understand the sources of identity of others.

MAKE THE CONNECTION WITH ... THE ZONE OF PROXIMAL DEVELOPMENT

- Each of the early years curriculum guidance documents across the UK sets out an aim that children are enabled to develop a positive outlook on their own cultural background, as well as begin to understand backgrounds other than their own. Focus on the words 'begin to ...'.

- Anti-bias practice in the early years is in the business of sowing seeds – not harvesting the entire crop. The aim is to stretch children's understanding a little beyond their own backyard, not confuse them with 'doing' a long list of celebrations that are without context.

- Three-, four- and five-year-olds are at the beginning of a learning journey. It can be valuable for adults to reflect on: 'How did I learn about my own culture?' and 'How did I learn about unfamiliar social or cultural groups?'.

- Reflect on what and how much you are trying to do in this area of learning. In what ways can children connect with planned activities – think about the zone of proximal development (page 178).

MAKE THE CONNECTION WITH ... A POSITIVE APPROACH TO BEHAVIOUR

- It is also important to address hurtful or unkind behaviour between children in ways that still follow a positive approach to behaviour. Look at the ideas in Chapter 1 of my book *Equal opportunities in practice* (1998).

- Reflect on your own setting. What are the details of the behaviour policy and what actually happens in practice?

- What happens if particular kinds of offensiveness become a more significant 'incident'? How do children feel about what has been described as a 'hierarchy of hurt'?

- Does such an approach help children to understand and change their behaviour? Or does labelling behaviour as 'sexist' or logging 'racist incidents' reassure adults that they are doing something?

Vulnerability and resilience

Families live within a broader society and the pattern of their lives is affected by social and financial circumstances. Children's behaviour and their development are not changed directly by social class or poverty. Children are affected by the attitudes, experiences and stresses that reach them through their parents, and other important adults in their lives – Bronfenbrenner's macrosystem (page 45).

- Mothers may have less easy access to pre-natal care which can increase the health risks to mother and child. Very poor families may live in areas that are realistically dangerous, so the children's play opportunities and experiences are restricted.

- Families with low financial resources are more likely to live in deprived areas with fewer services. When both parents have no option but to work, they may have to take poor quality childcare.

- Financial and other stress in the family may mean that parents have less time to play and talk with their children. They may turn to more authoritarian methods of child rearing out of exhaustion. This feature of family life can, of course, arise in time-poor but money-rich families.

All of these features combine to make for more negative outcomes for children's development. The Sure Start national programme in England was developed in recognition that alleviating the effects of poverty and social disadvantage on children required a network of initiatives.

After many studies of the impact of poverty and social deprivation, in the 1980s researchers became interested in those children who, against all the odds, emerged to do well in adulthood. Norman Garmezy, Michael Rutter and others developed the idea of resilience and relative vulnerability in children.

- Resilience in children seems to be developed when families are cohesive, they pull together and children feel confident of the support of their parents. Under tough social conditions, appropriate interventions, such as the well-funded US early education programmes (page 107), promote feelings of competence in children.

- The parent involvement part of the programmes appeared to strengthen family beliefs that challenges can be met. Resilient children tend to have parents who are loving and act in an authoritative way (page 202). The more resilient children felt a strong sense of attachment to their parents; they have an emotional grounding to protect against minor and more major disruptions through childhood.

Resilience is unlikely to be developed if parents protect themselves by believing their children are unaffected by high levels of family or neighbourhood stress. Rosie Burrows and Brid Keenan offer a good example of what can be done to support adults to be able in turn to support their children. *We'll never be the same again* is the report of a Barnardo's project in Northern Ireland, which arose from the pilot work in the project 'Parenting in a divided society'. The entire project has strong community roots yet is equally committed to the welfare of children. The work is also very supportive of adults, including parents, who cope with stressful conditions partly by hoping that their children are not seriously affected – when unfortunately children are very aware. The project blends theoretical perspectives with a practical resource (download from http://www.barnardos.org.uk).

The concept of resilience has strong links with other outlooks, such as positive dispositions (page 103) and an outlook of mastery for learning (page 107). Research about children's experiences in hospital has highlighted that even young children can vary in styles of coping with distressing experiences. Some children were more motivated to seek out information and this orientation can be encouraged. Health psychology and the importance of play in hospital has acknowledged much more that children's well-being in hospital is shaped by opportunities for them to understand and influence, where possible, what is happening to them.

TAKE ANOTHER PERSPECTIVE

- The concept of resilience is not used to mean that children tolerate random change and adults ignore their feelings and perspective.

- Watch out for phrases such as 'the children are so resilient', when observation would suggest that the children have given up on expecting their lives to be predictable and have learned to tolerate that life is chaotic.

- Robert Brooks and Sam Goldstein describe the concept of genuine resilience and the practical applications to families, but the ideas are equally relevant to practitioners. Look at their books *Raising resilient children* (2001) and *Nurturing resilience in our children* (2003). The first title describes the concept of resilience and the second offers practical advice in a question and answer format.

WHAT DOES IT MEAN?

Resilience: an outlook for children characterised by the willingness to confront challenges, with a sense of confidence that it is possible to deal with setbacks and a backdrop of emotional security that key adults will help.

If you want to find out more:

✫ **Barrett, Helen** 2003 *Parenting programmes for families at risk: a source book*. London: National Family and Parenting Institute.

Comprehensive review of programmes to support parents and the challenge for evaluation. Chapter 4 is also a useful discussion about research methods.

✫ **Haggerty, Robert; Sherrod, Lonnie; Garmezy, Norman** and **Rutter, Michael** (eds) 1994 *Stress, risk and resilience in children and adolescents: process, mechanisms and interventions*. Cambridge: Cambridge University Press.

Discussion of the research and ideas on how children may resist the impact of negative experiences and how this process may work.

✫ **Lindon, Jennie** 2006 *Equality in Early Childhood*. London: Hodder Arnold.

Good practice regarding ethnic group background, gender, disability and faith.

✫ **Lindon, Jennie** 2001 *Understanding children's play*. Cheltenham: Nelson Thornes.

Description of research, theory and concepts about children's play and learning in all parts of their life.

✫ **Lindon, Jennie** 2003 *Child care and early education: good practice to support young children and their families*. London: Thomson Learning.

Chapter 1 has some background to the UK services and Appendix 2 a list of organisations.

✯ **Mayall, Berry** (ed.) 1994 *Children's childhoods: observed and experienced*. London: Falmer Press.

A sociological approach to children and childhood. Other chapters are also thought-provoking, for instance, on children's health and health services.

✯ **Maybin, Janet** and **Woodhead, Martin** (eds) 2003 *Childhoods in context*. Milton Keynes: Open University.

Good chapter by the editors on placing the UK system in perspective by also discussing alternative approaches to an early years curriculum.

✯ **Moss, Peter** and **Petrie, Pat** 2002 *From children's services to children's spaces: public policy, children and childhood*. London: Routledge Falmer.

Discussion of how social values affect perceptions of childhood and how childhood services are developed and judged.

✯ **Pugh, Gillian; De'Ath, Erica** and **Smith, Celia** 1994 *Confident parents, confident children: policy and practice in parent education and support*. London: National Children's Bureau.

Reviews the wide range of approaches and attitudes within support for families from different services in the UK.

✯ **Smith, Peter** 1994 'Play and the uses of play'. In Moyles, Janet (ed.) *The excellence of play*. Buckingham: Open University Press.

Discussion of how play has been interpreted and valued within research and practice.

✯ **Sylva, Kathy** 1994 'The impact of early learning on children's later development'. In Ball, Christopher (ed.) *Start right: the importance of early learning*. London: Royal Society of the Arts.

Research review on impact of early years settings – USA and UK.

MAGAZINES

Many of the magazines listed here have a news page as well as features. Reports and features tend to give relevant website addresses, as well as references to books or articles. Even if you can buy a magazine over the counter, it is usually cheaper to take out a subscription if you want every issue. The websites of the magazines all tell you about the publication, but some offer other features, such as discussion online. There may be further sections accessible only to subscribers who have been given a password.

- *Children Now* weekly magazine – news, updates and features. Part of the National Children's Bureau subscription, otherwise pay by subscription. Tel. 020 8606 7500. http://www.childrennow.co.uk

- *Early Years Educator* – a monthly magazine with current issues and features published by MA Education Ltd. Tel.: 020 7738 5454. http://www.earlyyearseducator.co.uk

- *Nursery World* – weekly magazine providing articles, topic booklets and news. There are also regular supplements: *The Professional Nanny, Training, Nursery Chains, Nursery Equipment*. Available from newsagents or on subscription. Tel. 01454 642480. http://www.nursery-world.com

- *Practical Pre-School* – monthly magazine with news, features and practice inserts. Published by Step Forward Publishing, available on subscription and from newsagents. Tel. 01926420046. http://www.practicalpre-school.com

- *Practical Professional Child Care* – monthly magazine crossing the age range, with news, features and inserts. Also from Step Forward Publishing, on subscription or from newsagents.

- *Zero to Nineteen* – monthly free magazine with news and features, online updates of current news and research digests. Register online for the magazine or telephone 01444 475612. http://www.zero2nineteen.co.uk

USING THE INTERNET

If you are not yet confident to access the internet, now is the time to tackle this skill. Find someone who will be patient and not pronounce, 'But it's so easy!'. All major organisations and government departments now have websites and many have papers and reports you can download and print. From experience, I suggest checking the length of any document before you press the Print button! Longer reports often have a summary.

You need to be as careful with information from the internet as from any other source. The websites of known early years organisations or charities can be trusted but, of course, you still cannot assume that a site will give you every angle on a topic. If you do some 'fishing' through open searches, then you will bring in a mixed 'net'. Be ready to find another source, because there is no overall web authority that checks the validity of information or claims.

The internet is a far more manageable source of information with the arrival of website addresses and more sophisticated search engines. All addresses given here are correct at the time of writing but websites are re-organised, so the same route may not continue to apply. It can be tough to track something, even if there is a search facility on the site. Larger sites usually have an email address and I have experienced a good rate of reply to 'where is it?' queries.

Search engines such as Google or AskJeeves now let you avoid the huge lists that put me off my first sortie into the internet, but a general topic search will still bring up a lot. You can narrow a search by using more than one key word in the format of word + word + word. The worldwide web is a free range zone. There is undoubtedly some downright repellent material on the web, as well as good quality and reliable information.

These are useful sites for tracking research or keeping up to date. All the organisations listed also have websites, some of which are rich sources of information and material available to download.

- http://www.childpolicy.org.uk
  4 Nations Child Policy Network – updates on events in England, Wales, Scotland and Northern Ireland.

- http://www.dfes.gov.uk/research
  Large site with details of research in process and published. You can narrow the search by using key words such as 'early years' but it is easier if you have the full route.

- http://www.eduref.org
  The Educator's Reference Desk, current home of the huge database known as ERIC (Educational Resources Information Center). ERIC was being reorganised through 2004. It may come back as AskEric, but you will have to check. ERIC can be searched to find articles in educational journals and texts.

- http://www.eppi.ioe.ac.uk
  Evidence for Policy and Practice Information – group that aims to enable practitioners to access research more easily. Information and research reviews online. For example, a 70 page review of studies about impact of integrated care and education settings on children and families.

- http://www.ltscotland.org.uk
  Information about early years and school in Scotland, but valuable for anyone elsewhere in the UK. Online resources, including the news magazine *Early Years Matters*. Publications also by telephone (01382 443600).

- http://www.nerf-uk.org/bulletin
  National Educational Research Forum – aims to address links between research and practice. First online bulletin *Evidence for Teaching and Learning* summer 2004, more will hopefully follow. Bulletins can also be ordered from Prolog. Tel. 0845 6022260.

- http://www.nfer.ac.uk
  National Foundation for Educational Research – a portfolio of their projects, provides summary and contact details.

- http://www.puzzlemaker.com
  A tip passed on by a college tutor. Source for creative material to catch students' attention: puzzle formats, clip art, word search formats and brain booster stories or exercises. This site is free. There are other similar sites, but you only get tasters unless you subscribe.

- http://www.scotland.gov.uk
  Information about services in Scotland. Reports and research reviews can be downloaded.

- http://www.scre.ac.uk
  Scottish Centre for Research in Education – information and summaries of research undertaken in Scotland. The Spotlight section has downloadable research papers.

- http://www.skepdic.com
  Useful site that challenges some popular areas of research and 'everybody knows'. I encountered the site when researching the Mozart Effect.

- http://www.standards.dfes.gov.uk/research
  Includes The Research Informed Practice Site (TRIPS) – an online database to help access to academic research.

- http://www.teachernet.gov.uk/research
  Information about projects. Direct links with TRIPS and other online research information, not all directly relevant for early years.

- http://www.trainer.org.uk
  Website of Modular Trainers' Course (organisation that runs training skills for professionals) – many resources about learning by adults and key concepts.

USEFUL ORGANISATIONS

◾ *Barnardo's*, Tanners Lane, Barkingside, Ilford IG6 1QG, UK. Tel. 020 8550 8822. http://www.Barnardos.org.uk
National charity concerned with the well-being of children. The website has briefing papers that can be downloaded

◾ *Children in Wales (Plant yng Nghymru)*, 25 Windsor Place, Cardiff CF1 3BZ, UK. Tel. 02920 342434. http://www.childreninwales.org.uk
Works with organisations and professionals involved with children and their families in Wales.

◾ *Children in Scotland (Clann An Alba)*, Princes House, 5 Shandwick Place, Edinburgh EH2 4RG, UK. Tel. 0131 228 8484. http://www.childreninscotland.org.uk
Brings together statutory and voluntary organisations and professionals working with children and their families in Scotland.

◾ *Community Insight*, The Pembroke Centre, Cheney Manor, Swindon SN2 2PQ, UK. Tel. 01793 512612. http://www.communityinsight.co.uk
Mail-order company specialising in a wide range of publications about good practice with children.

◾ *Community Playthings*, Robertsbridge, East Sussex TN32 5DR, UK. Tel. 0800 387 457. http://www.communityplaythings.com
Production company of the Bruderhof community. They make good quality wooden play materials and furniture and work in consultation with settings to make the most of available space. Some free videos and booklets.

◾ *Daycare Trust*, 21 St George's Road, London SE1 6ES, UK. Tel. 020 7840 3350. http://www.daycaretrust.org.uk
Provides information about day care and publishes discussion and review papers.

◾ *Early Education*, 136 Cavell Street, London E1 2JA, UK. Tel. 020 7539 5400. http://www.early-education.org.uk
A focus on all aspects of young children's learning. The useful *Learning Together Series* can be downloaded.

◾ *IPPA: The Early Childhood Organisation*, Unit 4 Broomhill Business Complex, Broomhill Road, Tallaght, Dublin 24, Republic of Ireland. Tel. 353 (0)1 4630010. http://www.ippa.ie
IPPA works with early years practitioners and services in the Republic of Ireland (Eire).

◾ *Learning Through Landscapes*, 3rd floor, Southside Offices, The Law Courts, Winchester S023 9DL. Tel. 01962 845811. http://www.ltl.org.uk
LTL led a consultation approach about school grounds and valuing children's playtime in primary school. They now also work within early years settings.

■ *Letterbox Library*, 71 Allen Road, London N16 8RY, UK. Tel. 020 7503 4801. http://www.letterboxlibrary.com
Mail-order children's books, specialising in a non-sexist and multicultural list. Dual language books and posters.

■ *National Children's Bureau*, 8 Wakley Street, London EC1V 7QE, UK. Tel. 020 7843 6000. http://www.ncb.org.uk
The main organisation publishes books, reading lists, and the *Highlight* series. NCB members can access more services within their membership fee. The NCB encompasses many networks and groups at the same address and you can identify them from the website under fora and councils, and networks. Of direct interest for early years are:

   ■ *Children's Play Council*, http://www.ncb.org.uk/cpc: brings together national voluntary organisations working to promote children's play.

   ■ *Children's Play Information Service* (CPIS), http://www.ncb.org.uk/library/cpis: provides an information service as part of the NCB library.

   ■ *Early Childhood Unit*, http://www.earlychildhood.org.uk: information about early years practice, research and resources. The useful *Listening as a way of life* series can be downloaded.

■ *NCH*, 85 Highbury Road, London N5 1UD, UK. Tel. 020 7226 2033. http://www.nch.org.uk
National children's charity that undertakes projects, runs centres for children and their parents. Some material can be downloaded.

■ *National Family and Parenting Institute*, 430 Highgate Studios, 53–79 Highgate Road, London NW5 1TL, UK. Tel. 020 7424 3460. http://www.nfpi.org.uk
Independent charity offering support to families. Leaflets can be downloaded.

■ *NIPPA: the Early Years Organisation*, 6c Wildflower Way, Apollo Road, Belfast BT12 6TA, UK. Tel. 028 90 662825. http://www.nippa.org
Works with early years practitioners and services in Northern Ireland.

■ NSPCC (*National Society for the Prevention of Cruelty to Children*), 42 Curtain Road, London EC2A 3NH, UK. Tel. 020 7825 2500. http://www.nspcc.org.uk
Support and information about child protection and related issues. Briefings can be downloaded from the section on publications for professionals.

■ *Save the Children*, 17 Grove Lane, London SE5 8RD, UK. Tel. 020 7703 5400. http://www.savethechildren.org.uk
Supports a wide range of research projects and other units, such as on supporting children's rights.

■ *Tamarind Ltd*, PO Box 52, Northwood HA6 1UN, UK. Tel. 020 8866 8808. http://www.tamarindbooks.co.uk
A wide range of fiction, puzzles and posters that show children of different ethnic backgrounds, disabled children and books with non-sexist themes.

■ *Zero to Three*, part of the Center for Infants, Toddlers and Families in the USA. http://www.zerotothree.org
Wide range of information to download as well as to purchase online.

FINDING BOOKS

You may want to track other books, or further publications by the same author. There are several possible detective routes:

■ An internet search by name will bring up information about an author.

■ If you know the publishing company, then their website may help, providing the book is in print. *The Writers' Yearbook* (should be in the reference section of a public library) also gives contact details for UK publishers.

■ An internet site such as http://www.amazon.co.uk can provide information as well as a means to purchase.

■ A specialist mail order firm can often track titles or types of book. I have been greatly helped by Community Insight (Tel. 01793 512612, http://www.communityinsight.co.uk).

■ Everyone is well advised to use the resources of a college library while they are students, but do not overlook your local public library. Staff will often track a book around libraries in the same local authority area or further afield. If library staff judge a book is of general interest, they may buy the title you request (thank you Balham!).

■ You may also find that your local early years and childcare department has a resource centre that you can access.

SUGGESTED BOOKS

■ Acredolo, Linda and Goodwyn, Susan 2000 *Baby signs: how to talk with your baby before your baby can talk*. London: Vermilion.

■ Alderson, Priscilla 2000 *Young children's rights: exploring beliefs, principles and practice*. London: Jessica Kingsley.

■ Arnold, Cath 1999 *Child development and learning 2–5 years: Georgia's story*. London: Paul Chapman Publishing.

Arnold, Cath 2003 *Observing Harry: child development and learning 0–5*. Maidenhead: Open University Press.

Athey, Chris 1990 *Extending thought in young children: a parent–teacher partnership*. London: Paul Chapman.

Bain, Alastair and Barnett, Lyn 1986 *The design of a day care system in a nursery setting for children under five*. London: The Tavistock Institute of Human Relations, Occasional Paper No. 8.

Baron-Cohen, Simon 2003 *The essential difference: men, women and the extreme male brain*. London: Allen Lane.

Barrett, Helen 2003 *Parenting programmes for families at risk: a source book*. London: National Family and Parenting Institute.

Bee, Helen 1997 *The developing child*. Eighth edition. Harlow: Longman.

Bee, Helen and Boyd, Denise 2004 *The developing child*. Boston MA: Pearson Education.

Beyer, Jannik and Gammeltoft, Lone 2000 *Autism and play*. London: Jessica Kingsley.

Bilton, Helen 2002 *Outdoor play in the early years: management and innovation*. London: David Fulton.

Bilton, Helen 2004 *Playing outside: activities, ideas and inspiration for the Early Years*. London: David Fulton.

Bion, W.R. 1962 *Learning from experience*. London: Heinemann.

Blatchford, Peter and Sharp, Sonia (eds) 1994 *Breaktime and the school: understanding and changing playground behaviour*. London: Routledge.

Blythe, Sally Goddard 2004 *The well balanced child: movement and early learning*. Stroud: Hawthorn Press.

Bowlby, John 1965 *Child care and the growth of love*. Harmondsworth: Penguin.

Boxall, Marjorie 2002 *Nurture groups in school: principles and practice*. London: Paul Chapman Publishing.

Brennan, Carmel (ed) 2004 *The power of play: a play curriculum in action*. Dublin: IPPA.

Bronfenbrenner, Urie 1979 *The ecology of human development*. Cambridge MA: Harvard University Press.

Brooker, Liz 2002 *Starting school – young children learning culture.* Buckingham: Open University Press.

Brooks, Robert and Goldstein, Sam 2001 *Raising resilient children.* New York: McGraw Hill.

Brooks, Robert and Goldstein, Sam 2003 *Nurturing resilience in our children.* New York: McGraw Hill.

Bruner, Jerome 1990 *Acts of meaning.* Cambridge MA: Harvard University Press.

Bryman, Alan 2004 *Social research methods.* Oxford: Oxford University Press.

Buckingham, David 1996 *Moving images: understanding children's emotional responses to television.* Manchester: Manchester University Press.

Burrows, Rosie and Keenan, Brid 2004 *We'll never be the same again.* Barnardo's Northern Ireland. Download from http://www.barnardos.org.uk

Caddell, Dorothy 1998a *Numeracy in the early years: what the research tells us.* Dundee: Scottish Consultative Council on the Curriculum.

Caddell, Dorothy 1998b *Numeracy counts.* Dundee: Scottish Consultative Council on the Curriculum (also available from http://www.ltscotland.org.uk).

Caddell Dorothy 2001 *Working with parents: a shared understanding of the curriculum 3–5.* Glasgow: Learning and Teaching Scotland.

Call, Nicola and Featherstone, Sally 2003a *The thinking child: brain-based learning for the foundation stage.* Stafford: Network Educational Press.

Call, Nicola and Featherstone, Sally 2003b *The thinking child resource book.* Stafford: Network Educational Press.

Campbell, Robin 1999 *Literacy from home to school: reading with Alice.* Stoke-on-Trent: Trentham Books.

Carr, Margaret 2001 *Assessment in early childhood settings.* London: Paul Chapman Publishing.

Carter, Rita 1999 *Mapping the mind.* London: Orion Publishing Group.

Chang, Jung 1991 *Wild swans.* London: Harper Collins.

Charlton, Tony; Gunter, Barrie and Hannan, Andrew (eds) 2002 *Broadcast television effects in a remote community.* New Jersey: Lawrence Erlbaum Associates.

- Clark, Alison and Moss, Peter 2001 *Listening to young children: the Mosaic approach*. London: National Children's Bureau.

- Close, Robin 2004 *Television and language development in the early years: a review of the literature*. For the Literacy Trust, http://www.literacytrust.co.uk

- Clough, Peter and Nutbrown, Cathy 2002 *A student's guide to methodology*. London: Sage.

- Cole, Michael and Cole, Sheila 2000 *The development of children*. New York: Worth Publishers.

- Connolly, Paul; Smith, Alan and Kelly, Berni 2002 *Too young to notice: the cultural and political awareness of 3–6 year olds in Northern Ireland*. Belfast: Community Relations Council.

- Cousins, Jacqui 1999 *Listening to four year olds: how they can help us plan their education and care*. London: National Children's Bureau.

- Cremin, Hilary 2002 'Circle time: why it doesn't always work'. *Primary Practice 30*, 26–28.

- Dickins, Mary with Denziloe, Judy 2003 *All together: how to create inclusive services for disabled children and their families*. London: National Children's Bureau.

- Donaldson, Margaret 1978 *Children's minds*. Glasgow: Fontana/Collins.

- Donaldson, Margaret 1992 *Human minds: an exploration*. London: Penguin.

- Donaldson, Margaret; Grieve, Robert and Pratt, Chris (eds) 1983 *Early childhood development and education: readings in psychology*. Oxford: Blackwell.

- Dorman, Helen and Dorman, Clive 2002 *The social toddler: promoting positive behaviour*. Richmond: The Children's Project.

- Dreikurs, Rudolf and Soltz, Vicki 1995 *Happy children: a challenge to parents*. Melbourne: Australian Council for Educational Research (ACER).

- Dunn, Judy 1984 *Sisters and brothers*. London: Fontana.

- Dunn, Judy 1986 'Children in a family world'. In Richards, Martin and Light, Paul *Children of social worlds: development in a social context*. Cambridge: Polity Press.

- Dunn, Judy 1993 *Young children's close relationships beyond attachment*. London: Sage.

- Eckerman, Carol 1993 'Imitation and toddlers' achievement of co-ordinated actions with others'. In Nadel, Jacqueline and Camaioni, Luigia (eds) *New perspectives in early communicative development*. London: Routledge.

Edgington, Margaret 2002 *The great outdoors: developing children's learning through outdoor provision*. London: Early Education.

Edwards, Anna Gillespie 2002 *Relationships and learning: caring for children from birth to three*. London: National Children's Bureau.

Eisenberg, Nancy 1992 *The caring child*. Cambridge MA: Harvard University Press.

Elfer, Peter; Goldschmied, Elinor and Selleck, Dorothy 2003 *Key persons in the nursery: building relationships for quality provision*. London: David Fulton.

EPPE: *The Effective Provision of Pre-School Education Project* http://www.ioe.ac.uk/cdl/eppe

Evans, Betsy 2002 *You can't come to my birthday party: conflict resolution with young children*. Ypsilanti: High/Scope Press.

Fabian, Hilary 2002 *Children starting school*. London: David Fulton Publishers.

Fajerman, Lina; Jarrett, Michael and Sutton, Faye 2000 *Children as partners in planning: a training resource to support consultation with children*. London: Save the Children.

Ford, Gina 2002 *The new contented little baby book*. London: Vermilion.

Garmezy, N. and Rutter, M. 1983 *Stress, coping and development in children*. New York: McGraw Hill.

Gesell, Arnold 1954 *The first five years of life*. London: Methuen.

Gibbens, John 1950 *Care of children from one to five* (fourth edition). London: J&A Churchill Ltd.

Goldschmied, Elinor and Jackson, Sonia 2004 *People under three: young children in day care*. London: Routledge.

Goleman, Daniel 1996 *Emotional intelligence – why it can matter more than IQ*. London: Bloomsbury.

Gopnik, Alison; Meltzoff, Andrew and Kuhl, Patricia 2001 *How babies think: the science of childhood*. London: Phoenix.

Gottman, John and Declaire, Joan 1997 *The heart of parenting: how to raise an emotionally intelligent child*. London: Bloomsbury.

Green, Christopher 1990 *New toddler taming: a parent's guide for the first five years*. London: Vermilion.

Green, Christopher 2000 *Beyond toddlerdom: keeping five to twelve year olds on the rails*. London: Vermilion.

Grieve, Robert and Hughes, Martin (eds) 1990 *Understanding children: essays in honour of Margaret Donaldson*. Oxford: Basil Blackwell.

Haggerty, Robert; Sherrod, Lonnie; Garmezy, Norman and Rutter, Michael (eds) 1994 *Stress, risk and resilience in children and adolescents: process, mechanisms and interventions*. Cambridge: Cambridge University Press.

Hardyment, Christina 1995 *Perfect parents: baby care advice past and present*. Oxford: Oxford University Press.

Healy, Jane 1994 *Your child's growing mind: a practical guide to brain development and learning from birth to adolescence*. New York: Doubleday.

Henry, Margaret 1996 *Young children, parents and professionals: enhancing the links in early childhood*. London: Routledge.

Hewlett, Sylvia Ann 1993 *Child neglect in rich nations*. New York: UNICEF.

Holland, Penny 2003 *We don't play with guns here: war, weapon and superhero play in the early years*. Maidenhead: Open University Press.

Hughes, Anne and Ellis, Sue 1998 *Writing it right? Children writing 3–8*. Dundee: Scottish Consultative Council on the Curriculum.

Hughes, Martin 1986 *Children and number*. Oxford: Blackwell.

Humphreys, Margaret 1994 *Empty cradles*. London: Doubleday.

Hyder, Tina 2004 *War, conflict and play: working with refugee children in the early years*. Buckingham: Open University Press.

Isaacs, Susan 1929 *The nursery years*. London: Routledge and Kegan Paul.

James, Allison and Prout, Alan (eds) 1997 *Constructing and re-constructing childhood*. London: Routledge Falmer.

Karmiloff-Smith, Annette 1994 *Baby it's you: a unique insight into the first three years of the developing baby*. London: Ebury Press.

Kehily, Mary (ed.) 2004 *An introduction to childhood studies*. Buckingham: Open University Press.

Kindlon, Dan and Thompson, Michael 1999 *Raising Cain: protecting the emotional life of boys*. London: Penguin.

Kinney, Linda and McCabe, Jerry 2000 *Children as partners: a guide to consulting with very young children*. Stirling: Stirling Council.

Knopp, Guido 2002 *Hilter's children*. Stroud: Sutton Publishing Ltd.

Konner, Melvin 1991 *Childhood*. London: Little Brown and Co.

Learning and Teaching Scotland *Birth to Three: supporting our youngest children* 2005. Download from: http://www.ltscotland.org.uk/earlyyears/birthtothree.asp

Lindon, Jennie 1993 *Child development from birth to eight: a practical focus*. London: National Children's Bureau.

Lindon, Jennie 1996 *Growing up: from eight years to young adulthood*. London: National Children's Bureau.

Lindon, Jennie 1997 *Working with young children*. London: Hodder and Stoughton.

Lindon, Jennie 2006 *Equality in Early Childhood*. London: Hodder Arnold.

Lindon, Jennie 2000 *Early years care and education in Europe*. London: Hodder and Stoughton.

Lindon, Jennie 2001 *Understanding children's play*. Cheltenham: Nelson Thornes.

Lindon, Jennie 2003a (A set of three books) *What does it mean to be three? (four, five) A practical guide to child development in the Foundation Stage*. Leamington Spa: Step Forward Publishing.

Lindon, Jennie 2003b *Too safe for their own good? Helping children learn about risk and life skills*. London: National Children's Bureau.

Lindon, Jennie 2003c *Child protection*. London: Hodder and Stoughton.

Lindon, Jennie 2003d *Child care and early education: good practice to support young children and their families*. London: Thomson Learning.

Locke, Ann and Ginsborg, Jane 2003 'Spoken language in the early years: the cognitive and linguistic development of three- to five-year-old children from socio-economically deprived backgrounds'. *Educational and Child Psychology* 20(4), 68–79.

Maclellan, Effie; Munn, Penny and Quinn, Victoria 2003 *Thinking about maths: a review of issues in teaching number from 5 to 14 years*. Glasgow: Learning and Teaching Scotland.

MacNaughton, Glenda; Rolfe, Sharne and Siraj-Blatchford, Iram 2001 *Doing early childhood research: international perspectives on theory and practice.* Buckingham: Open University Press.

MacNaughton, Glenda and Williams, Gillian 2004 *Teaching young children: choices in theory and practice.* Maidenhead: Open University Press.

Mayall, Berry (ed.) 1994 *Children's childhoods: observed and experienced.* London: Falmer Press.

Mayall, Berry 2002 *Towards a sociology for childhood: thinking from children's lives.* Buckingham: Open University Press.

Maybin, Janet and Woodhead, Martin (eds) 2003 *Childhoods in context.* Milton Keynes: Open University Press.

Meggitt, Carolyn and Sutherland, Gerald 2000 *Child development: an illustrated guide – birth to 8 years.* London: Heinemann.

Miller, Judy 1996 *Never too young: how young children can take responsibility and make decisions.* London: Save the Children.

Miller, Linda and Devereux, Jane (eds) 2004 *Supporting children's learning in the early years.* London: David Fulton.

Miller, Sue and Sambell, Kay (eds) 2003 *Contemporary issues in childhood: approaches to teaching and learning.* Newcastle upon Tyne: Northumbria University Press.

Milner, David 1983 *Children and race: 10 years on.* London: Ward Lock.

Moss, Peter and Petrie, Pat 2002 *From children's services to children's spaces: public policy, children and childhood.* London: Routledge Falmer.

Moyles, Janet (ed.) 1994 *The excellence of play.* Buckingham: Open University Press.

Munn, Penny 1997a 'Children's beliefs about counting'. In Thompson, Ian (ed.) *Teaching and learning early number.* Buckingham: Open University Press.

Munn, Penny 1997b 'What do children know about reading before they go to school?'. In Owen, Pamela and Pumfrey, Peter (eds) *Emergent and developing reading: messages for teachers.* London: Falmer Press.

Murray, Lynne and Trevarthen, Colwyn 1985 'Emotional regulation of interactions between two-month-olds and their mothers'. In Field, T.M. and Fox, N.A. (eds) *Social perception in infants.* Norwood: N.J. Ablex.

Murray, Lynne and Andrews, Liz 2000 *The social baby*. Richmond: The Children's Project.

Nolte, Dorothy Law and Harris, Rachel 1998 *Children learn what they live: parenting to inspire values*. New York: Workman Publishing, or download the poem from http://www.EmpowermentResources.com

Ouvry, Marjorie 2000 *Exercising muscles and minds: outdoor play and the early years curriculum*. London: National Children's Bureau.

Ouvry, Marjorie 2004 *Sounds like playing: music and the early years curriculum*. London: Early Education.

Paley, Vivian Gussin 1984 *Boys and girls: superheroes in the doll corner*. Chicago: University of Chicago Press.

Paley, Vivian Gussin 1988 *Bad guys don't have birthdays: fantasy play at four*. Chicago: Chicago University Press.

Paley, Vivian Gussin 2004 A *child's work: the importance of fantasy play*. Chicago and London: Chicago University Press.

Pascal, Christine and Bertram, Tony 1997 (eds) *Effective early learning: case studies in improvement*. London: Hodder and Stoughton.

Pinker, Steven 1994 *The language instinct: how the mind creates language*. New York: Morrow.

Pipher, Mary 1994: Reviving Ophelia. London: Vermilion.

Pipher, Mary 1996 *The shelter of each other: rebuilding our families to enrich our lives*. London:Vermilion.

Play Scotland 2003 *School grounds literature review*. Contact theresacasey@playforlife.fsnet.co.uk or the website http://www.playscotland.org

Pugh, Gillian; De'Ath, Erica and Smith, Celia 1994 *Confident parents, confident children: policy and practice in parent education and support*. London: National Children's Bureau.

REPEY project *Researching Effective Pedagogy in Early Years: Brief No. 356* http://www.dfes.gov.uk/research/data/uploadfiles/RB356.doc

Ridler, Catherine 2002 'Teachers, children and number understanding'. Conference paper, British Psychological Society Psychology of Education Conference. University College, Worcester.

Riley, Denise 1993 *War in the nursery: theories of the child and mother*. London: Virago.

Roberts, Joy 2000 'The rhetoric must match the practice'. *Early Years Educator* 2(5), 26–27.

Robertson, James and Robertson, Joyce 1989 *Separation and the very young*. London: Free Association Books.

Robinson, Elizabeth and Robinson, Peter 1983 'Ways of reacting to communication failure in relation to the development of the child's understanding about verbal communication'. In Donaldson, Margaret; Grieve, Robert and Pratt, Chris (eds) *Early childhood development and education: readings in psychology*. Oxford: Basil Blackwell.

Rogoff, Barbara 1990 *Apprenticeship in thinking: cognitive development in social context*. Oxford: Oxford University Press.

Rutter, Michael 1972 *Maternal deprivation re-assessed*. London: Penguin.

Rutter, Michael 1999 'English and Romanian adoptees study (ERA)'. In Ceci, Stephen and Williams, Wendy (eds) *The nature–nurture debate*. Malden MA: Blackwell.

Schafer, Mechthild and Smith, Peter 1996 'Teachers' perceptions of play fighting and real fighting in primary school'. *Educational Research* 38(2), 173–181.

Schaffer, H. Rudolph 1998 *Making decisions about children: psychological questions and answers*. Oxford: Blackwell Publishing.

Severe, Sal 2004 *How to behave so your children will too* London: Vermilion.

Shaw, Sara and Hawes, Trevor 1998 *Effective teaching and learning in the classroom*. Leicester: Optimal Learning.

Sheridan, Mary 1960 *Children's developmental progress from birth to five years: the Stycar sequences*. Windsor: National Foundation for Educational Research.

Sheridan, Mary 1977 *Spontaneous play in early childhood: from birth to six years*. Windsor: National Foundation for Educational Research.

Shore, Rima 1997 *Rethinking the brain: new insights into early development*. New York: Families and Work Institute.

Skynner, Robin and Cleese, John 1997 *Families and how to survive them*. London: Vermilion.

Slaby, Ronald; Roedell, Wendy; Arezzo, Diana and Hendrix, Kate 1995 *Early violence prevention: tools for teachers of young children*. Washington DC: National Association for the Education of Young Children.

SPEEL 2002 *Study of pedagogical effectiveness in early learning Brief No. 363*. http://www.dfes.gov.uk/research/data/uploadfiles/RB363.doc

Spock, Benjamin and Palmer, Stephen 1997 *Baby and child care*. London: Simon and Schuster.

Sure Start/DfES 2002 *Birth to three matters: a framework to support children in their earliest years*. A substantial research review on the CD Rom.

Sutherland, Peter 1992 *Cognitive development today: Piaget and his critics*. London: Paul Chapman.

Sylva, Kathy 1994 'The impact of early learning on children's later development'. In Ball, Christopher (ed.) *Start right: the importance of early learning*. London: Royal Society of the Arts.

Tassoni, Penny 2002 *Planning for the Foundation Stage: ideas for themes and activities*. Oxford: Heinemann.

Thomson, J.; Tolmie, A.; Foot, H. and McLaren, B. 1996 *Child development and the aims of road safety education*. London: HMSO.

Titman, Wendy 1992 *Play, playtime and playgrounds*. Winchester: Learning Through Landscapes/World Wide Fund for Nature UK.

Titman, Wendy 1994 *Special places, special people: the hidden curriculum of school grounds*. Winchester: Learning Through Landscapes/WWF UK.

Tizard, Barbara 1986 *The care of young children: implications of recent research*. London: Thomas Coram Research Unit: Working and Occasional Papers No. 1.

Tizard, Barbara; Mortimore, Jo and Burchell, Bebb 1981 *Involving parents in nursery and infant schools*. London: Grant McIntyre.

Tizard, Barbara and Hughes, Martin 2002 *Young children learning: talking and thinking at home and at school*. Oxford: Blackwell.

Tobin, Joseph; Wu, David and Davidson, Dana 1989 *Preschool in three cultures*. Cambridge MA: Harvard University Press.

Tough, Joan 1976 *Listening to children talking*. London: Ward Lock.

Trevarthen, Colwyn; Barr, Ian; Dunlop, Aline-Wendy; Gjersoe, Nathalia; Marwick, Helen and Stephen, Christine 2003 *Meeting the needs of children from birth to three years*. Summary on http://www.scotland.gov.uk/library5/social/ins6-00.asp; full report on http://www.scotland.gov.uk/about/ED/IAC/00014478/page705680189.pdf

▨ Valentine, Marianne 1999 *The Reggio Emilia approach to Early Years education*. Dundee: Scottish Consultative Council on the Curriculum.

▨ Vygotsky, Lev 1962 *Thought and language*. Cambridge MA: MIT Press.

▨ Vygotsky, Lev 1978 *Mind in society: the development of higher psychological processes*. Cambridge MA: Harvard University Press.

▨ Ward, Sally 2004 *Baby talk*. London: Arrow.

▨ Whiting, Beatrice Blyth and Edwards, Carolyn Pope 1988 *Children of different worlds: the formation of social behaviour*. Cambridge MA: Harvard University Press.

▨ Wiseman, Michael 2004 *Did you spot the gorilla? How to recognise hidden opportunities*. London: Arrow.

▨ Wood, Elizabeth and Attfield, Jane 1996 *Play, learning and the early childhood curriculum*. London: Paul Chapman.

VIDEOS

This is a selection of videos that I personally find useful. Check the relevant organisation for current prices. Only the first two sets of videos are free.

▨ Community Playthings. Tel. 0800 387 457. This community-based organisation does not use conventional advertising but promotes their equipment and publications through their videos and booklets.

   ▨ *Roomscapes* – about use of space and the environment.

   ▨ *Children come first* – putting the focus on children and their needs.

   ▨ *Foundations: the value of unit block play* – using the opportunities of a set of wooden blocks for learning and creativity.

▨ From Prolog, the DfES publications centre. Tel. 0845 6022 260, both are free.

   ▨ *Sure Start – Birth to three matters: a framework to support children in their earliest years* 2002. Pack with poster, CD Rom, video, cards.

   ▨ *Foundation Stage* – video and leaflets for sharing with parents. This video has some useful footage to highlight what should be happening with and for 3–5-year-olds.

▨ From the National Children's Bureau. Tel. 020 7843 6000.

   ▨ *Tuning in to children* 1997 video and book.

- Elinor Goldschmied 1986 *Infants at work: babies of 6–9 months exploring everyday objects*.

- Elinor Goldschmied and Anita Hughes 1992 *Heuristic play with objects: children of 12–20 months exploring everyday objects*.

- From High/Scope UK. Tel. 020 8676 0220.

  - *The High/Scope approach for under threes* 1999.

  - *Supporting children in resolving conflicts* 1998 (when slightly older children have the words to talk about problems).

  - *It's mine! Responding to problems and conflicts* 2003 (about under threes).

- *Baby it's you*. Woodside Promotions. Tel: 01372 805000.

- *Key Times: a framework for developing high quality provision for children under three years old* 2001 Julia Manning-Morton and Maggie Thorp. A video and pack on good practice from Camden Early Years (tel. 020 7974 8188).

- *Learning together with babies*. From the PEEP centre, Peers School, Littlemore, Oxford OX4 6JZ. Tel. 01865 779779. A series of videos from PEEP, developed firstly for parents and used in groups for parents but with useful images and ideas for early years practitioners. Also *Learning together with ones* (*twos, threes* and *fours*).

- *We can work it out: parenting with confidence* 1999 Save the Children and Open School Network video and booklet about a positive approach to behaviour. Distributed by Plymbridge, tel. 01752 202301.

- *REAL Project Early Literacy Education with Parents: a framework for practice* 1996 Sheffield University. Tel. 0114 222 0400.

- *Rising Sun Woodland Pre-school Project* Sightlines Initiative 2001 Video and booklets about outdoor learning. Tel. 0191 261 7666, http://www.sightlinesinitiative.com

- *The social baby* 2004 The Children's Project and NSPCC. Tel. 020 8546 8750, http://www.childrensproject.co.uk

All of the above suggestions are videos that can be purchased. Some good television series are not on offer as commercial videos, for example the Channel 4 *Childhood* programmes. Schools and colleges should have an ERA licence (Educational Recording Agency, tel. 020 7837 3222) to use recordings that have been recorded to video direct from the television. If your educational organisation holds this licence, you can subscribe to the facilities of The Video Library of Richmond-upon-Thames College, which has a store of videos, including *Childhood*. Tel. 020 8607 8423, http://www.rutc.ac.uk – go through Facilities.

NAME INDEX

This index lists people whose ideas or research are discussed. If the name you are looking for is not here, try the 'If you want to find out more' sections at the end of each chapter or the 'Using further resources' section.